UNDERSTANDING
WORLD
CHRISTIANITY

Photograph by Rapur Bunupuradah

UNDERSTANDING
WORLD
CHRISTIANITY

The Vision and Work of
Andrew F. Walls

Edited by
William R. Burrows, Mark R. Gornik
and Janice A. McLean

ORBIS BOOKS
Maryknoll, New York 10545

Founded in 1970, Orbis Books endeavors to publish works that enlighten the mind, nourish the spirit, and challenge the conscience. The publishing arm of the Maryknoll Fathers and Brothers, Orbis seeks to explore the global dimensions of the Christian faith and mission, to invite dialogue with diverse cultures and religious traditions, and to serve the cause of reconciliation and peace. The books published reflect the views of their authors and do not represent the official position of the Maryknoll Society. To learn more about Maryknoll and Orbis Books, please visit our Web site at *www.maryknollsociety.org.*

Library of Congress Cataloging-in-Publication Data

Understanding world Christianity : the vision and work of Andrew F. Walls / edited by William R. Burrows, Mark R. Gornik, and Janice A. McLean.
    p. cm.
"Bibliography of the writings of Andrew F. Walls" –P.
Includes bibliographical references and index.
ISBN 978-1-57075-949-9 (pbk.)
    1. Walls, Andrew F. (Andrew Finlay) 2. Christian biography. I. Burrows, William R. II. Gornik, Mark R. III. McLean, Janice A.
BR1725.W293U53 2011
266.0092 – dc22   2011014799

To Doreen Mary Walls

August 13, 1919–October 11, 2009

Contents

vii

Introduction

WILLIMN R. BURROWS, MARK R. GORNIK,

AND JANICE MCCLEAN

In the Pauline usage, humility not only enables one to move more deeply into a life with God, but draws in others as well. This is at the heart of the gift that is Andrew Walls. Most certainly, he would object to the title of this volume, *Understanding World Christianity: The Vision and Work of Andrew F. Walls*. But to be clear, our ability to imagine what is now called "World Christianity" has been singularly shaped by his life and scholarship. Walls invites us to consider what God is doing in the world as the Gospel interacts with cultures and Christ becomes embodied in communities.

Fittingly, this volume is not a tribute to Andrew Walls in the traditional way of gathering interesting but unconnected essays. Instead, it is a serious and significant set of reflections on and engagements with his life, ideas, institutions, networks, publications, activities, and proposals.

Rather than foster his own career, Walls has endeavored to empower others, and from the journals he launched to the research centers he developed, he created a climate that fosters scholarly activity among a wide community. His life and scholarship are a model in another way. Listening to and absorbing what is happening on the ground, whether in Aberdeen, Freetown, or New York City, Walls is attentive to the signs of revival and life, wherever they are found. Consequently, this has led him to create new paths of scholarship. Like the manner by which he has proceeded, this introduction to Walls's work is intended to spur on not just closer interaction with his scholarship, but also to encourage new endeavors and lines of inquiry.

The contributors to this volume are friends, colleagues, and, in one fashion or another, all students of Andrew Walls. That the authors come from Africa, Asia, North America, and Europe, and are all creative leaders in helping to shape an understanding of World Christianity, is simply to hint at the influence of Walls. If for John Wesley the world was his parish, for Walls the world is his classroom.

Part I, "A Man with a Large Map," provides an introduction to Andrew Walls in his role as mentor, teacher, and preacher. To open, we are privileged to share the reflections of the remarkable African theologian and church leader Kwame Bediako. I. Howard Marshall, the internationally renowned New Testament scholar, introduces us to Walls the local preacher and a hymn writer with pastoral vocation in Aberdeen and beyond. From the Akrofi-Christaller Institute for Theology, Mission, and Culture in Akropong-Akuapem, Ghana, a home in so many ways for him, Allison Howell and Maureen Iheanacho offer an account of Walls as teacher.

In the next part, "Breaking Boundaries, Building New Ways of Scholarship," we see how Walls has not simply cultivated what is known as "World Christianity," but has labored to create new institutions and approaches that nurture our understanding of what this all means. In his chapter, Wilbert Shenk introduces the narrative that enabled Walls to rethink Christian history, the myriad of activities it produced, and the challenges it offers to the academy. Brian Stanley documents one of the most significant fruits of Andrew Walls, the Centre for the Study of Christianity in the Non-Western World at the University of Edinburgh. Jon Bonk shines a light on the way Walls's ideas on both mission and World Christianity studies have reshaped their fields. Within this framing of a new way of operating, Moon-jang Lee points out, the particularity of the transmission of faith that Walls stresses should directly influence theological education and entail a holistic spirituality.

With Part III, "Themes of the Transmission of Faith," translation, conversion, and ecclesiology are placed in the foreground of Walls's scholarship. Lamin Sanneh examines the Bible in translation, and as both he and Walls have demonstrated, this has been at the heart of the expansion of the Christian movement. William Burrows, who as editor has played a crucial role in bringing the scholarship of Andrew Walls to a wider reading public, indicates the central role that conversion plays in his thought. Stephen Bevans works to connect the dots in Walls's views of the church and, not surprisingly, relates its missionary dimension.

In Part IV, three essays consider the ways in which Walls has helped to rethink an understanding of history. In her chapter, Dana Robert shows how the historiography that guides Walls flows out of a history of scholars from the past. Mark Noll suggests in his chapter ways Walls can help reframe an understanding of Christianity in American history. Michael Poon moves historical matters out more broadly and significantly, showing how Walls calls for a commitment to document what is taking place in the church within a World Christianity framework.

Africa has not only helped to shape Andrew Walls; he has helped to reframe the place of Africa's past and present within the Christian story. In Part V J. Kwabena Asamoah-Gyadu reviews the richness of this contribution. Gillian Bediako helps us see not only some of what Andrew Walls has offered others through his encouragement of scholars and scholarship in Africa, but also how Africa influenced the course of his scholarship. Africa is on the move across borders, as Jehu Hanciles makes clear, and this too is something Walls gives us eyes to see, from both historical and theological perspectives.

What does World Christianity mean for theology? For the concluding essay, we again turn to the reflections of the late Kwame Bediako, who not only offers his own unique contribution, but does so in dialogue with his friend Andrew Walls. Finally, a bibliography of the work of Andrew Walls is provided, with material written about him included as well.

Much more can be said, but together, the essays in this book tell something of the remarkable life and contributions of Andrew Walls. In countless ways, Walls has changed the theological questions we ask and the frameworks we use to understand the church and mission. His quiet and unassuming manner belies the radical challenges he represents, and yet ironically, it is through such an approach that one comes to a deeper affirmation of the mystery of Christian faith across the ages and cultures.

In *Essays in Religious Studies for Andrew Walls,* a book offered in his honor in 1986 at the University of Aberdeen, his friend and colleague Harold Turner wrote of Walls:

> Of the special virtues of his spirit, the qualities of his thought and the distinctive features of his style I will not attempt to write. If the sign of an educated man is that he can do things he has never done before, Andrew exhibits the sign and had contributed to my own education at every turn. Who knows just where this versatile assembly of great qualities will lead us next?

In the present book we find both an answer to Turner's question and yet the question, remains. Where will the wealth of gifts of Andrew Walls lead next? The answers will no doubt surprise us and, as is appropriate, foster immense gratitude, wonder, joy, and perhaps no little upturning of patterns of thought.

Let us give the last word to Charles Wesley, whose hymns and prayers we hear echoed in the vision and life of Andrew Walls:

> Closer knit to thee, our Head,
> Nourished, Lord, by thee and fed,
> Let us daily growth receive,
> More in Jesus Christ believe,
>
> Never from thy service move,
> Needful to each other prove;
> Use the grace on each bestowed,
> Tempered by the art of God.
>
> Love, like death, has all destroyed,
> Rendered all distinctions void;
> Names, and sects, and parties fall:
> Thou, O Christ, are all in all.

Part I

A MAN WITH
A LARGE MAP

1

Andrew F. Walls as Mentor

KWAME BEDIAKO

The last public event Professor Kwame Bediako attended was the launching of the Andrew F. Walls Centre for the Study of African and Asian Christianity at Liverpool Hope University in the U.K., on May 24, 2008, at which he defied considerable weakness to give a "word of greeting," which lasted thirty minutes.

Professor Walls has indicated how it really was very difficult for us to come here, but as we looked at our program it was quite clear that we are not here simply to launch a Centre; we are also here because we have been brought together by a person whose pioneering role in the field of his investigations unites all of us in such a gathering, such an event, a great delight to us all.

For our part, Gillian and I, energy permitting, planned to be here whether or not I was able to give the regular lecture, which I wasn't able to do because of the illness that has been mentioned. We planned to be here, for an event honoring our beloved professor cannot be missed. So I bring greetings from our institute, where the professor serves as a senior research professor, and I bring salutations to Liverpool Hope University for the honor that is being given these two days but especially today to Professor Andrew Walls. Many of us here, if we were asked to bring greetings as I have been asked to do, each, I'm sure, would tell their story of how Professor Walls has influenced, has shaped, has had an impact on our lives. Well, this is my story.

I thought I might hold myself accountable to a number of points I have put on paper lest in the presence of my Methodist preacher brother, I make my greetings something of a Presbyterian Charismatic sermon.

Professor Walls, I will never forget the immensely liberating impact that you made on Gillian and me in the early spring of 1975, when as students at London Bible College, now London School of Theology, together with our friend John Howell from Australia, we invited you to be the keynote speaker at the college day conference on world mission. You discussed with us the shift in the center of gravity of Christianity, with particular attention to Africa's place in Christian history. I recall that moment with the realization of the fresh power that can come on such an occasion.

The year 1975 was just five years after my personal Damascus road experience in Bordeaux, France, and my transition from atheism through my exposure to Western culture, my passing through the gates of French intellectual culture, a transition into an awareness of the living Christ and the realization that the pursuit of the intellectual life without reference to the living God and the living Christ is futile. And as I reflected on what was happening to me it occurred to me that in becoming Christian, I was becoming African again.

As I listened to Professor Walls in 1975, my next destination after Damascus became clear to me. Three years later in October 1978, I would begin my apprenticeship under Professor Walls in Aberdeen. It was for me like Clement of Alexandria discovering his teacher, Pantaenus. Clement tells us that in an environment given to much self-advertisement among some teachers, that Sicilian bee was quietly working away and hacking away at forming minds and hearts of young scholars at the Alexandrian Catechetical School. As I began my apprenticeship under Professor Walls, I learned through firsthand observation the lessons of self-sacrifice in a scholarly life. Within the not too congenial environment of a public secular university our postgraduate seminar in Aberdeen became something of a community of scholars around seasoned teachers. Many would come and encourage us, and our beloved professor certainly was one of them in those heady days in Aberdeen. Yet our program was always fragile; it could all be brought to an end through a variety of circumstances as indeed eventually it was. Still the vision has not dimmed. Working with and learning from Professor Walls would continue for Gillian and me into the development of our institution in Ghana. Initially a study center serving the church and academy but with no academic status of its own, it is now a fully autonomous and chartered institute authorized to award postgraduate degrees, the first and only private theological institution in Ghana with presidential approval for a charter.

Professor Walls has continued to act in a formal capacity recognized by our council as a senior research professor. And this continued relationship would give further opportunity for learning even more fully yet other lessons about the life of scholarship. Hearing Professor Walls expound on the Scriptures in the context of our worship sessions in Akropong and hearing him intercede for us, we have heard a servant of the Lord, a servant of the Word of God. He taught us by example, as Origen did in his time, that at the heart of the scholarly life there lay prayer and worship. The professor openly prayed for his former students who had become professors and prayed for the students of the new professors.

In a recent doctoral seminar on "Slavery, Slave Trade, and Christianity" Professor Walls worked through the dilemmas facing the Christian conscience when confronted by the practice of institutional slavery. Professor Walls demonstrated through meticulous investigation and analysis that the study of Christian history is an exercise in cross-cultural experience, entering into another person's world and so learning to discern how against all odds the hidden influences of God are carried forward in each generation. I learned that the practice of Christian scholarship involves the discernment of community through historical research, finding hidden ancestors. It could be Jonathan Edwards, it could be John Calvin, it could be Richard Baxter. These are our kinsmen, and in our own generation the practice of Christian scholarship is the nurture of a living community of scholars and much less the nurture of one's individual career. When the time came to prepare our documents for government gazetting following the approval of charter status, we asked Professor Walls, who was then with us in Ghana, for a recommendation to write into the statutes we were about to submit to the Ministry of Education. Professor Walls wrote into our objectives in his own hand these words: "To maintain a community life marked by Christian mission and service."

From Aberdeen days to date, thirty years and more, Professor Walls would always give me offprints of virtually every article he wrote. But he is author of many more books that can't be listed on paper; I am one of those books.

On this occasion we honor our beloved professor, and we celebrate his pioneer role. We also salute and congratulate Liverpool Hope University for its part in recognizing and honoring him by appropriately naming its Centre for the Study of African and Asian Christianity after him. We honor this university for doing him this honor.

Perhaps one final idea in what was meant to be a word of greeting — see I have become a preacher! One final idea for a colloquium on the significance of African and Asian Christianity: might it be symbolic that at the birth of the Savior wise men came from Asia, having recognized through their own traditions the sign of the momentous event that was completely lost on the priests and teachers of Jerusalem? Might it be symbolic that when his infant life was threatened, Africa gave him sanctuary? That event has burned its way into the Coptic memory; it is a living memory for Coptic Christians in Egypt and it is in their liturgy. Might it be significant and symbolic that when the time came for him to die for the salvation of the world, Africa shared his burden by carrying his cross?

What might these signs mean as we consider and seek to reassess the significance of African and Asian Christianity in Christian history? May it be that in the context of a new Christian world in which the heartlands of the faith are yet again relocated in the South, as they were in the formative centuries of Christian history, that it may become more readily recognized, and recognized afresh that in fact they brought the Good News from South to North. May the Andrew Walls Centre for the Study of African and Asian Christianity at Liverpool Hope University flourish. Oh, may it flourish, flourish in ways that we may not yet imagine today. May the good hand of the Lord of Christian history, sovereign over history, be upon the Centre, upon the university, and upon all of us who feel a part of it and sense we are participants in that history.

Thank you very much.

2

Andrew F. Walls,
Methodist Local Preacher and Hymn Writer

I. HOWARD MARSHALL

As a friend who knows him well, I offer this brief comment on Andrew's activities as a preacher — and more.

Andrew Walls came to reside in Aberdeen in 1966. He was already since 1953 a Methodist "Local Preacher" — this is the Methodist nomenclature for those who would be called lay preachers or readers in some other denominations, and it is based on the distinction between so-called "itinerant" full-time ministers who move from one appointment to another every so many years and the local people who take their share in leading services and preaching while continuing their secular callings. He was therefore expected to play his part with the rest of the preachers in the Circuit in taking Sunday services on a regular basis.

The Circuit consists of nine (now eight) congregations, one in Aberdeen, and the others scattered along the northeast coast of Scotland from Peterhead in the east to Buckie further west. All of these preaching places are like points on the very rough arc of a circle with its center in Aberdeen, and the length of the radii varied from thirty-eight to sixty-two miles. So, unless it is in Aberdeen, a Sunday morning appointment usually means setting out by car somewhere around 9:00 a.m. At first, there were some places with afternoon and/or evening services, and so one might be out all day, not getting back home till about 9:00 p.m. in the evening. Preachers can expect to be "planned" about one Sunday per month or more. Sometimes two or three might all be planned simultaneously in different congregations, and if so they endeavor to travel in one carload. Several of the preaching places are fairly close together, so this is a convenient arrangement. One snag can be the weather in wintertime; some Sundays between December and March can be quite adventurous trips through the snow, but this danger has not been so common in recent years; with global "warming" the weather up here may become more severe.

11

Andrew undertook these duties with enthusiasm. The congregations outside Aberdeen are largely of fisherfolk (not quite so much in recent years with the decline of the industry); they owed their origins to the travels of John Wesley himself, and then gained fresh life from the 1859 revival and a small-scale revival in the area in the 1920s. Andrew is on their wavelength with his carefully prepared expositions of Scripture; his sermons always take the form of a biblical text carefully explained and applied in a way that is thoughtful and yet simple and comprehensible. There is never any attempt to lecture the congregation or give a display of scholarship. There is, needless to say, a depth of understanding in them that equally appeals to the more educated and theologically literate members of the congregations. Sometimes in Aberdeen he may include a hymn of his own composition alongside the traditional hymnody, which is generally in the Wesley-Watts tradition.

One of the side-blessings of all this, of course, for the rest of us is sharing the drive to Cullen or Banff or wherever with Andrew in the car and enjoying his stimulating conversation. His range of knowledge of the past and the present is utterly encyclopedic and available on instant recall. At first he naturally drove himself, and the journeys could be memorable for his passengers; there was the Sunday evening, for example, when the car was stuck in top gear and he did not dare stop anywhere, not even for traffic lights and halt (stop) signs, lest the car would not start again. In later years he has no longer been able to drive himself because of his poorer eyesight and has to be a passenger with others. Or he would take the bus. He bought a small house in Portessie to be a kind of holiday retreat, and this has enabled him to spend the occasional weekend with Doreen (who sadly passed away on October 11, 2009) on the coast.

And he is still doing it at a point when other people might cut down on their activities, and he has done it at times when he has literally arrived back in Aberdeen from Ghana on Saturday, preached on Sunday and then gone off on Monday (desperately early in the morning) to the United States or perhaps just to Edinburgh!

He is not just a preacher. He also is a hymn-writer, producing verses that have a certain amount of local color and therefore not always easily adaptable for use outside their local Aberdeen setting. Two examples show his hymn-writing skills.

FLIGHT INTO EGYPT

When first I learned what treasure lay in me
How my heart leapt! I magnified the Lord.
I cried aloud how blest it was to be
His servant. Never occurred
The thought of those rampaging soldiers sent
To pillage my treasure, rifle and destroy,
Licensed to smash and trample as they went
Pour spite and terror till they kill my boy —
O who could hate so, send them to such feats

O Lord, drag down the mighty from their seats!
How close behind, I wonder, are they now

At every crossing how I dread
The sight of armour. And on this rocky causeway, how
The poor child's jolted, even in his bed.
He's cold, too. But he's with me. My poor friends,
Martha, Hannah, Ruth in Bethlehem,
They all have lost their babies to the fiends.
What can I say to them

Lord, comfort weeping Rachel. King of kings,
When will you feed the hungry with good things

The border post at last. The sentry, half asleep,
Just nods us through. What does he care

How dark it is. How strangely deep
The silence, and how bare
The whole terrain. How long must we live here
How long this exile last

And yet the fear, the devastating fear
Of close pursuit is past.
Though in an alien land we have escaped the sword.
My child is safe. I magnify the Lord.

Andrew F. Walls © 1999

MAGNIFICAT (John Brown's Body)

With all my heart I praise the Lord, I've got to shout and sing!
Soon all will see he rescues me from every evil thing,
The helpless insignificant are friends of God the King,
Make great the name of God!

The Lord has done great things for me, and holy is his name!
In every generation he has always been the same,
He never lets his people down, nor lets them take the blame,
Make great the name of God!

Down from their mighty thrones he drags the governments and kings,
And those who have too much in life to emptiness he brings,
While those who are in want will get abundance of good things.
Make great the name of God!

He stretches out his mighty arm and scatters all the proud,
Their schemes and plans and policies will all be disallowed,
But poor downtrodden nobodies have cause to shout aloud,
Make great the name of God!

The God who keeps his promises, the God who won't forget,
The God who picked out Abraham remembers even yet,
The God of all poor nobodies will fight for his own set,
Make great the name of God!

Andrew F. Walls © 1989–90

One other aspect of his activity could be mentioned here also: his interest in politics. He was the unsuccessful Labour candidate for a parliamentary seat in Banffshire in 1970: the seat was a "safe" one for another party, but somebody had to be prepared to take up all the chores of a lost cause for the sake of the party, and Andrew did it because nobody else would. He served on the Aberdeen City Council and was convener of the committee that looked after museums and the art gallery. There was no need for him to do so, but with two or three friends he produced a series of "Lunchbreaks" at the Gallery where they performed in verse and prose readings and musical items on various themes. Andrew himself took part under the nom de plume of Finlay Anderson, and it was he himself who compiled the programs, based on his own omnivorous reading and displaying his sense of humor. So, for example, in January 1981 the theme was "The happiest days of your life" with readings about school and schoolteachers from such as John Betjeman, Charlotte Bronte, Elizabeth Barrett Browning, Henry Cockburn, Charles Dickens, Kenneth Grahame, Joyce Grenfell, and Sir Henry Newbolt. On another occasion the theme " 'The cup that cheers' — an anthology of tea-totalitarianism" included items composed by Andrew himself.

3

Andrew F. Walls as Teacher in Africa

ALLISON HOWELL AND MAUREEN IHEANACHO

Introduction

Known simply as Professor Walls by most of his students, Andrew Walls has been a teacher for most of his adult life. This demanding but rewarding work has taken him to many countries throughout the world. It has been the periods of teaching in Africa, however, that have most influenced the content and style of his teaching, resulting in directional changes in his scholarship.

Beginning in Sierra Leone in 1957, he taught church history at Fourah Bay College. It was here that he gained a new understanding of what was happening in the Christian faith in Africa. More significantly, it was also here that the story of Walls's own life was rewritten.[1] In 1962, he moved on to Nigeria to start the new Department of Religion at the University of Nigeria, Nsukka. The impact of this African experience would have profound implications not only for Walls's own life by defining his calling to the vocation of teaching in the West, but also for the teaching of Religious Studies in other Western universities.[2] Not surprisingly, back in Scotland, the period of his teaching at the University of Aberdeen (1966–85) culminated in the establishment of the Centre for the Study of Christianity in the Non-Western World (CSCNWW), which subsequently moved to the University of Edinburgh by 1986.[3]

The broad areas of Walls's teaching have been theology, mission, and church history. His African experience led him to reconfigure the teaching of church history as Christian history, for he realized that the content of the church history course at the time imposed serious limitations with its traditional emphases on Western Protestant church history. The rich depth

---

1. Andrew F. Walls, "Introduction," in *The Missionary Movement in Christian Faith: Studies in the Transmission of Faith* (Maryknoll, N.Y.: Orbis Books, 1991), xiii.

2. Ibid., xiii–xiv.

3. David Kerr, "Mission Studies in Edinburgh," in BIAMS (British and Irish Association for Mission Studies), *Newsletter*, no. 23 (2004): 2.

of Walls's long and fruitful career of more than half a century defies precise delineation. More of a practicing than a professional theologian, it is his extensive and insightful interpretation of Christian history that distinguishes him among his peers as a historian of religions and of Christian mission.[4]

Although Andrew Walls has taught in scores of public universities and institutions of ministerial training in many countries of the world, the focus of this chapter is his teaching role at the Akrofi-Christaller Institute of Theology, Mission, and Culture (ACI) in Akropong-Akuapem, Ghana. We are well aware that ACI may appear too narrow a representative sample of those institutions. Yet in many ways, it paradigmatically embodies his approach to teaching as a vocation, and as a calling. Furthermore, Walls's teaching at ACI represents for him a way of staying at the cutting edge of the emerging trends in an increasingly Christian Africa. This is not the mere reflection of an Africanist attitude, but because, as Walls has acknowledged,

> it is equally true that if you want to know something about Christianity, you must know something about Africa. The outstanding feature of twentieth-century religion is the southward swing of the Christian center of gravity which has made Christianity more a non-Western than a Western religion, as it has lost its hold on Europe and spread rapidly in Africa and the other southern continents.[5]

Teaching as a Way to Get Students "on Fire"

Andrew Walls has taught at all levels of university education. The experience includes sometimes having to mark volumes of assignments and examination scripts, as well as teaching numbers of students, many of whom show little commitment to or interest in the subject area. For many university teachers, it is an experience more to be endured than enjoyed, and for that reason, they avoid teaching fresh university students, if possible. However, unlike many of his university colleagues who tend to avoid first-year classes and leave them to their less experienced or younger colleagues, Walls's greatest enjoyment has come from teaching first-year undergraduate classes. He knows that in the first year, many students usually would choose a subject such as "Religious Studies 101" or "Introduction to Christian History"

---

4. Walls, "Introduction," in *The Missionary Movement*, xv.

5. Andrew F. Walls, "Of Ivory Towers and Ashrams: Some Reflections on Theological Scholarship in Africa," *Journal of African Christian Thought* 3, no. 1 (2000): 1. Even though it has been almost a decade since Walls's article, many in Africa continue to embrace Christianity.

without any real intention of pursuing that particular field of study. Conversely, Walls's perspective is that the best time to catch the interest of the students who have drifted into those subject areas and "get them on fire" is in the first year. Andrew Walls loves teaching, and his students soon realize this, especially those who, like his first-year university students, begin to sparkle with the confidence of new knowledge and understanding.

Walls's approach with his first-year undergraduate students has been successfully applied to other categories of "new" students. He has demonstrated this capacity to "get them on fire" in every institution where he has taught. Several decades since the 1950s, his ability to "catch their interest" has not waned, and he continues to positively influence people to move into new subject areas or to consider research on new aspects of any particular subject area. At the Akrofi-Christaller Institute, where Andrew Walls teaches annually, the same objective is integral to his teaching as he seeks to get his graduate students "on fire." Not surprisingly, many of them have found themselves interested in aspects of Christian history or in issues of Gospel and culture that they did not even know existed before they arrived at the Institute! All because they attended Walls's lectures or seminars, or read some of his writings.

Teaching through Curriculum Development

Andrew Walls's teaching involvement at ACI commenced in September 1997 as a member of the faculty for the Centre's newly designed M.Th. program in African Christianity.[6] In its foundational years, the program was offered conjointly with the University of Natal (now KwaZulu-Natal) which awarded the degrees. Andrew Walls's role was vital in the way he skilfully guided discussions on the development of curricula, academic procedures, and organizational matters, with his suggestions providing the much-needed momentum. His foresight and commitment to the program received affirmation many years later in the award of a presidential charter to ACI in 2006, making it possible for the Institute to award its own degrees.

Walls's role did not end with his participation and leadership in curriculum design; he subsequently taught the core course, "Aspects of World Christian History." A second core course, "Studies in Gospel and Culture," was co-taught with the founding director of the Centre, the late Kwame

---

6. At the time, ACI was known as the Akrofi-Christaller Memorial Center for Mission Research and Applied Theology (ACMC).

Bediako, a former student, friend, and colleague of Walls. As the program progressed, Andrew Walls also co-taught, again with Bediako, the elective courses "Early African Christianity" and "The Bible in African Christianity." The latter course was introduced with the commencement of Certificate and Diploma programs for students of the Summer Institute of Linguistics (SIL).

Preparing to Teach

One can be forgiven for thinking that with so many years' experience and the knowledge of global developments in his preferred subject areas, Andrew Walls would not need to prepare his lectures. Yet hardly any lecture of his takes place without adequate preparation. Take, for instance, the course "Aspects of World Christian History," which he has taught now for more than a decade. It does not matter how many times he may have previously taught the material. Anyone sitting through the course a number of times would consistently discover new elements or aspects, and fresh perspectives. There is no sense of déjà vu or the boredom of hearing the same material repeated or rehashed. Often, a completely new perspective is introduced.

This is because every year Andrew Walls revises his lectures to reflect fresh thinking and reflection, especially taking into account any current developments in the subject area. He lugs his heavy hand luggage all the way to Ghana, carrying his precious handwritten notes, gleaned from years of research and continually updated. Even if the lectures are prepared from his older notes, carefully stored in well-traveled and worn folders, Walls would always rework the material from new insights he has gained in between visits. If the material had already been published since the last time it was presented in lecture form, he would produce completely new material. As he often would say, the students can always read the old material in its published form. That is the distinction he makes between a lecture (with updated and current information) and a book or an article (already dated and permanently set in time).

That probably explains why, regardless of the many pressures and demands on him, Andrew Walls would never resort to reading extensive texts of books to his students during the lecture, especially not his own books. Nor, unlike some university professors, would he cite passages from other writers while passing them off as his own work. Any significant or noteworthy comment or observation is extracted, written out, and appropriately referenced within the lecture. He believes that students should learn to enter the minds of those who belong to the periods they study. Accordingly, most of his quotations are taken directly from the persons under study — the primary sources — and not from others' comments about them or references to the period. Since he considers primary sources the vital indicators of mission activity, he would rather cite documents from the specific periods.

An undeniably familiar sight in Akropong is that of Walls in his office, working late into the night, writing fresh notes for the next day's lectures while sipping his tea. Yet these nights of long and intense preparation are not times of isolation, for work never becomes an excuse to shut the door on divine interruptions. Whoever comes to see him, whether by appointment or not, is welcome. Andrew Walls would call out a greeting or a welcome and put his pen down almost gratefully, rise from his seat, move around from behind his desk, pull up another chair, and sit expectantly facing his guest. No desk is allowed to separate him from his visitor. Not that it can, in any case.

Teaching through Lectures

Andrew Walls's distinct teaching style shows him to be a storyteller par excellence. He structures most of his lectures by initially providing the background to the subject he is teaching on, or by linking it with a previous lecture. This enables students to locate themselves in the period of the subject and to follow the time line as well. He would then "tell the story" while highlighting the important features that emerge from the narrative.

The potential of this storytelling approach lies in the impact of the mind's direct engagement with the narrative. Walls's presentation of the material and poignant comments guide the students in their own enquiry and analysis. He encourages his students to discuss the material he presents and to ask questions, even if the questions seem unrelated to the subject matter. In true *magisterial* style, he is able to establish the hidden links with the subject matter. However, woe betide the Ph.D. student who sits complacently in Walls's two-hour class arms folded, not taking a single note. Yet should that arrogant student ask a question that reveals his inattentiveness, Walls will rebuke, albeit briefly and graciously. In Walls's incarnational style of teaching, the break period would be spent in deep reflection, seeking ways to resolve the problem of the student's lack of focus. At the start of the next lecture, the content of the lecture series may well be set aside while Walls expounds on the purpose of a Ph.D. as an apprenticeship for the scholarly life: it is not for acquiring status in the community or the church. His own commitment to this vocation is modeled in the way he applies himself to his teaching.

Even in his teaching, Walls is not afraid to be vulnerable, although he would not use any inconvenience to his person as an excuse for shoddiness. Whatever the group dynamics, he is able to guide his audience along the right paths like the experienced shepherd that he is. Teaching a class of graduate students of different nationalities, Walls's attitude is that "everyone is a teacher and everyone a student."[7] Both Walls and his students have the role to "uncover not only their own, but one another's Christian history."[8] To the nervous and insecure students, therefore, he gives compassionate attention and encouragement, a virtue that is lacking in many erudite scholars in our world. In affirming the brilliant but cocksure students, he does not allow them to monopolize the discussions or suppress the other students with their knowledge.

It is perhaps Walls's affectionate respect for Africa that is most clearly communicated in his teaching at ACI. His stance is that teaching "African Christianity" is not so much teaching African students to be better Christians as it is tracing together with African brothers and sisters the footsteps of the God of history and mission in their part of the world.

Always humble and unafraid to admit that he does not know everything, Walls once confided to his World Christian History class that earlier on in his own scholarship, he made the decision to learn Old Norse in order to study the pre-Christian primal religions in Europe. Not one to miss a good learning opportunity, he took advantage of having colleagues in Syriac studies to check his own information in that field. His earnestness yields dividends as a modest knowledge of Syriac and Old Norse was added to Latin and Greek, a working knowledge of French, and just enough of two African languages (Igbo and Krio) to be able to "connect" with co-pilgrims of the Christian faith from Nigeria and Sierra Leone respectively. His conviction is that Christian scholarship cannot be divorced from Christian mission since both are valid responses to the call of Christ by his followers.

Since Andrew Walls does not use PowerPoint presentations in his teaching, it is easy to conclude that he is very much of the old school. "It

---

7. Walls, "Introduction," xvi.
8. Ibid.

[PowerPoint] takes away from a lecture," he once remarked, when asked his view on the use of PowerPoint presentations in lectures. In other words, it limits rather than enhances the content of a lecture. Students either become preoccupied with copying what appears on the slides or else cease all note-taking, while hoping for the eventual "hand-out" of printed copies of the slides. As a result, they do not stay focused on the ensuing discussions nor are they able to engage with the lecture material.

So he would rather use conventional visual aids, such as maps, which he brings along from Aberdeen. The different shades of scotch tape and thumbtack piercings on the maps evidence their repeated use over the years. Wide sweeps of either hand indicating the movement of Christianity and mission activity "from here...to here...and over here" require alertness and close attention from the students. Thus, he is able to demonstrate that the global nature of Christianity in the twentieth century was not a recent phenomenon, but already was a feature of the sixth century.

Occasionally Walls would take students through a piece of interactive reading of primary source documents, explaining the segments as he goes along. This exercise, by no means a substitute for an unprepared lecture, is a vital component of his teaching and is used to encourage students to enter into the spirit of the period. Otherwise, as Walls insists, it is impossible, for instance, for them to understand the thinking of Al-lo-pen[9] or Matteo Ricci[10] in their respective periods in China. Following their adept guide, Walls's students would thus attempt to enter into the Celtic world of Patrick speaking through his *Confession,* or that of King Clovis's struggles with conversion through the narrative of Gregory of Tours,[11] or that of an indignant Father António Montesinos denouncing his congregation for their "cruel and horrible slavery" of the Indians of South America.[12]

It is possible to discern the mission of God through Andrew Walls's lectures. In the course "Aspects of World Christian History," for instance, students are usually amazed at the vast expanse of lands that feature in Walls's intellectual landscape. His lectures demonstrate a deep knowledge and understanding of the Christian faith and mission in countries with

---

9. John Foster, *The Church of the T'ang Dynasty* (London: SPCK, 1939), 138.

10. Matthew Ricci, *China in the 16th Century: The Journals of Matthew Ricci 1583–1610,* trans. Louis J. Gallagher Jr. (New York: Random House, 1992).

11. Gregory of Tours, *The History of the Franks,* trans. Lewis Thorpe (Baltimore: Penguin, 1974), 2:20–22.

12. Bartolomé de Las Casas, *História de las Índias,* vol. 2, 441–42 of *Latin American Civilization: History and Society, 1492 to the Present,* 7th ed. trans. and ed. Benjamin Keen (Boulder, Colo.: Westview Press, 2000), 65–67.

sometimes unpronounceable names and whose locations on the atlas would require an entire geography lecture! Yet even though understanding of the material may come sometimes rather slowly, Walls's lectures are far from drab. History, linguistics, religions, Scripture, poetry, literature, and current events are all ingredients of the rich experience of his lectures, like the rain that cleanses the land of dust and debris.

Teaching by Inclusion

At the graduate level (M.Th. and Ph.D.), much of Walls's teaching is done through seminars, workshops, and colloquia. Rather than teaching the same course every year, Walls has preferred this mode of teaching in his "active" retirement. If students' minds are not stretched enough in Walls's lectures, the seminars stretch them even further. His choice of topics is influenced not only by the immediate needs of an institution, but equally by an attempt to reflect current events and trends. His view of teaching is that of a shared experience of learners together on a journey. This is expressed in his inclusion of others in teaching seminars, such as the seminar he led at the Institute on "Working with Archives" (2005) and a symposium on "Christianity, Slavery, and the Slave Trade" (2007). In seminars where he gives the plenary papers, his selection of study documents aims to encourage participants to reflect deeply on rather disturbing issues. One such seminar series in 2005 was on "Jews, Christians, and Muslims." Long-held and sometimes inaccurate notions about Protestant mission history were shattered when Walls examined the challenge of "Understanding the Western Missionary Movement" (2006). Equally stimulating was the experience of his audience when Walls expanded on the theme of "Mission in Scholarship: Scholarship in Mission: Some Passages of Christian Intellectual History" (2006). For in Walls's perspective, there is no contradiction or dichotomy between mission and scholarship.

Teaching through "Readings in Greek"

It is only natural to expect rest and recuperation at the end of a long day of teaching, reading, marking students' essays, and meeting with various members of the ACI community. Strangely though, rest hardly features in Andrew Walls's visits to the Akrofi-Christaller Institute. Apart from the regular lectures and seminars, he always offers students the opportunity to "read Greek" with him for an hour before supper. The Greek class sits outside in the fading sunset, which compensates for the darkened classroom when the power supply is interrupted. The level of proficiency in Greek does not matter as interested students and faculty cluster around Walls, each armed with a copy of the Greek New Testament. He would encourage them to take turns reading the study passage out loud. He would usually explain the grammar and meaning of words and expressions as the group slowly progresses through a segment of John's Gospel. Students with more advanced Greek may find themselves studying the Septuagint together, while working through a similar process.

Teaching through Mentoring Relationships

Some of the most difficult aspects of a teacher's work include marking written assignments and grading term papers. They form part of a process of giving feedback to students. Like any other senior academic, Walls knows well the constraints of reading and marking students' papers. A multitude of commitments and extensive travel usually push these aspects of his teaching down the order of priorities. This is by no means intentional, and he would profusely apologize to students who come to him to enquire about papers submitted to him. For Walls, marking a student's paper is as much a part of the discipline of teaching and mentoring as his face-to-face teaching. However, when he is at the Akrofi-Christaller Institute, it is not unusual to find Andrew Walls reading students' papers, or even a dissertation or thesis in his spare time. Nor is this a perfunctory exercise, for papers are not returned with simply a mark or grade on them. On the contrary, he would make notes throughout the paper and, depending on the quality of the submitted work, comment on the strengths and weaknesses of the paper, as well as indicate areas where the paper could be improved.

Regardless of the frustrations of reading a poorly written or presented paper, Andrew Walls's gentle but firm approach in pointing out its weaknesses ensures that the student is neither disgraced nor shamed. Students may thus emerge from such meetings feeling they have to work harder but at the same time grateful for a renewed sense of direction.

Walls is respected and loved by all his students. They appreciate his generous investment in their lives. They are grateful for his listening ear when he assumes his characteristic head-in-the-hand or bowed-head pose, as well as his readiness to offer prayerful counsel and willingness to adjust his schedule to read that thesis chapter, journal article, or paragraph of creative writing.

Most of all, Walls is carried in the hearts of his students in thankful appreciation for his friendship — a friendship which for many has transcended the confines of the classroom and traversed many cultural frontiers and denominational boundaries in a bond of continuing fellowship and service to their one Lord and Master, Jesus Christ.

Teaching through Communal Participation: Mission in Context

That self-giving generosity that marks Andrew Walls's relationship with both his students and colleagues also undergirds his scholarship and reflects his conviction that the God of mission meets us in community. Since there can be no community without participation, Walls sees his participation in the ACI community as part of his own mission to Africa and in Africa. God continues to fulfill promises he made back in those early years of the late 1950s and early 1960s in Sierra Leone and Nigeria. We, at ACI, are grateful for the privilege of having Andrew Walls as a valued member of our community. He is more than a staff member: he is teacher, mentor, exemplar, team leader, friend, counsellor, adviser, guide, co-pilgrim, father, and brother.[13] He is one of us, and he is not ashamed of that.

By far Andrew Walls's greatest impact has been in his calling to Christian scholarship as a layperson. He holds his own as a lay preacher and scholar simply because he understands his calling, first as a follower of Christ and second as a Christian scholar. He believes that he is called by Christ, to Christ, and for Christ, for service through scholarship. It is in this understanding of the superior calling of Christ that sacrifices, including those related to his commitment to ACI, are borne graciously. It is perhaps this paradox of being an active participant in the church without being a church "politician" that allows him room for objectivity. He is able to maintain a "distance" from the church while at the same time being able to clearly discern the emerging currents and trends of Christianity. In other words, Walls maximized the advantage he saw in not "pontificating" but in rather simply observing what is going on.[14]

---

13. Cf. Staff and students of Akrofi-Christaller Institute of Theology, Mission and Culture, "In Appreciation of Andrew F. Walls," *Journal of African Christian Thought* 9, no. 2 (2006): 51–55.

14. Walls, "Introduction," xiii.

Invariably, Andrew Walls's definition of the community of the faithful extends beyond the Institute. One constant companion to Akropong is his small black Twi Bible. It follows him to the daily weekday morning devotions at ACI and to the Sunday forenoon service at the Presbyterian Christ Church, Akropong. Usually and whenever flight bookings allow, Walls arranges to arrive on a Saturday so that he can attend the Sunday service the next day. We always marvel at how those Sunday services, even though mostly conducted in Twi, seem to enable as well as sustain his conversations with various persons in between visits. They also provide him with a few more brushstrokes to apply to the canvas of mission in context.

Andrew Walls would always try out his modest Twi vocabulary and does not mind the laughter caused by his mispronunciations. Understandably, his primary mission is not to impress anyone with native proficiency. His desire is rather to communicate the essential humanity that says, "I am with you here and now, and I want to be able to share in your experience of God's mission in His world." His empathy goes beyond the recommended niceties taught to most Western missionaries on how to relate to the "natives." More than anything else, Walls desires to connect with his interlocutor and to put the other person at ease. He is always striving for that possibility of communing in the things that make them both human. In this, he shares in the experience of thousands of other missionaries, having to feel many times

> ...the need to speak someone else's language, the consciousness of doing it badly or even laughably, being unsure of etiquette, constant fear of giving unintended offence, realization of the vast depth and complexity of another community's traditions and history, and thus identity.[15]

Thus, each "laughable" incident becomes for Walls an opportunity to live on terms set by his host, whether they affect people or events. Of course, an anecdote or snippet would usually follow to relate how another "stranger" in history responded to a similar situation. Whether it is the very abridged story of a Robert de Nobili professing to be an "Italian Brahmin,"[16] or a Yoruba-speaking Ajayi Crowther, writing the first book in Igbo![17] Sometimes

---

15. Andrew F. Walls, "Christianity in the Non-Western World," in *The Cross-Cultural Process in Christian History: Studies in the Transmission and Appropriation of Faith,* ed. Andrew F. Walls (Maryknoll, N.Y.: Orbis Books, 2002), 41.

16. Robert de Nobili, "A Letter of Fr. Robert de Nobili to Pope Paul V," *Indian Church History Review* 2, no. 2 (1968): 85.

17. Andrew F. Walls, "Samuel Ajayi Crowther (1807–1891): Patterns of African Christianity in the Nineteenth Century," in *The Cross-Cultural Process in Christian History* (Maryknoll, N.Y.: Orbis Books, 2002), 161.

Walls's quips at himself would lead his hearers or interlocutors to unconsciously reflect on their own reactions to similar linguistic embarrassments. One mark of Walls's teaching style is undoubtedly his ability, or perhaps willingness, to laugh at himself while allowing others to learn vital lessons through his disconcertment.

Take, for instance, the red palm oil stains that often would appear on his shirt after a good lunch of his favorite Ghanaian dish of *fufu* and chicken light soup specially served up for him at the Institute's cafeteria. "Now Victoria [the staff person in charge] knows how much I enjoyed my lunch!" he says without the slightest tinge of self-consciousness. He chooses to compliment both the person and all the consideration that has gone into preparing such a treat for him. Andrew Walls would rather make an exception to his no-lunch policy and eat all his *fufu,* even if he has to struggle to keep both himself and his students awake during the afternoon lecture sessions. Again, he is the first to admit his fallibility in a standard joke with students: "I have even gone to sleep in my own lectures!"

On a more serious note, though, it must be said that mealtimes provide Walls with ample opportunities for continuing those life-transforming conversations and explorations into new subject areas often launched in class. They may take the form of his own answers to students' questions or their outspoken self-probing shared in the confidence of his reliable guidance. Whatever the topic of conversation, mealtimes become the crucibles of crucial decisions and choices that sooner or later are reflected in the topics of essays, the titles of dissertations and theses, or even more enduringly, in a response to the call to scholarship. Indeed, many of Walls's students discover that in whatever field of endeavor they find themselves after their studies, their understanding of mission has been honed by his mentoring influence as they have responded to their own calling to Christian mission.

Teaching about Life by Sharing Life

Teaching for Andrew Walls thus takes place everywhere: in the formal setting of the lecture room but also in the informal classroom of life in the community, wherever that might be. Lessons abound when life touches life. The mission of scholarship is not divorced from the daily challenges that confront us in life. Whether he is reminiscing in lines from George Herbert or recalling a couplet from Justin's *Dialogue with Trypho,* praying for coherence in a student's thesis chapter or recommending a visit to the specific archives that hold the key to a dissertation topic, Walls's incarnational teaching has touched and enriched many lives on the African continent.

As far as he is concerned, it is, indeed, in these mundane yet significant snapshots of life that we recognize that Jesus Christ is "at home" in all our cultures. That is to say that Christ can live within our particular social, linguistic, and cultural contexts, as Walls insists, "in the persons of his followers, as thoroughly at home as he once did in the culture of first-century Jewish Palestine."[18] One feature of work and study at ACI is its multicultural representation despite the Institute's location in Akropong, Ghana. In fact, this multicultural distinctive of the community ensures that the Gospel is always confronting our various cultures and forcing us to think as a community. Therefore, in Walls's view, it is vital that we all determine to be perpetual students of life, not in its abstracted form, but in true discipleship and service. He demonstrates this himself and would never allow anyone to do for him what he believes he can manage himself: he wants to carry his heavy hand luggage, he will always wipe the white board clean at the end of every lecture, and, unlike many "great men of God" on the continent, Walls insists on carrying his books and papers himself! His standard response is, "That's very kind of you, but I think I can manage. Thank you very much."

It is not difficult to see how Andrew Walls's painstaking involvement in both the work and life of his students inspires in them the kind of confidence that enables them to believe in themselves. One never knows how he is able to find out about those family difficulties and ministry challenges that plague the students' minds. Yet he does know and takes all that into consideration, often without the students' themselves either realizing that he knows or that the anxieties caused by their personal struggles are discernible in their academic performance.

Understanding the Vision That Informs Andrew Walls's Teaching

Although conscious of fulfilling the present urgent need for theological formation on the African continent, Walls's perspective has an eschatological dimension. Mission, like Christian history and theological scholarship, is

---

18. Andrew F. Walls, "The Translation Principle in Christian History," in *The Missionary Movement in Christian Faith: Studies in the Transmission of Faith* (Maryknoll, N.Y.: Orbis Books, 1991), 29.

neither the simple means of livelihood nor its destination. They are only parts of the same continuing story of conversion and redemption. So Walls's Christian vocation is apparent not only in his World Christian History classes, but also constitutes for him and for his students the preparation for a future culmination when "we live with the Lord in love and peace forever and ever!" This is not a fairy tale, but the true story of a promise fulfilled.

Andrew Walls believes that even when all appears to be inert and silent, like the grain of mustard seed in the soil, something is happening. The fact that it is not (yet) visible does not mean that nothing is happening. It is reminiscent of the stream running through cracks in the rocks and underground, weaving through thick vegetation and appearing in the valley as a river or on the mountainside as a waterfall. Although initially hidden from sight, it is always moving, persisting in its flowing journey. The stream is never the same: gathering whatever it finds along the way, washing, cleansing, swelling here and trickling there. The life-giving water with its vital essence appears to be flowing forward, but in reality it is flowing back to its Source of everlasting life.

It is that eschatological vision that marks Walls's teaching. He sees beyond the confused questions and faltering answers of his students and guides them to the crack in the wall through which they can see just a sliver of the light that shines outside. He teaches them to listen for the sound of the stream. He urges on their intellectual curiosity to want to see more and, in the process — why not? — to also enjoy the warmth of the sunshine out there or catch the drops of water. Even the shadows tell us something about the brightness of the sun, about those who have no way of sheltering from its scorching heat, about the acute dryness of thirst at high noon, and about the unbearable bite of the burning, sandy ground on bare feet. Similarly, the wetness of the soil and vegetation under our feet tells us that we are close to a body of water.

Conclusion: Teaching as Discipleship

It is clear that Walls does not consider teaching as a mere transmission of facts and information or the explanation of things past. Scholarship — Christian scholarship — is essentially about the healing of the nations — the various nations represented by the students (and staff) of ACI in his formal and informal classes. It is not the quest for knowledge for its own sake or the desire to acquire degrees and paper qualifications and prestige. The scholarly vocation is about knowledge that leads to faith and affects the understanding of one's calling. In Walls's consideration, because it involves discipleship, it is serious business. In short, scholarship is a matter of life and death.

If Christian scholarship is understood in terms of discipleship, then it is possible to see that it is no different from ministry. The "secular" work of teaching is a sacred calling after all. In other words, scholarship is ministry, at least, as modeled by Andrew Walls. Scholarship is not simply the mission of teaching, writing, and sharing knowledge. It "follows Christian mission and derives from Christian mission."[19] Thus, scholarship *is* mission, and Christian scholarship is Christian mission, because it is in the service of the Gospel of Jesus Christ and not of individuals. Walls's model of scholarship is a means of "*discipling* the nations"[20] as his students are equipped for mission to and in their countries. He invites us to share in his hope for Africa as, indeed, for the rest of the world when he states that

> ... there is a need for scholarship to be perceived and lived as a Chris-tian vocation, and for scholarship to develop in the service of mission and, indeed, as a component of mission. Vocation implies dedication to many years of intense, scrupulous, all-consuming toil in research and teaching. Scholarship as a vocation requires passionate commitment. It is not a hobby or a job but a life-long occupation.[21]

Our affirmative response to Walls's invitation may well lead us to the enrich-ing discovery of our own calling. And we may get there through very rough roads. After all, "Theology is always a hazardous business!"[22]

---

19. Andrew F. Walls, "Christian Scholarship in Africa in the Twenty-First Century," *Journal of African Christian Thought* 4, no. 2 (2001): 44.

20. Cf. Andrew F. Walls, "The Translation Principle in Christian History" in *The Missionary Movement*, nn. 3, 27; 48–51. Note Walls's careful distinction between the making of human disciples and the task of "making disciples of all nations."

21. Andrew F. Walls, "Scholarship, Mission and Globalization: Some Reflections on the Christian Scholarly Vocation in Africa," *Journal of African Christian Thought* 9, no. 2 (2006): 37.

22. Walls, *The Cross-Cultural Process in Christian History*, 45.

Part II

BREAKING BOUNDARIES, BUILDING NEW WAYS OF SCHOLARSHIP

4

Challenging the Academy,
Breaking Barriers

WILBERT R. SHENK

Some years ago a seasoned academic dean remarked, with evident resignation, "The one thing that has not changed in two hundred years is the theological curriculum." Schleiermacher's syllabus has cast a long shadow indeed and the modern theological program has proved to be "a mighty fortress." Only the foolhardy, or perchance the doughty iconoclast, has dared to plot and carry out attacks on such an impregnable institution. Here I shall attempt to show that Andrew Finlay Walls has worked doggedly and imaginatively for such reform, convinced that theological education has the potential to play a constructive role in the contemporary world Christian movement provided it shakes off its antiquated habits of thought and embraces the new reality.

My introduction to Andrew Walls came about in what at first appeared to be pleasant but unremarkable circumstances. In retrospect, I came to realize that it was accompanied by portents and signs of things to come. In October 1965 I paid my first visit to Nigeria for the purpose of meeting Mennonite Mission field staff for whom I had recently become administratively responsible. I spent a weekend in Enugu, Eastern Nigeria, with colleagues. They announced that on Sunday we would go to Nsukka for worship and to meet friends at the university.

Upon arrival at Nsukka we went directly to the worship service that was held in the large campus auditorium. It was a dazzling sight with hundreds of women decked out in their enormous colorful head scarves. The congregation was fully engaged in worship. I was told that this was a significant occasion inasmuch as the service was being conducted for the first time according to the liturgy prepared for the much anticipated union of Anglicans, Methodists, and Presbyterians. Alas, after years of preparation those negotiations were to break down a few months later, aborting formation of the United Church of Nigeria.

35

An Anglican priest was presiding at the service. Just as the benediction was announced I noticed two men in the front row get up and make their exit. The presiding priest pronounced the benediction and the congregation dispersed. My colleagues told me that we would be going to the home of Andrew and Doreen Walls for tea. Harold and Maude Turner would also be there.

When we arrived at the Walls's home, the two men were engaged in animated conversation about what had happened in the final moments of the service. Contrary to what had been agreed by the committee that drafted the new liturgy for the United Church, the priest had insisted on reverting to Anglican practice by facing away from the congregation as he pronounced the benediction. Harold Turner and Andrew Walls would have no part of it. The officiant had not kept faith with the scheme of union.

The following January the Walls family returned to Scotland, and Andrew accepted appointment as lecturer in church history at the University of Aberdeen. The thirty-eight-year-old who became lecturer in Aberdeen's Divinity Faculty in 1966 was not the same person who had arrived in Sierra Leone in late 1957. Had the Aberdeen appointment been made in 1957, an Oxford trained Patristics scholar of uncommon ability would undoubtedly have left his mark on the field of church history within the time-honored curriculum. According to this regime, students preparing for the Christian ministry studied church history three years: the first year covered the early church, year two concentrated on the Reformation, and the third was sensibly devoted to Scottish church history. The churches growing in Africa and Asia had no recognized place in church history. If treated at all, these "younger churches" would be part of a course in missions. A British lecturer in church history would teach the history of the church in Africa or Asia using the same syllabus, ensuring that African and Asian seminarians were introduced to normative church history with the expectation they would appropriate it for themselves.

In the years following World War II Europeans were debating the future of religion. It was widely agreed that the outlook was bleak and that with good reason. For a century the churches in Europe, measured in terms of active participation, had been steadily declining. Among scholars the theory of secularization had acquired the status of dogma: the secular would inevitably triumph over religion. Western scholars were largely ignorant of the vitality of religion in other continents, but especially Africa, with new forms and movements emerging all the time.

Providentially, Andrew Walls's journey to Aberdeen went by way of Sierra Leone and Nigeria. The Walls family arrived in Sierra Leone in late 1957 where he took up appointment as a lecturer in the Fourah Bay University College Theology Department. Sometime later he had an experience that shattered the classical framework he had so conscientiously imbibed at Oxford. Concerning this transforming moment he later remarked:

> I still remember the force with which one day the realization struck me that I, while happily pontificating on that patchwork quilt of diverse fragments that constitutes second-century Christian literature, was actually living in a second-century church. The life, worship, and understanding of a community in its second century of Christian allegiance was going on all around me. Why did I not stop pontificating and observe what was going on?[1]

This was the kind of experience that one did not shake off. It set in motion a radical rethinking of Christian history. The possibility that present-day African Christian experience could shed light on what had happened in earlier periods of Christian history suggested there were new ways of interpreting the Christian movement. On empirical, theological, and historical grounds the entrenched verity that the post-Reformation church was foundational for all subsequent Christian development had to be jettisoned. The story of the people of God demanded a much broader historical canvas. The conceit that Western Christendom was the lens through which all of Christian history and theology was to be viewed was nothing more than a self-deluding provincialism.

It was clear that if one were to take this insight seriously a comprehensive new research program was needed. This would require that the primary source materials be collected, catalogued, and made available for scholarly use. The fact that much of this material was in danger of being devoured by white ants or deteriorating for lack of proper storage in the tropics added a sense of urgency. But it was not easy to get institutional support for such a new venture. The disdain of the Western academy for missions and missionaries, on the one hand, and widespread ignorance of the churches emerging in the South Pacific, Asia, Africa, and Latin America, on the other, represented a persistent drag. Only extraordinary tenacity combined with

---

1. Andrew F. Walls, "Introduction," in *The Missionary Movement in Christian History: Studies in the Transmission of Faith* (Maryknoll, N.Y.: Orbis Books, 1996), xiii.

intellectual brilliance might have a chance against these odds. Fortunately, other scholars were making similar discoveries and this began to lead to collaboration in various ventures.

Harold W. Turner had begun teaching at Fourah Bay University College in 1955. On a family outing to a Freetown beach in 1957 he encountered a leader in one of these movements engaged in prayer. His curiosity piqued, Turner struck up a conversation with this Nigerian apostle. Later he acknowledged, "Even in my second year of teaching in Sierra Leone I was still completely ignorant of what are commonly called the new religious movements of Black Africa."[2] Turner was so impressed with what he saw that he undertook a scientific study of this group. He had stumbled onto what would become his major preoccupation for the next three decades.

Setting out to research this movement, Turner discovered that little scholarly research of this phenomenon had been published.[3] In 1958 only a handful of articles were in print describing aspects of these religious movements. Two book-length empirical studies had been published, both by Scandinavian scholars. Bengt Sundkler produced a seminal pioneering sociological study in 1948, *Bantu Prophets in South Africa,* which attracted some attention; but Efraim Andersson's 1958 *Messianic Popular Movements in the Lower Congo* went largely unnoticed.[4] A comprehensive survey of these movements for Africa was still a decade away.[5]

This meant that research tools needed to be developed and bibliographies compiled. Over the next decade Turner concentrated on a comprehensive scientific study of this Nigerian apostle's church, which already had congregations in four West African countries. To conduct this research he developed models, typologies, and theories drawn from the history and

---

2. Harold W. Turner, *Religious Innovation in Africa: Collected Essays on New Religious Movements* (Boston: G. K. Hall, 1979), ix.

3. See "Special Bibliography," in Bengt Sundkler, *Bantu Prophets in South Africa,* 2nd ed. (London: Oxford University Press, 1961), 375–76, which lists all the books and articles on these movements published from 1902 to 1945. Generally, these early studies were unsympathetic toward such movements, regarding them as "breakaway" and reactionary.

4. Ibid. Sundkler's landmark work is regarded as the starting point for scholarly study of these movements. He identified some eight hundred churches that self-identified as African Independent Churches (the term used in this early stage) in South Africa. A revised edition in 1961 included a thirty-five-page report of subsequent developments, 1945–60, which confirmed many of his original findings. But Sundkler also indicated that he had revised his original conclusion, i.e., that the "Bantu Separatist Church [was] a bridge to a religion of the past, a bridge leading people back to 'African spiritism' " (1961: 302). By 1961 he no longer regarded this conclusion to be tenable.

5. Cf. David B. Barrett, *Schism and Renewal in Africa: An Analysis of Six Thousand Contemporary Religious Movements* (Oxford: Oxford University Press, 1969).

phenomenology of religion. He wrote up his findings in a series of scholarly essays that were published in various journals. His two-volume study of the Church of the Lord (Aladura), *African Independent Church,* was published in 1967.[6] This remains the most comprehensive study of a single movement that has been published.

Andrew Walls and Harold Turner recognized that they were living in the midst of a dynamic situation of which the Western academy in the 1950s was largely ignorant. To study this uncharted world, tools and resources had to be developed. How could the Western university legitimately claim to be a *university* if it closed its eyes to these burgeoning developments in Africa, the South Pacific, Latin America, and Asia? Among other things, this phenomenon was calling into question the leading theories about religion and secularization. Furthermore, the way the modern university curriculum was increasingly dominated by specialization in every field of study posed problems. To study phenomena like new religious movements the resources of multiple disciplines were needed.

Instrumenta and Institutions

Already at Fourah Bay Walls began to identify the new *instrumenta* that would be needed to support the kind of research program that was emerging: professional societies, journals, bibliographies, archives, and new university-based departments and research centers that would encourage wide-ranging scholarly investigation of religious history and movements, all the while developing new generations of scholars drawn from across the world that would carry the cause forward in their own nations. In the future he would elaborate, extend, and refine the vision, but its essentials have remained constant.

Less than two years after his arrival at Fourah Bay, Walls launched a new journal, the *Sierra Leone Bulletin of Religion.* This inaugural issue also carried the first article he wrote from Africa, "The Nova Scotian Settlers and Their Religion."[7] Here Walls retrieved the long forgotten and remarkable story of 1,131 ex-slaves from the American South, who had moved to Nova Scotia

6. Harold W. Turner, *African Independent Church, vol. 1: History of an African Independent Church: The Church of the Lord (Aladura);* vol. 2 *African Independent Church: The Life and Faith of the Church of the Lord (Aladura)* (Oxford: Clarendon Press, 1967).

7. *Sierra Leone Bulletin of Religion* 1 (1959), 19–31. Walls returned to this topic later: Walls, "A Christian Experiment: The Early Sierra Leone Colony," in *The Mission of the Church and the Propagation of the Faith: Papers Read at the Seventh Summer Meeting and the Eighth Winter Meeting of the Ecclesiastical History Society,* Studies in Church History 6, ed. G. J. Cumming (Cambridge: Cambridge University Press, 1970).

and then, assisted by the Sierra Leone Trading Company, a project of British evangelical activists engaged in the anti-slavery movement, migrated to the "province of freedom" in 1792.[8] The Nova Scotians arrived as congregations of Methodists, Baptists, and Countess of Huntingdon's Connexion.

It was hoped this new journal would stimulate African scholars to research and write from their own situations about religious history and contemporary developments. The next issue of the *Bulletin* carried another article by Walls that gave further guidance as to the way forward: "Documentary [Materials] for the Study of Sierra Leone Church History."[9] It was essential that every local church learn to value its own history and take steps to preserve its records. That a Western scholar acknowledged the legitimacy of indigenous materials and encouraged the writing of *Sierra Leone church* history gave added weight. In 1962 Walls led in organizing the Society for African Church History and the *Bulletin of the Society for African Church History.*

Aided and abetted by Turner, Walls was dreaming of grander schemes. Then an opportunity came in 1962 to give institutional form to his emerging vision: Walls was invited to establish the Department of Religious Studies at the new University at Nsukka in Nigeria. Turner was appointed a lecturer in the department. The new location was propitious in two ways. First, Walls was able to establish a department along the lines he deemed necessary. "In its curriculum and its range of research there was nothing like it anywhere else in Africa."[10] The department quickly became a center for a range of research projects related to indigenous religious movements, mission-founded churches, and Islam. Second, whereas several West African countries had few new religious movements in the 1960s, southeastern Nigeria was a veritable factory for religious activity, and this had been going on for many decades. But scholars had largely ignored the plenteous phenomena to be found in this region. From the beginning the department reached out to local religious leaders, opening channels of dialogue and exchange. In one case this resulted in an extensive survey of churches in Ibibio country where African Initiated Churches had been especially prolific.

In late 1958 a Mennonite missionary couple, Edwin and Irene Weaver, arrived in southeastern Nigeria in response to an appeal from a group of

---

8. "The Nova Scotian Settlers," 20.

9. Walls, *Sierra Leone Bulletin of Religion*, 57–61.

10. Harold W. Turner, "Andrew Walls as Scholar," in *Essays in Religious Studies for Andrew Walls*, ed. J. Thrower (Aberdeen: University of Aberdeen Department of Religious Studies, 1986), 1.

churches to help them train their pastors and establish the usual complement of medical and educational institutions that a proper church must have.[11] The Weavers and Harold Turner had chanced to meet at a guesthouse in Lagos in 1961. Turner was pursuing his research into the history and life of the Church of the Lord (Aladura) and the Weavers had recently been given notice to leave the country for lack of a proper visa. In conversation the Weavers and Turner soon discovered they were trying to understand the same bewildering phenomena. Eventually, the Weavers secured their visas and, as already noted, Turner moved to the University of Nsukka in 1963. Before long the Department of Religious Studies formed a partnership with Edwin Weaver, who organized a team of local church members that gathered data on the profusion of churches in that district while Turner and Walls spearheaded the scholarly analysis of the growing mass of data.[12] Sadly, all of this activity was disrupted by the outbreak of the Biafran War in 1967, and it was not possible to resume the work after the war ended in 1970.[13] Yet this brief experiment had demonstrated the synergy that can be achieved through this kind of collaboration.

Storming the "Bastille"

Andrew Walls returned to Great Britain brimming with ideas for what ought to be done to revitalize the study of Christian history, religions, theology, and mission studies. His experience in Africa had been formative — stirring

---

11. Edwin and Irene Weaver had served in India twenty years, witnessing India's independence in 1947. They were in fully sympathy with the decolonization movement and concerned not to revert to the colonial model even though it seemed to them this was what these Nigerian churches expected of them.

12. For example, one survey carried out in a five-mile radius around the town of Abak showed 250 congregations of fifty different denominations were crowded into this area. The results of this survey were issued by the Department as *The Abak Story* (1967). These early developments were recorded as vignettes and later published as *The Uyo Story* by Edwin and Irene Weaver (Elkhart, Ind.: Mennonite Board of Missions, 1970). See also Wilbert R. Shenk, "Go Slow through Uyo: Dialogue as Missionary Method," in *Fullness of Life for All: Challenges for Mission in Early Twenty-First Century*, ed. Inus Daneel, Charles Van Engen and, Hendrik Vroom (Amsterdam: Rodopi, 2003), 229–40. Unfortunately, much of the research was destroyed as a result of military action in 1967. Several of the reports, such as *The Abak Story*, survived since copies had been sent abroad.

13. Virtually all expatriates in Eastern and Southeastern Nigeria, the regions directly affected by the war, were forced to leave the country. Many of them were not granted visas to return after the war ended in 1970. See Andrew F. Walls, "Structural Problems in Mission Studies," *International Bulletin of Missionary Research* 15, no. 4 (1991): 151, where the impact of this episode is assessed. Walls refers to the same incident and its consequences for creating scholarly resource collections in "Globalization and the Study of Christian History," in *Globalizing Theology: Belief and Practice in an Era of World Christianity*, ed. Craig Ott and Harold A. Netland (Grand Rapids: Baker Academic, 2007), 80–81.

the imagination, compelling action. But he soon encountered the academy's formidable resistance to change, with which he would do battle for the next four decades. This demanded the tenacity of purpose and the canniness of the effective politician, qualities with which he was endowed.

By 1967 he had founded the *Journal of Religion in Africa/Religion en Afrique,* published by E. J. Brill. Walls would serve as editor of the *JRA* for its first eighteen years of publication. The editorial board was made up of scholars from a number of African countries, Germany, United States, and Great Britain. During the first year after his return to Great Britain he also led the way in organizing the Scottish Institute of Missionary Studies with thirty-four member institutions and agencies.[14] Walls envisaged a drag-net operation that would gather mission materials, much of it still in private

---

14. The *Bulletin of the Scottish Institute of Missionary Studies* (1967) listed the following members:

> Africa Evangelical Fellowship;
> Archdiocese of Glasgow;
> Archdiocese of St. Andrews and Edinburgh;
> Baptist Missionary Society and Baptist Union of Scotland;
> Bible and Medical Missionary Fellowship;
> Bible Training Institute, Glasgow;
> Center of African Studies, University of Edinburgh;
> Christ's College, Aberdeen;
> Church of Scotland Overseas Council;
> Department of Church History, University of Aberdeen;
> Department of History, University of Aberdeen;
> Department of Religious Studies, University of Aberdeen;
> Department of History, University of Edinburgh;
> Department of Arabic and Islamic Studies, University of Edinburgh;
> Edinburgh Medical Missionary Society;
> Episcopal Church Overseas Committee;
> The Leprosy Mission;
> Library of the University of St. Andrews;
> Methodist Missionary Society and Methodist Church, Scotland District;
> National Bible Society of Scotland;
> National Library of Scotland;
> New College, Edinburgh;
> St. Andrew's College, Drygrange;
> St. Colm's College, Edinburgh;
> St. Mary's College, St. Andrews;
> St. Peter's College, Cardross;
> Scotland Central Library;
> Scottish Churches' Council;
> Scottish Congregational College;
> Scottish National Council of YMCAs;
> Society for African Church History;
> Theological College of the Church of Scotland;
> United Pentecostal Mission;
> United Society for Christian Literature;
> The University of Stirling.

hands, for deposit and preservation in official archives. Typically, these were held by descendants of missionaries who had little appreciation of the value of primary documents for historical research. Indeed, these holdings were in danger of being lost for lack of proper storage. Walls saw the value in materials that others regarded as ephemera. He established a special collection of nineteenth- and twentieth-century missionary periodicals that were generally unknown and largely unavailable.

Official archives of missionary agencies, church bodies, and universities, with a few exceptions, had not yet properly organized their holdings for the use of research scholars. One had to start by raising the awareness of librarians, directors of archives, and institutional administrators concerning the value of these materials for the massive new research program being envisioned.[15] Of course, bibliographies had to be compiled in all fields related to mission studies.[16] These would be made available, along with scholarly articles, in the *Bulletin of the Scottish Institute of Missionary Studies*.[17] Again, this was an interuniversity organization that provided a rallying point for scholars in African studies, church history, and mission studies who typically had no colleagues who shared these interests. It was a maneuver based on one of Walls's strategic principles: use all means possible to "spoil the Egyptians" in order to accomplish goals that would otherwise not be achievable. And there was more to come.

In May 1967 a conference of Scottish university divinity faculties was hosted by King's College, Aberdeen. Walls delivered a paper entitled "Missionary Studies and the Scottish Theological Faculties." Appropriately, he began with the efforts of Alexander Duff, illustrious Scottish missionary to India, who upon his retirement to Scotland worked to found the first chair in mission studies anywhere in the world.[18] In 1867, despite his ill health,

15. Cf. Walls, "Why Mission Studies Librarianship Is Different: Responsibilities and Opportunities," *Bulletin, Association of British Theological and Philosophical Libraries* 2 (November 1990): 25–33.

16. Walls has compiled the quarterly annotated bibliography published by the *International Review of Mission* since 1972.

17. The *Bulletin* was published from 1967 to 1976. It resumed publication in 1982, with the last issue being published in 1994.

18. In 1992 Walls presented a paper entitled "Missiological Education in Historical Perspective," in which he gave a more complete account of the Duff initiative and the subsequent fits and starts in getting mission studies established. Among other themes, he touched on "the parochialism of Western theological education, holy subversion, i.e., the tactic of enticing other disciplines to engage with mission studies, and, hence, the need theological education has for mission studies. See *Missiological Education for the Twenty-First Century*, ed. J. Dudley Woodberry, Charles E. Van Engen, and Edgar J. Elliston (Maryknoll, N.Y.: Orbis Books, 1996), 11–22.

Duff himself was installed in this chair at New College, Edinburgh. But the chair did not survive long. The Duff Missionary Lectures, delivered intermittently over the years, are the only remaining vestige of that noble venture a century earlier.

Walls examined the role that mission studies had in the training of candidates for ministry in the Scottish churches and showed how meager it was. He then set in place the fulcrum for his argument: *the center of gravity of the Christian movement worldwide is shifting decisively.* Given the trends evident already in 1967 it was clear that the majority of Christians would soon be located in Africa, Asia, and Latin America. The growth rates among Christians in other continents presented a sharp contrast with the declining membership "in the lands of the setting sun." Sub-Saharan Christianity had been increasing "in geometrical progression."[19] European Christians must now adjust to this rapidly changing situation and accept the fact that the vast majority of Christians would in the future be found on other continents.

This sea change suggested an urgent question to divinity faculties: "What effect is this to have on the theological curriculum?" Walls asked rhetorically.[20] In view of these trends, he gibed, "the Churches of Scotland are ludicrously overstaffed, criminally overbuildinged, are grotesquely over-divinity schooled."[21] No right-thinking business person would allocate resources the way the church has done. Walls proposed that the divinity faculties be reoriented to serve the worldwide Christian movement by offering their "one remaining resource" to the global church. Western divinity schools ought to place at the disposal of the churches on other continents "Christian technology: communities of Christian scholars, a long tradition of disciplined study of the Bible, of Christian history, of the data of the Christian revelation."[22] These communities have at their disposal the physical facilities, splendid libraries, well-trained scholars, and academic resources to assist the churches on other continents to train the future generations of leaders.

As he presses his argument, Walls is sensitive to the irony that the church in the West, despite its wealth of resources, is itself decaying from the inside out. What is to insure that the churches from other continents will escape the same fate if they allow their future leaders to be trained in the West?

---

19. Andrew F. Walls, "Missionary Studies and the Scottish Theological Faculties," a paper read May 5, 1967, at the Conference of the Scottish University Divinity Faculties, held at King's College, Aberdeen (unpublished), 4.
20. Ibid.
21. Ibid.
22. Ibid., 5.

Obviously, the West needs the help of the churches in the South if it is to recover vitality. In reply he put forward three recommendations that require interdependent action. If carried out such an approach could lead to a basic reorientation of global theological education.

First, open up Western institutions and research resources for the training of students from other continents to become first-class scholars. Second, the curriculum studied by Western students must be overhauled so that those being trained for the ministry in the West become familiar with the *world* Christian movement. Such revision ought to begin with a thorough reformulation of the church history syllabus so that the churches on all continents are covered. The West must outgrow the mind-set that holds that Christian history means *Western* Christian history and everything else is covered in a throwaway chapter entitled "history of missions." Third, by reorienting the curriculum toward the world Christian movement, nontheological students preparing to work overseas can benefit from certain courses. All of this ought to be done by drawing on the rich resources in libraries and archives that the Scottish Institute of Missionary Studies proposed to make available for research. The challenge presented was worthy but daunting. To accomplish it would require a new level of cooperation among the various faculties and departments.

Walls had thrown down the gauntlet to the Scottish divinity faculties; but there is no recorded response to his challenge. In 1967 senior divinity faculty at Aberdeen still donned their academic robes when lecturing; change would be an unwelcome interloper. Yet the vision kindled by Africa shone with ever greater intensity and gave Walls no rest.

On another front Walls was working with British evangelical mission leaders to take up mission studies. Addressing a group in London in January 1968 on "Missionary Studies — Why and What?" he set forth a threefold argument. In the first place, it was impossible to understand either the contemporary world or the church without the aid of mission studies. A survey of the changes in church and world between 1568 and 1868 showed that distribution of the Christian population worldwide had changed little. But in the century since 1868 a momentous transformation had occurred. In 1900 Christianity in Africa was still negligible but by 1967 the trends were that Africa was rapidly becoming the continent with the largest Christian population. Failure to understand this massive southward shift was to misunderstand the emerging new world. Historical Christendom as a territorial reality was rapidly disintegrating.

Second, mission studies ought to be promoted because they clarify and deepen our understanding of the world as it is and is becoming. World evangelization cannot be effective if missionaries do not understand the context of the people with whom they are trying to communicate. Here history can be our tutor. Take the example of linguistic science. Much of the pioneering work that laid the foundation for modern linguistics was done by missionaries. These missionaries realized that they must study the cultures of the peoples if they were to learn their languages. Christian history is replete with insights that we will need if we are to continue the task of evangelization.

A third reason why mission studies are necessary is that scholars from other disciplines — history, sociology, anthropology, economics, political scientists — are researching and writing scholarly monographs and articles that draw on mission materials. They do not always understand and interpret accurately what they are treating. Sharing of resources would be to the benefit of all. Walls concluded with three practical admonitions: "(1) Let us spoil the Egyptians . . . (2) Let us make full use of our resources . . . (3) Let us work in fellowship."[23]

In 1970 Walls was appointed head of a new Department of Religious Studies at the University of Aberdeen. The new department was affiliated to the Divinity Faculty but students took work in other departments as their programs required. Walls had already had a taste of the possibilities of such a department at Nsukka. The Department of Religious Studies at Aberdeen quickly began attracting research students from all continents investigating topics that would not have readily fit into traditional categories; but these were the questions of importance to Christians in other parts of the world. In 1982 Walls established the Centre for the Study of Christianity in the Non-Western World for the purpose of collecting and making available research materials for the study of global Christianity. The Center was housed in the department and proved a valuable ally in defining the new agenda that Walls had worked so assiduously to introduce to the Western academy.

In the 1980s the Thatcher government set out to reform and rein in British universities. Academic programs that did not line up with the government's priorities were to be eliminated or severely curtailed. Religious studies fell in the expendable category. Andrew Walls, following two heart attacks, was

_____

23. Andrew F. Walls, "Missionary Studies — Why and What?" A paper to a group considering evangelical missionary studies. London, January 1968 (unpublished).

forced to retire on health grounds. Since there was no supervision for the department's graduate students in primal religions and non-Western Christianity, he returned at once to the university in an honorary capacity to supervise these students as director of the Centre for the Study of Christianity in the Non-Western World. Several years later the University of Aberdeen discovered that Walls's Department of Religious Studies was the one department that was turning a profit for the University due to the unusually large number of international students it was attracting. Fortunately, by 1986 Walls had found a new home for the Centre at New College, Edinburgh, where the program continued to thrive as it served the global Christian movement.

Reprise: The Future of Mission Studies

In January 1991 Walls gave the keynote address at a consultation entitled "The Future of Mission Studies." The overarching concern was the revitalization of mission studies. Walls approached the consultation theme from the angle of "The Structural Problems in Mission Studies."[24] All the elements are present here that were put forward in 1967, but two decades of experience gave added authority and urgency. The same apostolic passion enlivens the argument. Familiar obstacles continue to block the path of genuine reform of theological education. And the intervening years have amply confirmed that the "structural problems" are not simply a matter of physical facilities. The problems with which Walls was concerned were embedded in patterns of blinkered thinking combined with a neuralgic reaction to change.

The Christian movement was at a watershed. In the last century two contrasting developments had taken place. One continent, Africa, had experienced the largest accession of new Christians in eight hundred years while the West, the historic heartland of Christianity, at the same time, sustained the largest recession in membership since Islam appeared on the scene. But what Western Christian historian or theologian registered these historic changes?[25] In the late 1960s the eminent Cambridge church historian

---

24. Andrew F. Walls, *International Bulletin of Missionary Research* 15, no. 4 (1991): 146–55. Republished in *The Missionary Movement in Christian History*, 143–59.

25. Walls, "Globalization and the Study of Christian History." "All over the Western world, ministers are being trained and future theological scholars are being identified and taken to doctoral levels and beyond without any idea of what the church of today, in which they are called to serve, is really like" (78).

Owen Chadwick published an erudite two-volume history titled *The Victorian Church*.[26] This work contains no direct reference to the modern mission movement even though Great Britain furnished the largest number of missionaries of any country throughout the Victorian period. Chadwick was not antagonistic toward missions. He had already written an appreciative biography of Bishop Charles MacKenzie, who led the missionary party that established the work of the Universities' Mission to Central Africa in 1861 and, subsequently, revised Stephen Neill's *History of Christian Missions* (1986).[27] Rather this observation points to the enduring power of categories, even when they no longer approximate reality. Church history and mission history have too long remained worlds apart. More than ever we must seek to understand and interpret Christian history.

From the vantage point of 1991, Walls could take some satisfaction in changes in the Western academy. When he joined the British African Studies Association, he was one of only four members specializing in religion. That field had undergone considerable change. Africanists have embraced a new appreciation of the central role of religion, including Christianity, in African culture and history. Now Walls could speak more confidently — even impatiently — of a new era in mission studies. The global scale of the task, the inadequacy of primary resources, the need for a greatly expanded corps of well-trained scholars drawn from "all the tribes and tongues," and the challenges of creating institutions where this ongoing work could be done were daunting. He appealed for a threefold response.

In the future this work must be thoroughly *international*. Resources are distributed haphazardly and unevenly across the globe, but we need to keep the *ecumene* always in view. There is no institution or nation that is self-sufficient in this regard. Any scholar or institution that is self-satisfied in its provincialism will be of little help to the world Christian movement. Today's world is dynamically linked. No one lives or dies to oneself.

A renaissance in mission studies will require an *integrative* approach. The modern idea of specialization must give way to a methodology that brings together the resources needed from various disciplines to plumb the depths of the data at hand. The great Harvard sinologist John King Fairbank observed that Christian missions represent the most sustained experiment in

---

26. Owen Chadwick, *The Victorian Church*, vol. 1 (London: Black, 1966, vol. 2, 1970).

27. Owen Chadwick, *MacKenzie's Grave* (London: Hodder & Stoughton, 1959); Stephen Neill, *A History of Christian Missions*, rev. ed. Owen Chadwick (London: Penguin, 1984).

intercultural interaction in history. If we think in these terms, we soon realize that no single discipline will be sufficient to study such a complex reality. Walls has argued, for example, that we will begin to grasp the "fullness of Christ" only as we bring together the insights that can be gained through comparative historical and comparative theological studies — Greek and Hebrew, Germanic and Latin, second-generation African Christian experience and second-century Gentile Christian faith. The attempt to explain the Christian faith using the thought categories and idioms of a particular culture will be unlike that of any other culture and language. Taken together, these various attempts enrich, stimulate, and illuminate, thereby filling out what is lacking when we are dependent on only one or two.

Third, in the future mission studies will depend on *cooperation* among scholars and institutions. Work must be done at multiple levels and on all continents. Everyone needs the help of someone else. While the southern continents are still getting their archives established and collections organized, there are substantial stores of primary source materials in Europe and North America that are largely unknown and unused by scholars. Several years ago a doctoral student used the archives of German missionary societies in gathering data for her dissertation. She was surprised to learn that she was the first person who had ever requested access to these well-organized and carefully preserved records.

Retiring from Edinburgh in 1995, Walls became visiting professor at Princeton Theological Seminary. As a peripatetic lecturer on all continents, he had an unparalleled opportunity to observe academic programs across the world. At a curriculum development workshop at the Akrofi-Christaller Center in Ghana in 1997, Walls spoke "Of Ivory Towers and Ashrams."[28] He made clear that his criticism of the Western academy still had not been addressed; it was not a universal model to be emulated on other continents. Emerging academic centers in Africa, Asia, and Latin America should explore the potential in alternative models for training indigenous persons to their own cultures, such as the Indian ashram. Always an encourager and enabler of the work of others, he emphasized that what was needed was the courage to explore and pursue promising alternative paths in theological and missiological training.

---

28. Andrew F. Walls, "Of Ivory Towers and Ashrams: Some Reflections on Theological Scholarship in Africa," *Journal of African Christian Thought* 3, no. 1 (2000): 1–4.

Much scorn and criticism has been heaped on the modern missionary movement by the Sydney Smiths of this world.[29] But the last word has yet to be spoken or written. Andrew Walls has been a seminal figure both in his brilliant reinterpretation of Christian history as well as his ceaseless efforts to create new *instrumenta* and institutions that will sustain and carry the work forward. In spite of repeated disappointments, he has kept his eye on "the prize." It is appropriate, once again, to let Walls have the last word: "The aim will be to raise the quality, the range and the depth of our scholarly work; the rigor and comprehensiveness of its method, its fidelity to sources, its attention to detail, its vision and insight, its sense of holy vocation. In the providence of God a renaissance of mission studies could be the prelude to the reordering of theology and the refreshment of the human and social sciences."[30]

---

29. Rev. Sydney Smith (1771–1845), writer and Anglican clergyman, wrote regularly for the *Edinburgh Review,* heaping special scorn on religious "enthusiasts" but especially missionaries.
30. Wall, "Structural Problems in Mission Studies," 154.

5

Founding the Centre for the Study of Christianity in the Non-Western World

BRIAN STANLEY

The Centre for the Study of Christianity in the Non-Western World (known since 2009 as the Centre for the Study of World Christianity), from its successive homes in the universities of Aberdeen and Edinburgh, has exercised an influence in the shaping and bibliographic resourcing of the new academic field of "World Christianity" that is arguably without parallel. That extraordinary and enduring influence derives in large measure from the single-minded vision and dogged persistence in the face of many institutional obstacles of Andrew Finlay Walls, O.B.E.[1] His own experience as a theological educator in Sierra Leone and Nigeria from 1957 to 1966 had left him in no doubt that the immediate future of Christianity lay in the southern hemisphere. But he had also become increasingly aware that this new and exciting chapter in Christian history could not be adequately written in the years to come unless some serious and urgent initiatives were taken to document and interpret the rapid growth and rich diversification of southern Christianity. The Centre for the Study of Christianity in the Non-Western World developed from Andrew's awareness of this compelling need.

In 1970 Andrew was promoted from his post as senior lecturer in church history in the Faculty of Divinity at the University of Aberdeen to become head of the new Department of Religious Studies (reconstituted from an existing Department of Biblical Studies) at the university. Funding was provided by a bequest for the provision of a lectureship or chair in comparative religion from a local schoolmaster, William Riddoch, who had died in 1942.[2] The fledgling department was to be independent of the Faculty of Divinity and was dedicated particularly to the study of religion in "primal societies"

---

1. He was awarded the Order of the British Empire in 1986 for his public service, especially to the arts in Scotland.

2. James L. Cox and Steven J. Sutcliffe, "Religious Studies in Scotland: A Persistent Tension with Divinity," *Religion* 36 (2006): 1–28 (reference at pp. 5–6).

(a contested term that Andrew has always resolutely defended as carrying no implications of primitivism) and non-Western expressions of Christianity. Influenced by the pioneering example set in the University of Ibadan by another Methodist missionary and scholar of African religion, Geoffrey Parrinder, Andrew's broad vision was of a department dedicated to "the study of religion, in its own terms and in its social, phenomenological and historical aspects."[3] Andrew soon attracted a number of highly distinguished academics to join him on the teaching staff.[4] They included: from 1973 to 1981, Harold W. Turner, a New Zealand colleague of Andrew's from both Freetown and Nsukka days and a pioneering scholar of African new religious movements; from 1976 to 1982, Adrian Hastings, the Catholic historian and interpreter of African Christianity; and from 1978 to 1981, Lamin Sanneh, a Gambian convert from Islam to Christianity, who later went on to hold chairs at Harvard and Yale. With such a gifted team, a steady stream of postgraduate students from Africa and elsewhere soon made their way north to Aberdeen. Andrew's own Ph.D. students in the Aberdeen years included such subsequently celebrated names as Kwame Bediako, Jonathan Bonk, James L. Cox, Edward Fasholé-Luke, David Shank, and Godwin Tasie.

The setting up of the Centre within the department at Aberdeen was a logical next step from Andrew's existing energetic activities as academic supervisor, journal editor, and bibliographer in the fields of mission studies and African religions. He was the founding editor of two new journals that had first appeared in 1967 — the *Bulletin of the Scottish Institute of Missionary Studies* and the *Journal of Religion in Africa* (*JRA*). The former publication continued, a little irregularly, in two series, the first running from the inception of the Scottish Institute of Missionary Studies in 1967 until 1976, and the second from the creation of the Centre in 1982 until 1994. For a period the *Bulletin* was accompanied by a bibliographical supplement (on microfiche) of Current Literature on Christian Mission and on Christianity in the Non-Western World. The *JRA* remained under Andrew's editorial guidance until Adrian Hastings took over in 1985: it continues to flourish to this day as the premier academic journal in its field.

---

3. James L. Cox, "From Africa to Africa: The Significance of Approaches to the Study of African Religions at Aberdeen and Edinburgh Universities from 1970 to 1998," in *European Traditions in the Study of Religion in Africa*, ed. Frieder Ludwig and Afe Adogame (Wiesbaden: Harrassowitz Verlag, 2004), 255–64 (quotation at p. 255).

4. See the comments of Adrian Hastings, "African Christian Studies, 1967–99: Reflections of an Editor," in *European Traditions in the Study of Religion in Africa*, ed. Frieder Ludwig and Afe Adogame (Wiesbaden: Harrassowitz Verlag, 2004), 265–74 (reference at p. 269).

While at Aberdeen, Andrew also assumed additional responsibilities in the sphere of the bibliography of World Christianity. The first volume of the *JRA* contained nearly fifty pages compiled by Andrew as the first installment of the Bibliography of the Society for African Church History.[5] The intention that this should appear annually was not fulfilled, though a similar but more comprehensive objective was fulfilled from January 1972, when Andrew took over as compiler of the bibliography on mission studies that had been published in each quarterly issue of the *International Review of Mission* (*IRM*) since its foundation in 1912 as the *International Review of Missions*.

The establishment in 1982 of the Centre for the Study of Christianity in the Non-Western World thus marked the natural culmination of Andrew's academic work at Aberdeen. The Center had relatively modest beginnings as a base for the collection of documentation on Christianity in the non-Western world. Integral to this goal was Andrew's work as compiler of the *IRM* bibliography, a role that from October 1995 was shared with Margaret Acton, the librarian of the Centre, and that he continued to exercise until the bibliography ceased publication (it is hoped only temporarily) in 2009. Andrew's passion for bibliography over such a wide field is a function of his commitment to the catholicity of the church and also indicative of the generosity of his spirit: as bibliographer and teacher he has anonymously shaped a far wider range of publications than he himself has authored.

In light of the fact that a regular flow of income from university sources was never a realistic prospect, the Centre adopted as its central principle of operation the international exchange of periodical literature and bibliographic information. In return for complimentary copies of the *Bulletin of the Scottish Institute of Missionary Studies,* or as an integral part of the bibliographical function of *The International Review of Mission,* church bodies, mission agencies, and study centers throughout the globe would send their periodicals, newsletters, and other publications to the Centre. On this basis the Centre developed within its first five years a remarkable library of some seven hundred current periodical titles, in addition to a further thirteen hundred noncurrent titles. A collection of some sixty-five hundred to seven thousand books also accrued from a variety of sources, mainly as donations or review copies, or as items sent for the *IRM* bibliography, whose categories of classification, deriving originally from the eight study

---

5. "Bibliography of the Society for African Church History," *Journal of Religion in Africa* 1 (1967–68): 46–94.

commissions at Edinburgh 1910, provided the basis of classification for the Centre library. The Butler collection on non-Western Christian art added an important visual dimension to the Centre's holdings.

The future development of the Centre from the mid-1980s onward was dictated by the convergence of two entirely unrelated forces: Andrew's precarious health and the cold winds of rigidly utilitarian approaches to higher education then blowing from the Conservative government of Margaret Thatcher (winds that have sadly continued to blow under successive administrations of different political complexion). In 1985 Andrew suffered a second and severe heart attack, which necessitated his retirement from his salaried post as head of the Department of Religious Studies. At the same time the department suffered drastic financial cutbacks. For the academic year 1985–86 Andrew endeavored to develop the Centre in Aberdeen as a quasi-autonomous base for his activities, but it became clear that a new home for the Centre had to be found.

Happily the University of Edinburgh was able to extend its hospitality, first in 1986 to Andrew himself and then, in September 1987, to his Centre, which was, over a period of some months, relocated in New College as part of the University of Edinburgh's Faculty (later School) of Divinity. This was a highly appropriate venue. New College was the institution which in 1867 had appointed the former India pioneer missionary Alexander Duff to a chair of "Evangelistic Theology" — the first academic chair in the study of missions anywhere in the world. Although that chair ceased to exist as a permanent post in 1892, the coming of the Centre to Edinburgh in 1987 can be interpreted as a late second flowering of Duff's vision of making New College into an institute of missionary studies.[6] Furthermore, it was in the same complex of buildings on the Mound that the celebrated World Missionary Conference had taken place in June 1910, giving birth, inter alia, to the *International Review of Missions* and its bibliography, for which Andrew was now responsible. Shortly before the move to Edinburgh, work began on compiling an electronic database containing the cumulative bibliography of the *IRM* from 1912 with the aid of a substantial grant from the World Council of Churches; this rapidly grew to over sixty-five thousand records. The WCC grant made possible the employment of a Research Fellow, Dr. A. Christopher Smith, who accompanied Andrew from Aberdeen

---

6. See Duncan Forrester, "New Wine in Old Bottles," in *Disruption to Diversity: Edinburgh Divinity 1846–1996*, ed. David F. Wright and Gary D. Badcock (Edinburgh: T. & T. Clark, 1996), 259–76 (reference at p. 271).

and was able to contribute significantly to the Centre's M.Th. teaching program. Dr. Andrew C. Ross, senior lecturer in ecclesiastical history in the Faculty of Divinity, was also appointed deputy director of the Centre.

The flow of doctoral students from the non-Western world was now progressively diverted from Aberdeen to Edinburgh to work under Andrew as honorary professor, and it continued to accelerate. His global reputation was signaled by the award of an honorary doctorate in divinity from the University of Aberdeen in 1988. Undergraduate teaching also reaped the benefit of the Centre's expertise, with "primal religions" appearing for the first time on the Edinburgh curriculum. Initially the University of Edinburgh was able to supply little more than space for the Centre's collections, and even that proved hard to find, but Andrew's success in attracting to the university both overseas postgraduate students and project funding soon made it possible for funded staff to be appointed to work alongside Andrew and Doreen, who for long worked as honorary publications secretary of the Centre (in addition to being an invariably welcoming host to the Centre's students). In 1988 Margaret Acton was appointed by the University of Edinburgh as the first (and, so far, the only) full-time librarian of the Centre, and she remained in post until 2007, when the post was axed for financial reasons. The Centre's expertise in the teaching of African Christianity was bolstered by two appointments. In 1993 Dr. Jack Thompson, a former Irish Presbyterian missionary to Malawi, moved from the Selly Oak Colleges in Birmingham to become lecturer in mission studies, on secondment from the Overseas Board of the Presbyterian Church in Ireland. He would later, from 2005 to 2008, serve as director of the Centre. In 1991 the university funded the post of associate director, and appointed Dr. John Parratt, an expert in African theology, who had been professor of theology and religious studies at the University of Botswana, and also had teaching experience in Malawi, India, and Papua New Guinea. In 1999 Dr. Parratt was appointed to a chair at the University of Birmingham.

The most notable externally funded project secured by the Centre was the African Christianity Project (ACP), established in 1992, and funded by The Pew Charitable Trusts of Philadelphia through two successive grants of $500,000 and $425,000.[7] It was under Andrew's overall direction in tandem with his former Aberdeen doctoral student, Dr. James L. Cox, who

---

7. For a summary of the activities and achievements of the ACP see James L. Cox, "Setting the Context: The African Christianity Project and the Emergence of a Self-Reflexive Institutional Identity," in *Uniquely African? African Christian Identity from Cultural and Historical*

joined the Centre from the University of Zimbabwe in 1993 and served as Co-ordinator of the Project to its conclusion in 1998. The ACP involved the Centre in collaboration with an eventual total of eight institutions on the African continent in the promotion of research, publication, and the compilation and exchange of bibliographical information, on African Christianity.[8] The project gained its own librarian based in the Centre, Elizabeth Leitch, in 1993. As the project proceeded, the emphasis progressively shifted from an Edinburgh-based program to one in which the institutions on the African continent increasingly took the lead. Of particular significance from 1987 onward was the partnership with the recently established Akrofi-Christaller Center for Mission Research and Applied Theology at Akropong in Ghana. This was directed by another of Andrew's former doctoral students, Kwame Bediako (1945–2008), an outstanding African theologian. Dr. Bediako became a visiting lecturer in African Theology at the Centre in Edinburgh, teaching for a term each year and funded by the African Christianity Project, while Andrew made frequent visits to teach at the Centre in Ghana. Dr. Bediako's visiting lectureship was funded initially by the Duff Missionary Lectureship[9] and then by the African Christianity Project.

The move to Edinburgh was followed in December 1990 by the signature of a formal agreement with the University of Edinburgh, which clarified the status of the collections, as belonging, for the most part, to the university. These developments greatly stimulated the stream of library and archival accessions to the Centre. Shortly after the move from Aberdeen, the Church of Scotland deposited its mission reference library on permanent loan in the Centre. This included a unique collection of pamphlets on India compiled by Alexander Duff, which has subsequently been microfilmed by Adam Matthew Publications. From Providence Seminary in Manitoba came the Ida Grace McRuer collection of North American evangelical mission periodicals and newsletters. Other deposited collections included works on Hindu literature from Dr. Eric Lott and on nineteenth-century China from Dr. George Hood. In addition, the Centre built up a unique range of contemporary pamphlets and ephemera ("gray material") from Africa, Asia, and the Pacific. A

Perspectives, ed. James L. Cox and Gerrie ter Haar (Trenton, N.J., and Asmara: Africa World Press, 2003), 1–7; see also Cox, "From Africa to Africa," 261–63.

8. The eight institutions were the Universities of Malawi; Zimbabwe; Botswana; Sierra Leone; Namibia; Eduardo Mondlane University in Mozambique; the University of Ghana, Legon; and the Akrofi-Kristaller Center in Ghana.

9. The Duff Missionary Lectureship Trust was established in 1879 by William Pirie Duff, son of Alexander Duff, in memory of his father, to provide for a quadrennial course of public lectures on some aspect of foreign missions, to be delivered in Edinburgh or Glasgow.

very significant body of manuscript and other archival material also began to find its home in the Centre. A rich collection of documentation on Christianity in the Himalayan region was deposited in 1990, comprising the archives of the United Mission to Nepal, the International Nepal Fellowship and the Nepal Church History Project; this has now been transferred to Yale Divinity School Library. Other extremely important missionary collections were acquired that remain in the Centre to this day. Those of the Regions Beyond Missionary Union (RBMU), incorporating the archives of the Livingstone Inland Mission and the Congo Balolo Mission, were deposited in 1991. They were followed by the archives of the Sudan United Mission (SUM) and Latin Link (formerly the Evangelical Union of South America). Most of the RBMU and SUM archive is now available on microfilm from Adam Matthew Publications. There are in addition a considerable number of private missionary papers from all parts of the world, though China is particularly well represented.

In addition to the close partnership with the Akrofi-Christaller Center in Ghana, under Andrew's leadership the Centre also forged strong links with Yale University Divinity School, where Lamin Sanneh was in 1989 appointed D. Willis James Professor of Missions and World Christianity, and professor of history, and whose archival and library holdings in non-Western Christianity were unrivalled. These links were formalized through the inception in March 1992 of the Yale-Edinburgh Group on the History of Missions and World Christianity, formed at a conference held at Yale. Beginning as a small informal gathering of invited friends of Professors Walls and Sanneh, the Yale-Edinburgh conference has, without losing its informal character, grown over the years into probably the most significant annual academic event in its field, alternating between the venues of Edinburgh and New Haven. The Overseas Ministries Study Center, a near neighbor of Yale Divinity School, has provided valued financial support.

A further significant development was the inception in April 1995 of a new academic journal, *Studies in World Christianity: The Edinburgh Review of Theology and Religion,* published by Edinburgh University Press. By the time of Andrew's "second retirement" from Edinburgh in 1996, the study of World Christianity in the university had attained a degree of permanence sufficient to enable the university to establish a funded chair in World Christianity, to which Professor David A. Kerr, a specialist in Christian-Muslim relations, was appointed. Andrew remained as honorary curator of the Centre's Collections and as an honorary professor of the University of

Edinburgh, although from 1998 new responsibilities as guest professor of ecumenics and mission at Princeton Theological Seminary had to be accommodated within his schedule. In late 1997 the library, postgraduate reading room, and offices for Centre staff were moved to premises owned by the Free Church of Scotland on Bank Street, adjacent to New College. It was entirely fitting that, on the suggestion of the then dean of the Faculty of Divinity, Professor Duncan Forrester, the library in its new home in what became known as Thomas Chalmers House was given the official title of "The Andrew F. Walls Library." The bulk of the Centre's accommodation remained in Thomas Chalmers House until 2007, when the Centre, with its library and archival collections, moved back into New College.

Although the original vision behind the creation of the Centre focused primarily on the collection of bibliographical resources for the study of non-Western Christianity, it is possible that its most substantial and enduring achievement will prove to have been its promotion of high-quality postgraduate research within the field. The faculty lists of universities and theological colleges throughout the non-Western world bear eloquent testimony to the uniquely influential role that the Centre has played in the provision of postgraduate education in the fields of non-Western Christian history, contextual theology, and African and Asian religious studies. Over the years an immense number of research students flocked from all quarters of the globe, but above all from Africa, to Aberdeen and later to Edinburgh, to work under the supervision of Andrew and his colleagues on topics in the history of missions and non-Western Christianity. By 1997 about one-third of the postgraduate student body of the Faculty of Divinity was affiliated with the Centre — a remarkable testimony to Andrew's work and worldwide reputation. Although his globe-trotting lifestyle made him sometimes physically elusive, his postgraduate students found they could count on his devoted attention in their supervisions and his intense loyalty ever after. As few students from the developing world had the necessary education to commence Ph.D. studies immediately, a one-year M.Th. degree course in Christianity in the Non-Western World was offered during the Aberdeen years, and the Edinburgh version was approved in 1987 and has flourished ever since. Many went on from the M.Th. to study at M.Litt. or Ph.D. levels.

By the first decade of the twenty-first century, the Centre could count some 129 M.Th. and 65 Ph.D. theses in its archives. Their authors have gone on to become some of the best-known names in the fields of World Christianity and mission studies. In addition to the examples from the Aberdeen years cited earlier in this chapter, the following names and their current spheres of service could be mentioned by way of illustration: Siga Arles (director of the Centre for Contemporary Christianity, Bangalore, India); Jehu Hanciles (associate professor of history of Christianity and globalization, Fuller Theological Seminary); Jooseop Kim (secretary, Council for World Mission and Evangelism, World Council of Churches, and editor of the *International Review of Mission*); Esther Mombo (deputy vice-chancellor, St. Paul's University, Limuru, Kenya); Cyril Okorocha (Anglican bishop of Owerri diocese in Nigeria); Diane Stinton (dean of students and associate professor of mission studies, Regent College, Vancouver); and Timothy Tennant (president of Asbury Theological Seminary). Many others, though not necessarily so well known internationally, are exercising key roles in national church leadership or theological education in their own countries. The geographical range of the topics covered is truly impressive, encompassing not simply the more "obvious" countries such as Nigeria, Ghana, India, China, or Korea, but also less well-worked territory, such as Namibia, the Malay peninsula, Burma, or Peru.

If there has been one disappointment in Andrew's hopes for the Centre that he founded in Edinburgh, it is that a large and complex university has proved unable in straitened economic times to provide the resources for the professional archival and library care of the Centre's special collections that their importance merits. In 2008 a new Andrew Walls Centre for the Study of African and Asian World Christianity was opened at Liverpool Hope University, whose vice-chancellor is Gerald J. Pillay. Some of the Edinburgh Centre's runs of English periodicals, and the Butler collection of non-Western Christian art, have been transferred to the Liverpool Centre. However, despite rumors to the contrary, the great majority of the printed book, pamphlet and archival holdings of the Centre remain intact in Edinburgh and available to researchers. The University of Edinburgh demonstrated its continuing commitment to the work that Andrew began by renewing the post of director of the Centre on Jack Thompson's retirement in 2008 and appointing Brian Stanley, not simply as director but also as the third professor of World Christianity. Andrew Walls has left his mark on the lives of two British universities, and, in his eighties, is now devoting his energies to a third. All students of World Christianity will be in his debt for decades to come.

6

Changing the Course of
Mission and World Christian Studies

JONATHAN J. BONK

The invitation to contribute to this festschrift arrived on August 5, 2008. The instructions stipulated that the essay should overview "ways in which Andrew Walls has helped to redefine the field of mission studies and world Christian studies." A measure of his influence may be deduced from the audacity of the assignment itself. Is there anyone else, still alive, whose influence would elicit let alone warrant such a request?[1]

Thanks to Walls, *mission* and *World Christianity* are of a piece. They can no longer be seen as discretely autonomous entities. The missionary movement from the West is one episode in the much grander drama of World Christianity. And it is not the central act. Those whose scholarship and outlook unabashedly reflect his influence, include former students, missionaries, church leaders, missiologists, and historians who have come under the spell of his lectures and published essays. Among these — who by no means represent any historiographic mainstream (even if there were such a thing) — his impact has been quietly, steadily, and profoundly revolutionary. This essay, it will soon be clear, is not so much an academic assessment as it is a synopsis of opinions and observations by several dozen well-known academics in the field whose advice I solicited before setting out to write this short tribute.[2]

---

1. On September 14, 2011, a simple Google of "Andrew Walls" yielded 93,900 results in less than one second.
2. Having accepted the invitation to contribute an essay to this volume, on September 4, 2008, I wrote to approximately one hundred academics whose research, writing, and teaching intersect with the study of mission and World Christianity. These include members of the Yale-Edinburgh Group for the Study of Missions and World Christianity as well as his former colleagues, collaborators, publishers, and students. Where I quote directly from their remarks, I so indicate.

The Influence of His Ideas

If Walls is notorious for his modesty, his devotees — including former students, professorial colleagues, and academic peers — tend to be effusive in their admiration of the man. For some, their encounter with Walls is expressed in terms ordinarily reserved for religious conversion. He was their academic epiphany.

"Andrew turned my life around," recalled Frederick Norris. "When I met Andrew at OMSC," he wrote, "I had been a history of theology major for eleven years and four degrees, including the Yale Ph.D. I had taught historical theology, theology, and ethics in all eras for five years in a provincial seminary. He made everything I had studied new: some things turned upside down, others related to events, persons, and writings I had not considered. *Never had I seen such insight into the nature and history of the Gospel, culture, and the church.* I stopped the project I was working on and turned to the history of World Christianity."[3]

"Andrew Walls," observed Philip Jenkins, "is a much maligned man. Everyone accuses him of just being a brilliant scholar on African Christianities in the modern world. . . . I still think the ideas expressed very briefly in his essay 'Eusebius Tries Again' should be enough to keep any decent history department on their toes for several years."[4]

In an interview about his book *The New Shape of World Christianity: How American Experience Reflects Global Faith* (InterVarsity 2009), historian Mark Noll acknowledged the transformative role played by Andrew Walls in his own thinking: "The missiologist Andrew Walls has written profoundly about the huge impact of voluntary societies on World Christianity," he said; "*My book is, in a sense, only an extended footnote on Walls's very important insights* (italics added)." Noll then went on to urge readers of his book to familiarize themselves with Walls's *The Missionary Movement in Christian History: Studies in the Transmission of Faith.*[5]

---

3. Frederick W. Norris in a personal email to Jonathan Bonk, dated September 11, 2008. Norris attributes his own *Christianity: A Short Global History* (Oxford: Oneworld Publications, 2002) to the influence of Andrew Walls.

4. Philip Jenkins to Jonathan Bonk, in a personal email September 5, 2008, referring to Andrew F. Walls, "Eusebius Tries Again: Reconceiving the Study of Christian History," *International Bulletin of Missionary Research* 24, no. 3 (2000): 105–11.

5. Justin Taylor, "An Interview with Mark Noll about The New Shape of World Christianity" first appearing in *Faith, Books and Culture* (June 8, 2009). *http://thegospelcoalition.org/blogs/justintaylor/2009/06/08/interview-with-mark-noll-about-new/* (accessed Aug. 30, 2010).

Daniel Bays, a leading academic interpreter of Christianity in China, recalls being "struck by the freshness of his approach and the cogency of his case for the need to reconceptualize both Western and non-Western Christianity" the first time he heard Walls lecture more than twenty-five years ago. "In the years since then," he wrote, "my own approach to issues in the history of Christianity in China has been heavily influenced by his insights.... For years now, I have been employing concepts coined by him as tools to enhance my own understanding of the historical dynamics of Christianity in the global East and South, and as examples of creative historical thinking. Andrew has almost single-handedly transformed the moribund field of 'mission studies' or 'missiology' into a lively arena of Christianity's interface with culture and cross-cultural transmission of faith."[6]

One would be hard pressed to write a credible history of World Christianity today without using ideas, themes, and orientations traceable to Walls. His ability to see connections, analogies and hitherto overlooked links across the spectra of time, ideas, practices, and places has often reenergized and even redirected serious historians. Scottish historian David Bebbington referred to Walls as "the leading pioneer of his generation in writing the academic history of Christian missions. His writing," he went on to say, "depicts the modern missionary movement as a phase in the grand sweep of global Christian history and he has illuminated with particular clarity the relationship between the Christian faith and its host culture."[7] In the words of evangelical historian Mark Noll, "No one has written with greater wisdom about what it means for the Western Christian religion to become the global Christian religion.... By tracing the current movement of Christianity from the post-Enlightenment North to the animistic South, Walls [shows] how much the twentieth century has resembled the second century, when Christianity moved out from its Judaic origins into the Hellenistic Mediterranean, and also its seventh and eighth century of northward migration from that Greco-Roman world into the Germanic regions of Europe."[8]

---

6. Daniel H. Bays, in a personal email to Jonathan Bonk dated September 26, 2008. Bays's best known book is *Christianity in China: From the Eighteenth Century to the Present* (Stanford, Calif.: Stanford University Press, 1996). Bays is professor and history director in the Asian Studies Program at Calvin College. His latest book, co-edited with Ellen Widmer, is *China's Christian Colleges: Cross-Cultural Connections, 1900–1950* (Stanford, Calif.: Stanford University Press, 2009).

7. David W. Bebbington to Jonathan Bonk, in a personal email dated September 4, 2008.

8. Mark A. Noll, "Andrew F. Walls: The Missionary Movement in Christian History (1996)," *First Things: A Monthly Journal of Religion and Public Life* (March 2000): 55–56.

The venerable Robert Frykenberg, preeminent Indian historian and professor emeritus of Asian Studies at the University of Wisconsin, frankly acknowledges the influence of Walls on his thinking since their first encounter at a conference in 1986. "The sheer breadth and depth and mind-expanding sweep of [his] ideas, as these have helped me to reformulate my own perspectives on Christian Missions and World Christianity, have been breathtaking," he wrote. "Indeed, his ideas enabled perspectives on the growth of Christianity in India, from its earliest beginnings to the present, that would not have been otherwise possible. For this alone I owe him a huge debt of gratitude."[9]

Commenting on David Barrett's prescient conjecture in 1970 that the growth surge in African Christianity portended that "African Christians might well tip the balance and transform Christianity permanently into a primarily non-Western religion," the late Kwame Bediako pointed out that it was Andrew Walls who realized that "what happens within the African Churches in the next generation will determine the whole shape of church history for centuries to come; what sort of theology is most characteristic of the Christianity of the twenty-first century may well depend on what has happened in the minds of African Christians in the interim."[10]

A prominent academic in Anabaptist circles with special expertise in Christendom's origins and subsequent impact upon World Christianity,[11] Alan Kreider acknowledges that Walls "has helped the world church to teach me, and I would suspect, many others, not least by continuing, learnedly but lightly, to make connections with the area of his own expertise — patristics. The dialogue between the new churches of the early centuries A.D. and the new churches of today is transformative. It has altered the way I understand and teach the early church; it has also given my students new perspectives on the ways that we can view the churches worldwide today.... A 'new Eusebius,' [his] awareness of the people of God across space and the centuries has both depth and breadth. His unerring eye for the tell-tale person or incident has provided specifics which have enabled me to see the huge

9. Robert Eric Frykenberg in a personal email to Jonathan Bonk, September 24, 2008. Frykenberg's most recent book is his highly acclaimed *Christianity in India: From Beginnings to the Present* (Oxford: Oxford University Press, 2010).

10. Kwame Bediako, *Christianity in Africa: The Renewal of a Non-Western Religion* (Maryknoll, N.Y.: Orbis Books, 1995), viii, citing David B. Barrett, "AD 2000: 350 Million Christians in Africa," *International Review of Mission* 59, no. 233 (1970): 39–54, and Andrew F. Walls, "Toward an Understanding of Africa's Place in Christian History," in *Religion in a Pluralistic Society*, ed. J. S. Pobee (Lieden: E. J. Brill, 1976), 180–89.

11. See, for example, his edited volume, *The Origins of Christendom in the West* (Edinburgh: T. & T. Clark, 2001).

movements of accession and recession across the centuries. . . . I have found his vision of the various forms that Christianity has taken in many settings historically and today to be both humorous and liberating."[12]

Similar stories have been recounted with such frequency on all five continents that it was not only appropriate but inevitable that the American Society of Church History should have honored him with its Distinguished Career Award in January 2007, in recognition of his impact on the field.[13]

Research and Documentation

The key role played by Walls in encouraging and stimulating the collection and preservation of often overlooked materials that retrospectively turn out to be indispensable to the collective memory known as "church history" cannot be overestimated. In an article appearing in the July/August 2010 issue of *Discover Magazine*, David Freedman examined the impact of what scientists refer to as "The Streetlight Effect" on medical and scientific theory and practice. "Researchers tend to look for answers where the looking is good, rather than where the answers are likely to be hiding," he observed, just like the old drunk who was found on his hands and knees crawling around under a street light. Asked by a police officer what he was doing, he said that he was looking for his keys. "Are you sure this is where you lost them," the policeman asked? "I lost them on the other side of the street," the man replied. "Then why are you looking for them here?" queried the puzzled officer. "Because," responded the man impatiently, "the light is better here. There is a streetlight."[14]

The streetlight effect has its analogue in the study of church history. Researching outside the beam of the streetlight — where Christianity is growing most rapidly and where theologies are proliferating as the Bible is brought to bear on questions and issues never anticipated by either its authors or its emissaries — is tedious, time consuming, and sometimes frustrating, so scholars go to the places where the streetlights shine: university and mission libraries, archives and materials in Western lands. There is, of course, nothing wrong with such histories, except that they no longer tell the story of the world church. Key elements of that story can be found only

---

12. Alan Kreider in a personal email to Jonathan Bonk, September 25, 2008.

13. URL: *www.churchhistory.org/researchgrants.html* (accessed October 20, 2010).

14. David H. Freedman, "The Streetlight Effect," *Discover Magazine* (July/August 2010): 55–57.

elsewhere, beyond the reassuring beam of the streetlight. And it is there that Walls has pioneered in both the search itself, in the documentation and interpretation of what is discovered, and in the creation of tools essential to the preservation of the record.

At the inaugural meeting of the International Association for Mission Studies (IAMS) in 1972, Walls initiated the Documentation, Archives, and Bibliography (DAB, now DABOH) Mission Study Group. Gerald Anderson, a contemporary, collaborator, and close friend of Walls, hailed him as "one of the Founding Fathers of IAMS, along with Myklebust, Gensichen, Arnulf Camps, S.J. Samartha, and Paul R. Clifford." Anderson went on to recall that "In the pre-history of...the founding of IAMS in 1972 at Driebergen.... [Walls] was at the important consultation in 1968 at Selly Oak Colleges, Birmingham...[although] he was not at the two preliminary meetings held in Hamburg in 1955 and 1966, because he was in Africa and returned to Scotland only in 1966 to teach at Aberdeen."[15]

In personal notes made at the follow-up conference in Oslo in 1970, Anderson recorded:

Andrew Walls reported in the business meeting that a group of participants had met to discuss concerns about bibliographical, documentation, and information services. They concluded that there was a need for more information about existing resources and services, and requested the Provisional Committee to sponsor a questionnaire to this end, "and that future conferences should provide for news and discussion of documentation and other instruments studiorum for mission studies." This was the beginning of what would become a major continuing project and initiative of the IAMS, known as DAB or DABOH." DABOH: "Documentation, Archives, Bibliography and Oral History.[16]

---

15. In a personal email to me on October 21, 2010 Anderson recalled that when Prof. Myklebust retired and stepped down from his position as general secretary and treasurer of IAMS at the conference in Frankfurt in 1974, Andrew was elected as the second general secretary [a separate person was elected as treasurer] of the Association, in which office he served until 1976.

16. Ibid. "DABOH," according to its official Web site, "exists to help rescue the memory of our people by: promoting the documentation (with due emphasis on recording personal memoirs through oral history and other means) of the mission of the Christian church around the world, especially in regions where infrastructures do not exist for such endeavors; (2) encouraging the support, development, and use of archives for mission; (3) stimulating the preparation and distribution of material to enable mission studies and other researchers to identify, locate, and access primary material on the mission of the church in their own country and worldwide;

Walls has continued to be an animating influence in meetings and projects undertaken by the DAB/DABOH. He played a leading role, for example, in the DAB consultation on "Mission Studies and Information Management" held in Rome in 1980 and in a subsequent DABOH consultation held in Rome in 2002 on the theme "Rescuing the Memory of Our Peoples." Among the tangible fruits of the 2002 consultation was a sixty-page "how to" archives manual compiled by Martha Smalley and Rosemary Seton. This widely used resource is now freely available online as a PDF in seven languages.[17]

More than most, Walls has understood that "A people is defined and unified not by blood but by shared memory.... Deciding to remember, and what to remember, is how we decide who we are."[18] And for decades he has acted practically, resourcefully, and without fanfare on that conviction. He is widely known for his work as editor of the long-running "Bibliography on Mission Studies" series that has been a regular feature of the *International Review of Mission* since 1982.[19]

Less conspicuous but possibly of greater ultimate significance have been his efforts to stimulate local documentation and collections. Where others saw junk mail, he saw the treasures of social history. So common as to escape scholarly notice at the time, such humble nonacademic materials become indispensable to a future generation's understanding of their ancestors. His eye for the important but generally overlooked category sometimes known as "gray literature" was evident in the voluminous but quirky collection of pamphlets, booklets, letters, flyers, tracts, printed memorabilia, and miscellanea that he accumulated over the years, and to which he would refer his students at Aberdeen and Edinburgh universities. He instilled in his students and inspired in his peers an appreciation for nonscholarly printed materials.

---

and (4) networking with individuals and groups with related concerns, and facilitating multilateral, ecumenical, intercultural and international conversation to further our understanding of worldwide Christianity." *http://missionstudies.org/index.php/study-groups/daboh/* (accessed October 15, 2010).

17. *Rescuing the Memory of Our Peoples: Archive Manual* (IAMS and OMSC, 2003) is available in English, French, Spanish, Portuguese, Korean, Swahili, and Chinese. It can be downloaded at *www.omsc.org/Links.htm* (the OMSC Web site) or at *www.library.yale.edu/div/RTMmanuallinks.html* (the Yale Divinity School Web site).

18. Robert Pinsky, "Poetry and American Memory," *The Atlantic Online* (October 1999), URL: *www.theatlantic.com/issues/99oct/9910pinsky.htm* (accessed October 21, 2010).

19. The title of this long-running series has evolved over time, beginning in January of 1972 as "Bibliography on World Mission and Evangelism," continuing until October 1987 as "Bibliography on World Mission," until finally settling on "Bibliography on Mission Studies" in January 1988. Margaret M. Acton has served as co-editor of the bibliography since April 1996.

It is only with the passage of time that such materials come to be appreciated as a clear window — unobscured by scholarly processing — into the world as seen, experienced, and articulated by those who lived and moved in earlier times.

Robert Schuster, director of the Billy Graham Center Archives at Wheaton, expressed his indebtedness to Walls "for his contributions, over more than a quarter of a century, to the task of ensuring that the record of Christ's church be preserved for the church as well as scholars and the general community. He has always stressed the need for the documents to be used as well as saved," wrote Schuster, "and for the historical resources to be as easily available in Africa, Asia, and Latin America as in Europe and North America."[20]

While on leave from St. Andrew's College in Kabare, Kenya, in 1988, Bishop Graham Kings recalls meeting Walls in Cambridge, where he was giving the Henry Martyn Lectures. "The importance he gave to...church archives in Nigeria was highlighted when he told me that the ones he had collected were destroyed in the Biafran war. This was the inspiration behind founding an archive center at St. Andrew's College,...which was opened in November 1992 and has the archives of Archbishop David Gitari and the Diocese of Mount Kenya East and a collection of material culture. Later on, his encouragement led to the founding of the Henry Martyn Centre for the study of mission and World Christianity in Cambridge in 1996, and our collaboration on the North Atlantic Missiology Project, led by Brian Stanley."[21]

He also figured significantly in facilitating Harold W. Turner's New Religious Movements collections when they were colleagues at the University of Aberdeen. It was as a colleague of Walls that Turner published his remarkable six-volume *Bibliography of New Religious Movements in Primal Societies* (G. K. Hall, 1977–92).[22] Walls did not see these movements as ephemeral desiderata on the margins of some timelessly "normative"

---

20. Robert Schuster in a personal email to Jonathan Bonk, September 18, 2008.

21. Canon Dr. Graham Kings, vicar of Islington, in a personal email to Jonathan Bonk, September 26, 2008. Dr. Graham Kings was appointed Bishop of Sherborne in Dorset in April 2009.

22. The Turner Collection is now a part of the Research Unit for New Religions and Cultures at the University of Birmingham. According to the Web site, "The collection is a record of Harold Turner's research into the phenomenon of new religious movements arising out of the interaction between traditional cultures and religions with biblical teaching, and with other religions on all continents, including Asia. The origin and emphasis of the documentation has been whether this phenomenon is widespread and how the proliferation of these movements raised important pastoral and theological issues for Christian mission." *www.asiamap.ac.uk/collections/collection.php?ID=174&Browse=Region&Region=1* (accessed October 21, 2010). The collection consists of some twenty-eight thousand items.

European Christian map. Rather, they were and are a crucial "older testament," indispensable to an understanding of the massive demographic shift taking place in World Christianity. It was these primal religions that made widespread appropriation of Christian faith across Asia, Latin America, Macronesia, and Africa over the past century possible, perhaps even inevitable. Andrew Walls grasped their significance decades before most of his peers. In an interview in 2007, Lamin Sanneh — an early colleague of Walls at the University of Aberdeen — noted that he was "one of the few scholars who say that African Christianity was not just an exotic, curious phenomenon in an obscure part of the world, but that African Christianity might be the shape of things to come."[23]

In my own case, the Ida Grace McRuer Mission Resource Center collection at Providence College and Theological Seminary was a direct result of Walls's pamphlet collection in Aberdeen. Neither mandated nor oriented to research, this nondenominational school in southern Manitoba became home to a collection of prayer letters and booklets, bulletins, in-house promotional materials and publications, pamphlets, etc. from some fourteen hundred North American mission societies — both independent and denominational. The collection grew until it filled five rooms, and occupied a handful of part-time student assistants just to keep up with the classifying and filing of the materials. The center received more mail each day than the cumulative aggregate of the entire staff and administration. Over time the value of the collection — comprised almost entirely of the sort of materials that almost inevitably ends up in the trash — became more and more evident, and scholars began to look to the materials to discover mission or missionary self-representation in a bygone era. It was the stuff of social history.

Thanks to Walls, scores of unlikely collections in similarly implausible locations now exist across the continents, each doing its part to ensure that later generations of scholars will have access to available primary-source materials that would otherwise have been discarded or shredded.

Networking and Collaboration

In addition to his key role in founding the International Association for Mission Studies (IAMS) as noted above, Walls was instrumental in co-founding

---

23. Tim Stafford, "Historian Ahead of His Time: Andrew Walls May Be the Most Important Person You Don't Know," posted February 8, 2007. *www.christianitytoday.com/ct/2007/ February/34.87.html* (accessed October 15, 2010).

with Lamin Sanneh "The Yale-Edinburgh Group on the History of the Missionary Movement and World Christianity," an informal group of scholars
who convene annually "to facilitate discussion and exchange of information
about historical aspects of the missionary movement and the development
of World Christianity, with special emphasis on the sources for documentation. It is a forum where viewpoints from the fields of political, social,
diplomatic, and religious history can converge to reassess the significance
of the missionary movement and its worldwide effects."[24] Like many other
worthwhile things, the group was begun somewhat accidentally. Martha
Smalley recalls that Andrew Walls and Lamin Sanneh thought it would be
appropriate to hold an event in 1992 to commemorate the two hundredth
anniversary of William Carey's departure for India, marking the symbolic
beginning of the modern missionary movement from the West. There were
two meetings that first year, one in Yale and one in Edinburgh. These meetings were so successful that the group decided to meet annually, alternating
between Yale University and the University of Edinburgh.

With twenty meetings behind it, this academic group serves as a venue
for both emerging and established scholars in the field, who come from all
over the world each year to present papers and engage in discussions ger-
mane to World Christianity. The influence of Walls's ideas on the way these
scholars approach and teach their subject is evident. Indeed, it is difficult
to imagine an informed discussion of either the missionary movement or
World Christianity taking place anywhere without the use of language and
concepts traceable directly to Walls.[25]

Lectures and Publications[26]

Anyone who has listened to his lectures and read his essays soon becomes
familiar with the recurring themes, emphases, and orientation that permeate

---

24. URL *www.library.yale.edu/div/yaleedin.htm* (accessed October 20, 2010).

25. See his essay "Afterword: Christian Mission in a Five-hundred-year Context," in *Mission in the Twenty-First Century: Exploring the Five Marks of Global Mission*, ed. Andrew F. Walls and Cathy Ross (Maryknoll, N.Y.: Orbis books, 2008), 193–204. Among the most frequently cited of the many essays in which he makes this point in extraordinarily imaginative ways are the first two chapters in his book *The Missionary Movement in Christian History: Studies in the Transmission of Faith* (Maryknoll, N.Y.: Orbis Books, 1996), 3–25: "The Gospel as Prisoner and Liberator of Culture" and "Culture and Coherence in Christian History."

26. I combine these two categories because Walls is a superb essayist, and because most of his essays began as lectures. As he writes in the preface to his best known collection of essays, *The Missionary Movement in Christian History,* "Most were originally prepared for oral delivery" (xi).

his vast scholarly written and oral corpus. The bibliography of his known publications numbers in the hundreds of articles, reviews, interviews, and books. It is hard to imagine another scholar whose publications appear in such an eclectic range of journals:

Theology;
Sierra Leone Bulletin of Religion;
Novum Testamentum;
Evangelical Quarterly;
New Testament Studies;
Vigiliae Christianae;
Tyndale House Bulletin;
Studia Patristica;
Bulletin of the Society for African Church History;
Journal of Religion in Africa;
Proceedings of the Wesley Historical Society;
Anglican Review;
Kingdom Overseas;
Hokhma;
Trivium;
Journal of the Scottish Branch of the Wesley Historical Society;
Religion;
International Review of Mission;
Evangelikale Missiologie;
Occasional Bulletin of Missionary Research;
Mission Focus;
Religions in Education;
International Bulletin of Missionary Research;
Faith and Thought;
Bulletin of the Scottish Institute of Missionary Studies;
Scottish Journal of Religious Studies;
Bulletin, Association of British Theological and Philosophical Libraries;
Mission Thrust;
Word and World;
Transformation;
Christian History;
Princeton Seminary Bulletin;
Journal of Presbyterian History;

Christian History Institute's Glimpses;
Yes Magazine;
The Bible Translator;
Covenant Quarterly;
AICMAR Bulletin;
Swedish Missiological Themes;
Word and Context;

and on it goes. Not surprisingly, personal interviews and articles *about* him likewise appear in unlikely places — Christian and missionary magazines, newspapers, hinting at the range of his influence.

It is a safe conjecture that his unpublished works may be as voluminous as those gracing the scores of journals, books, and encyclopedias in which he has left his trail, since he is famously averse to signing off on essays that fall short of his standard. As editor of the *International Bulletin of Missionary Research* and director of an organization that has for at least thirty years been a regular stop in his annual cycle of travels and lectures, I speak from firsthand experience. In my possession are manuscripts and lecture transcripts that have yet to be published. At our invitation, Walls prepared nineteen lectures on the Social History of the Western Missionary Movement, delivered at OMSC between 2005 and 2008. Under the rubric "Understanding the Western Missionary Movement," the lectures were organized under four subthemes: (1) Developments in a Formative Phase; (2) The Middle Years of Western Missions; (3) Western Missions Move into the Twentieth Century; and (4) The Second World War and the Old Age of the Western Missionary Movement. No lecture series in the history of OMSC has drawn as much outside interest, or so many Walls devotees.

Margins as Center

Walls is not the first to reflect on the encounter between Christianity and Islam. Robert Louis Wilken has written eloquently and persuasively about the difference between Christian and Muslim patterns of geographic expansion.[27] Until the advent of Islam, Christian growth and expansion was more-or-less steady, seemingly inexorable. By A.D. 600, the known world

---

27. See his essay "Christianity Face to Face with Islam," *First Things: A Monthly Journal of Religion and Public Life,* no. 189 (2009): 19–26.

that mattered was interconnected by churches, Christianity was an honored and necessary contingent to the state, and the future seemed assured. But by the eighth century, Islam had made remarkable progress in making distant, once-Christian regions across North Africa and the Middle East and eastward throughout Asia Minor a part of the Muslim *umma*. Christianity throughout the regions conquered by Islam gradually atrophied and often disappeared. In the eleventh century Asia Minor was thoroughly Christian; five hundred years later, Christianity had virtually disappeared. These lands were never recovered by Christianity, and remain Muslim to this day. As Wilken observes, "Set against the history of Islam, the career of Christianity is marked as much by decline and extinction as it is by growth and triumph.... Most of the territories that were Christian in the year 700 are now Muslim. Nothing similar has happened to Islam. Christianity seems like a rain shower that soaks the earth and then moves on, whereas Islam appears more like a great lake that constantly overflows its banks to inundate new territory. When Islam arrives, it comes to stay — unless displaced by force, as it was in Spain."[28]

Walls, while fully cognizant of the asymmetries marking the two faiths — the inexorable, irreversible expansion of Islam, on the one hand, and the decline and even extinction of once securely Christian territories, on the other — offers a profoundly theological interpretation of the phenomenon. Christian expansion, he is known to observe, is not *progressive,* but *serial.*[29] In an essay entitled "The Western Discovery of Non-Western Christian Art," Walls noted that "Christianity is in principle perhaps the most syncretistic of the great religions. Unlike Hinduism, it does not have a unifocal religious culture belonging to a particular soil; nor, like Islam, does it have a common sacred language and a recognizable cultural framework across the globe. Historically, Christian expansion has been serial, moving from one heartland to another, fading in one culture as it is implanted in another. Christian expansion involves the serial, generational, and vernacular penetration of different cultures."[30] "Do the resiliency of Islam and the vulnerability of Christianity reflect something of the inherent nature of the two faiths?" he

---

28. Ibid., 23.

29. Andrew F. Walls, "Christianity in the Non-Western World: A Study in the Serial Nature of Christian Expansion," in *The Cross-Cultural Process in Christian History: Studies in the Transmission and Appropriation of Faith* (Maryknoll, N.Y.: Orbis Books, 2005), 27–48.

30. Walls, *The Missionary Movement in Christian History,* 173. This essay first appeared in *The Church and the Arts,* Studies in Church History 28, ed. Diana Wood (Oxford: Blackwell 1992), 571–85.

asks. "Does the very freedom of response inherent in the Christian gospel leave it open to ultimate rejection?"[31]

Christianity and Christendom are not synonymous, Walls reminds us. Indeed, he observes, "the dissolution of Christendom made possible a cultural diffusion that is now in process of transforming it.... Christendom is dead, and Christianity is alive and well without it."[32] In an interview appearing in the *Christian Century* Walls explained that Christianity does not maintain its hold on its converts the way Buddhism or Islam do.[33] "One must conclude," he said, "that there is a certain vulnerability, a fragility, at the heart of Christianity. You might say that this is the vulnerability of the cross. Perhaps the chief theological point is that nobody owns the Christian faith. That is, there is no 'Christian civilization' or 'Christian culture' in the way that there is an 'Islamic culture,' which you can recognize from Pakistan to Tunisia to Morocco."[34] Repeatedly, insistently, and imaginatively, Walls points out that in its earliest days, while it was still a Jewish sect, followers of the Way concluded that new life in Christ could not follow tribal lines. The Good News was conversion to a new way, not proselytism to the Hebrew tribal religion. The cultural identities and lifestyles of new converts were to be transformed from the inside out.[35]

Man of the People

Although he is an active and honored member of many learned societies — British Association for the Study of Religions, International Association for Mission Studies, Aberdeen Artists' Society, and Deutsche Gesellschaft für Missionswissenschaft, to name a few — it is clear that he is not now and has never been an "ivory tower" intellectual, carrying on a private conversation with an elite group of insiders. He is as comfortable with undergraduates and modestly educated missionaries and church leaders as he is with fellow dons. Insofar as posterity may judge him to have transformed the course of mission and world Christian studies — and those of us in the field believe

31. Andrew F. Walls, "A History of the Expansion of Christianity Reconsidered: Assessing Christian Progress and Decline," in Walls, *The Cross-Cultural Process in Christian History,* 3–26 (13).

32. Andrew F. Walls, "Christianity in the Non-Western World: A Study in the Serial Nature of Christian Expansion," in ibid., 27–48 (34).

33. August 2–9, 2000, pp. 792–99.

34. Ibid.

35. Andrew F. Walls, "Converts or Proselytes? The Crisis over Conversion in the Early Church," *International Bulletin of Missionary Research* 28, no. 1 (2004): 2–6

that he has — it is as much a result of his generosity with the "least of these" as it is his nimble pen and encyclopedic knowledge. There are few who can recall him saying "no" when invited to give a lecture or write a paper, no matter how obscure the invitee or unimpressive the venue.

Added to academic achievements is his lifelong involvement in public service. He has served as an Aberdeen city councilor, as chairman of the Aberdeen Art Gallery and Museums Committee, the Council for Museums and Galleries in Scotland, the Committee on Arts and Recreation, and as chairman of the Disablement Income Group, Scotland. He contributed an article titled "Access Considerations for Handicapped Visitors" to the book *Museums and the Handicapped,* published in Leicester in 1976. David Bebbington tells of his surprise at seeing Andrew Walls at the University of Stirling on once occasion. "I asked him if he was attending some church history conference of which I had not heard, but the answer was no, he was there as a trade unionist. The Association of University Teachers, I inquired? No, he represented Unison, the union of the manual laborers in the universities. They are the poorest paid, he asked, are they not? And there was obvious point in the reply. Andrew is the rare sort of person whose remarks of this kind one remembers."[36]

His remarkable interest in what even the most unpromising student has to say sets him apart from most academic mentors. Whether in a personal conversation, an academic gathering, or a seminar, students and fledgling academics can count on his genuine appreciation for their modest efforts. At the weekly postgraduate seminars at the University of Aberdeen in the late 1970s, a particularly brilliant professor was feared by all of us, since he could be unsparing and unflattering in his criticism of our faltering efforts. Not so Andrew Walls! He encouraged even those of us most feebly endowed intellectually, finding ways to surprise and credit us and our modest research accomplishment with insights that were concealed from our own consciousness! He often understood, in ways that we could not, what it was we were stumbling upon, what it was we were trying to say, and how all this fit into the grand drama of World Christianity. Little wonder that his students flourished!

I have a list of seventy postgraduate students — men and women from around the world — whose dissertations have been supervised by Walls. There are doubtless many more, but each of these represents some sphere of

---

36. David W. Bebbington to Jonathan Bonk, in a personal email dated September 4, 2008.

academic or ecclesiastical influence, local, regional, national, or even international. Each is the center of a modest or even substantial intellectual, ecclesiastical or missional sphere now infused with the ideas and the spirit of Walls. Laughingly referred to several years ago by Orbis editor William Burrows as "The Walls Mafioso," these protégés can now be found in every substantial research center devoted to the study of World Christianity on all five continents.

Some, like the recently deceased Kwame Bediako — possibly the most brilliant student ever mentored by Walls — have made extraordinarily substantial contributions to the way we think about African, and indeed *world,* Christianities.[37] Several serve as editors of prestigious journals in the field; others serve as professors in some of the world's leading centers of historical research and intellectual thought; some are leaders of flourishing denominations in Africa and Asia. Others teach in more modest seminary and Bible college settings on all the continents, where aspiring ordinands or missionaries receive their training, imbibing a perspective on mission and World Christianity that has been heavily influenced by Andrew Walls. Still others serve as missionaries or as mission executives, as directors of modest research centers, or as research scholars whose influence is exerted on the subterranean foundations of what we know, how we know it, and why this matters. Walls's influence — from New Zealand to Nigeria, from Ghana to Grenada, from the Vatican to the Church of the Lord Aladura — is worldwide.

A Cloud as Small as a Man's Hand Is Rising from the Sea

This short essay can only hint at the impact of Andrew Walls on the way we think about mission and world Christian studies. His influence ripples outward through modestly influential, widely scattered devotees — numbering in the hundreds — around the world. His seminal ideas permeate the classrooms, publications, research, archives, and academic gatherings where World Christianity is the subject or the object of interest. Those of us who have been permanently and profoundly transformed by his ideas in turn affect those in our own modest orbits of influence. In this way, probably

---

37. For his immensely moving tribute to his friend, see Andrew F. Walls, "Kwame Bediako and Christian Scholarship in Africa," *International Bulletin of Missionary Research* 32, no. 4 (2008): 188–93.

more than it is possible to tell, the "structural problems in mission studies" so illuminatingly outlined by Walls in an essay written twenty years ago[38] are being addressed in scores of Bible schools, seminaries, research centers, and university departments around the world, especially beyond Christendom's old heartlands. Church history syllabuses are being subverted, non-Western Christian thought is being taken seriously, and emerging generations are becoming cognizant of realities on the ground. This is how Andrew Walls has changed the course of mission and world Christian studies.

We are far too close to Andrew Walls as a friend, mentor, and exemplar to properly assess his long-term impact on the way academics think about mission and World Christianity. Such a study will better be undertaken fifty or a hundred years from now. What we *do* see, however, are intimations — "a cloud as small as a man's hand is rising from the sea" — and those who have eyes to see believe that rain is on the way!

---

38. Andrew F. Walls, "Structural Problems in Mission Studies," *International Bulletin of Missionary Research* 15, no. 4 (1991): 146–55.

7

Theological Education as Embodiment of Jesus

MOONJANG LEE

As Andrew Walls has helped us to see, there was a shift in the center of Christian gravity from the West to the non-Western world during the twentieth century, though the implications of this shift have not been fully grasped by Asian theologians as well as those in the West. Walls observes that the expansion of Christian faith in the world has been serial, not progressive.[1] In this serial advance of Christianity, a previous center of Christian gravity became a periphery, and a periphery emerged as a new center. He further explains that the emergence of a new center of Christian gravity resulted from Christianity crossing the cultural frontiers, which in turn allowed the formation of new ways to express the Christian faith.[2] He also anticipates that new forms of theology will emerge in the process of the encounter between the Gospel and the thought-world of the non-Western peoples, and he even says that "the future of Christian theology and theological scholarship as a whole" depend on that encounter.[3] At the same time, he does not fail to point out that the geographical expansion of Christianity in the last century was not accompanied by the expansion of theology that would represent a local understanding of Christianity and direct a new way of being a Christian. His observation is meant to highlight the current situation in which the theologies produced in the West dictate the goals, tasks, and methods of Christian studies in the non-Western world, and to emphasize

---

1. Andrew F. Walls, "Rethinking Mission: New Direction for a New Century," *Mission and Theology* 8 (2001): 257.

2. Andrew F. Walls, "Culture and Coherence in Christian History," in *The Missionary Movement in Christian History: Studies in the Transmission of Faith* (Maryknoll, N.Y.: Orbis Books, 1996), 22–25.

3. Andrew F. Walls, "In Quest of the Father of Mission Studies," *Trinity Theological Journal* (1989): 26–27.

the necessity for local Christians to initiate a reorientation of the way we conduct theological studies in a specific locality.[4]

In conducting this reorientation, Walls's emphasis on conversion, culture, and the incarnation of Christ is integral in that it reminds us that theology is formed in the process of interacting with the particular questions of life in a particular society at a particular time. It therefore follows that the transmission of the theology shaped in one region cannot be accompanied by the transmission of the original life situation that gave birth to the theology. Thus, for Asian theologians and Christians, theology must be related to the concrete reality of our life and must penetrate into our real situations. In other words, theology must be incarnate in our contexts, providing insights and principles for Christian thinking and living, and also addressing the real issues arising in our life situations.[5]

Given this challenge not only to develop an Asian theology that represents the ethos of Asian Christians but also a model of theological learning I offer the following proposals for theological education in the Asian context. My theme is that theological education is to be an embodiment of Jesus. In this essay I will describe the new environment that demands a new approach in theological education in the global context. First, I will reaffirm the ultimate goal of theological education to be the embodiment of Jesus and accordingly reconceptualize the way theological students are trained. Then I will explain what it means to achieve Christlikeness through theological education and suggest how to achieve that goal.

Expansion of Christianity:
A New Christian Scholarship

At the beginning of the twenty-first century we celebrate the dawning of global Christianity, accompanying the shift of the center of Christian gravity from the West to the non-Western world. It seems, however, that the ramifications of this shift have not yet been fully grasped and reflected in theological education.[6] It may be partly due to the habit of thought that was formed during the Christendom era, but we anticipate that the future of global Christianity will see new initiatives in three areas.

---

4. Moonjang Lee, "Re-Configuration of Western Theology in Asia," *Common Ground Journal* 6, no. 2 (2009): 79.

5. Ibid., 83.

6. Cf. Andrew F. Walls, "Christian Scholarship in Africa in the Twenty-First Century," *Journal of African Christian Thought* 4, no. 2 (2001): 44–52.

First, a new biblical scholarship will be formulated. The traditional Western critical biblical scholarship has been criticized for its "a-political detachment, objective literalism and scientific value-neutrality."[7] Biblical scholars have devised various tools for the study of the Bible, and in recent years contextual and ideological readings have been experienced. We cannot fail to notice that all these scholarly attempts follow the rules and guidelines of biblical scholarship within the academia. However, we hear new voices that seek a new orientation in the study of the Bible. In early 1970s, Walter Wink suggested a new paradigm for biblical study, claiming that the critical approach to the Bible was bankrupt.[8] He emphasized that the Bible should be studied with an eye to human transformation. In the Asian theater, some have attempted to overcome the "scientistic ethos of value-free, detached inquiry" that lies behind Western biblical scholarship. George Soares-Prabhu has asserted that in the Asian religious milieu the Bible as a sacred text is read for personal transformation, and the traditional historical-critical reading method is not effective.[9] Personal transformation means the acquisition of practical wisdom and the ability to discern God's will in our daily walk. Through biblical studies, our eyes are to be opened to the way of God, as the psalmist said: "Your Word is the lamp on my footstool and the light in my path." If biblical studies is to be reoriented to serve the purpose of personal transformation, a new reading method to effectuate that goal needs to be devised.

Second, the goal of Christian scholarship will have to be revised to achieve a nondualistic embodiment of Christian teachings that will overcome any subject-object dichotomy. It is noteworthy that in the Eastern religious traditions the expectation and purpose of those who commit to religious studies is to achieve the highest stage of human perfection through spiritual and religious cultivation. As Fung Yu-Lan put it, "The ultimate purpose of Buddhism is to teach men how to achieve Buddhahood — a problem vital to the people of that time. Likewise, the ultimate purpose of Neo-Confucianism is to teach men how to achieve Confucian Sagehood."[10] Christian scholarship as developed in the West has focused mostly on the cognitive understanding

---

7. Elisabeth Schüssler Fiorenza, "The Ethics of Interpretation: De-centering Biblical Scholarship," *Journal of Biblical Literature* 107 (1988): 10.

8. Walter Wink, *The Bible in Human Transformation: Toward a New Paradigm for Biblical Study* (Philadelphia: Fortress Press, 1973).

9. George M. Soares-Prabhu, "Towards an Indian Interpretation of the Bible," *Bible-bhashyam* 6 (1980).

10. Cf. Fung Yu-Lan, *A Short History of Chinese Philosophy* (New York: Free Press), 271.

(orthodoxy) of the Christian truth based on scientific, rational, and historical studies. Beyond orthodoxy and orthopraxis, however, theological training should help students to achieve personal religious/spiritual transformation. The limitation of Western theological training was well illustrated in an essay written by African theologian John Mbiti. In his article, Mbiti describes how a young African theologian who returned home with a doctoral degree in theology after ten years of theological training in Europe failed to meet the religious expectations of the local villagers.[11] When asked to do something for his sister possessed by an evil spirit, he was found to be powerless. Through this semi-fictional story Mbiti showed that theological training in the West is not religious enough to transform students and equip them with the expected spiritual qualities. Christian scholarship in the twenty-first century will have to be realigned to accommodate the spiritual and religious felt needs of non-Western people.

Third, in the area of Christian mission a new approach will need to be implemented. It has been observed by mission scholars that the old paradigm of mission has ended and a new paradigm is expected to emerge. Missiologists are busy identifying the changed mission environment that requires a new strategy and tactics for global engagement. Among other things, the religious nature of the Christian mission will be reemphasized, and the spiritual quality of the Gospel-bearers will become a major concern. This is particularly important as the Christian mission is bound to face the challenges from other resurging religious communities. The image of Christian mission and the old mission practices need to be replaced by the biblical pattern of mission as exemplified by Jesus and his disciples. When Jesus sent out his disciples to spread the Gospel, he gave them this instruction: "Heal the sick, raise the dead, cleanse the lepers, cast out demons; freely you received, freely give. Do not acquire gold, or silver, or copper for your money belts, or a bag for your journey, or even two tunics, or sandals, or a staff; for the worker is worthy of his support" (Matt. 10:5, 8–10). Given the spiritual authority to proclaim the Gospel and the gifts and powers to heal and cast out demons, the disciples could have made a fortune exercising their gifts and powers. That was why Jesus warned them not to receive any money from the local people but to give, i.e., exercise their power freely. The disciples didn't need fund-raising for their missionary outreach. Today

---

11. John Mbiti, "Theological Impotence and the Universality of the Church," in *Mission Trends 3: Third World Theologies,* ed. Gerald Anderson (Grand Rapids: Eerdmans, 1976), 6–18.

a missionary candidate first has to find a sending church to secure funds to live and work overseas. What we see in the Bible is a very different picture of a missionary. If Christian workers in the twenty-first century regain such spiritual authority and power, we will see the advancement of the Gospel in the global context.

Christian Scholarship as Religious Formation

In the areas of biblical scholarship, theological discourse, and missionary training, Christian scholarship is pressed in the global context to reorient its discourse to train highly qualified Christian workers with religious and spiritual transformation.

One of the chronic problems of theological education today is that students are not quite ready to receive academic or vocational formation. It is wrong to assume that all those whose applications are accepted by a theological institution have the required personal Christian formation sufficient to qualify them for formal academic and vocational training. If students are not qualified enough to receive a formal academic and vocational training, theological schools need to provide a religious and spiritual formation for the students in the first place.

In recent years, an increasing number of theological schools have become aware of the importance of spiritual formation of their students. Almost all theological schools today offer degrees and courses in the area of spiritual formation. But courses on spiritual formation are perceived as necessary supplements to the existing curriculum, not as the ultimate goal of theological training. Nor is spiritual formation seen as the very foundation upon which the whole of theological education is standing. We cannot say that all the courses in the curriculum are taught to help students to achieve religious and spiritual formation.

Theological training should make religious and spiritual formation the basis for a sound Christian scholarship. Through theological training we come to comprehend the Christian truth, answer the questions that people raise in everyday life, defend the Christian truth in a hostile world, and proclaim the Gospel. All these theological activities can be reduced to mere cognitive exercises if the person engaged in theological studies does not have a proper personal religious and spiritual formation. Thus, as Edward Sands asserts, it will be most advisable to make personal formation dominant and biblical and theological studies subdominant in the curriculum.[12] The best arrangement will be that biblical and theological studies plus other disciplines are taught to serve the development of Christian spirituality.[13] This reconfiguration of the curriculum will help integrate religious and spiritual formation with vocational and academic formation. For a proper and relevant theological training in the twenty-first century, Christian scholarship should find ways to achieve religious and spiritual formation. In this way the dichotomy between theory and practice will be bridged in theological education.

Theological Education as Embodiment of Jesus

Sometimes I ask students what they expect to happen to them after receiving theological training for three years at the seminary. Students bring their own expectations, goals, and visions to equip themselves with the necessary skills and knowledge for their future ministry or academic career. I notice that most of the expectations are ministry-related, and I never met a student who said that he or she came to the seminary to achieve Christlikeness. Even though most theological institutions have in their mission statement the goal to teach students to become more like Jesus, we cannot say that most of the courses in the curriculum are designed and taught for that purpose.

Christian scholarship should teach people how to achieve religious and spiritual formation, i.e., to embody Jesus and become like him. Therefore, theological education should provide various ways to achieve embodiment of Jesus before engagement in ministry or in social works. Theological schools are to produce church leaders who imitate Jesus and achieve Christlikeness.

The ultimate goal of Christian scholarship and theological education should be to provide concrete theoretical and biblical steps to become like Jesus. Once the ultimate goal is affirmed, theological education must effectuate a constant transformation. The objective of Christian studies should be to find ways to change ourselves. Then theological education becomes a consistent process to discover, become aware of, and eventually change ourselves. Theological education should offer concrete ways to upgrade who we are, what we are, and where we are through self-change, self-transformation,

---

12. Edward Sands, "What Is Your Orientation? Perspectives on the Aim of Theological Education," *Journal of Christian Education* 44, no. 3 (2001): 7–19.

13. Brian V. Hill, "Do Theological Studies Foster Spirituality?" *Journal of Christian Education* 44, no. 3 (2001): 33–42.

and self-renewal. In this sense, theological education is to produce genuine practitioners of Christian teachings and faithful followers of Jesus.

After being born again, we are to grow not only in our theological knowledge but also in our holistic spiritual maturity. We are to grow in our thoughts, words, and deeds to the full stature of Christ. Christian scholarship should serve the purpose of achieving Christlikeness, and future leaders of the church will be those who are immersed in the Bible, integrate theological insights, and embody Christian spirituality. For this, theological education will have to be reconfigured to enable students to embody the four main features in the Christian tradition: an intimate relationship and mystical union with God (monastic tradition), thorough study and immersion in God's Word (modern biblical scholarship), practice of self-denial and self-mortification (Puritan spirituality), and gifts and powers of the Holy Spirit (Pentecostal-Charismatic movement).[14] The historical Jesus himself demonstrated these four features through his life and ministry.

First, theological education must teach students to develop an intimate relationship and mystical union with God, based on a experiential knowledge of God. Theological education is to train us to experience God and deepen our intimate relationship with God. We are to acquire first a thorough cognitive knowledge of God through the Bible and then to encounter the living God in person. We should become familiar with the nature, power, plan, and love of the triune God. As the central theme of the Bible is God himself and the unfolding of his redemption through Jesus Christ, we will be enlightened to the self-revelation of the triune God through biblical studies. The more we come to know God, the deeper will become our experience of God's presence. As many spiritual leaders have advised, we need to be trained to hear the voice of God and feel God's presence in our daily walk. Our response to the living God will then be characterized by faith, dependence, and complete trust. Acknowledging God in any circumstance will become real, and we will live free of worries under God's sovereign care. The mystical union with God should be guided by biblical insights, so biblical scholarship should enable us to acquire ways to deepen our intimate relationship with God.

Second, theological education must teach students to die to our flesh. Theological education is to teach us how to achieve self-denial and how to

---

14. Moonjang Lee, "Future of Global Christianity," in *Atlas of Global Christianity*, ed. Todd Johnson and Kenneth Ross (Edinburgh: University Press, 2010), 104–5.

take up our cross as Jesus demanded of those who want to follow him and become his disciples. Self-denial is to kill our fleshly desires, wage a spiritual warfare, die to our flesh and empty or cleanse our heart. Self-denial is a process of emptying our heart until we come to have the mind of Christ (Phil. 2:5). With the training in self-denial and dying to the flesh, we will learn to live according to the guidance of the Holy Spirit. Without the renewal of the inner life and emptying of our heart, we cannot achieve spiritual growth. Self-denial and dying to our flesh are the way to achieve Christlikeness, because without these we may not be able follow Jesus. Theological education should provide step-by-step guidelines to practice self-denial and emptying of the heart.

Third, theological education must teach students to immerse themselves in the Bible, acquire practical wisdom and spiritual insights, and learn to discern God's will. While on earth, Jesus followed God's will faithfully. As servants of Christ, we need to live according to God's will, the heavenly mandate. The eyes to discern God's will can be obtained through the study of the Bible. Theological education should teach us how to live and practice God's will. Modern biblical scholarship has accumulated lots of useful historical and literary research on the Bible. Built upon such academic findings, we are to learn how to interact with the Bible to gain spiritual awakening. Beyond academic interest to obtain exact information, we should learn to embody the biblical teachings and thus be transformed.

Fourth, theological education must teach students to receive the gifts and power of the Holy Spirit as recorded in the Bible. Jesus was the *charisma* incarnate as well as the *logos* incarnate. Jesus said, "Truly, truly, I say to you, he who believes in me, the works that I do, he will do also; and greater works than these he will do; because I go to the Father" (John 14:12 NASB). Spiritual experiences that we read aboout in the Bible need to be actualized today in the life of the global church. The history of early Christianity began with the descending of the Holy Spirit on the day of Pentecost. The spiritual gifts and powers are to be taught and cultivated at theological schools.

A Methodological Reorientation: Cognitive, Experiential, and Spiritual Knowing

There are three stages of knowing in Christian studies: cognitive, experiential, and spiritual. Theological training needs to incorporate all three stages to facilitate the embodiment of Jesus.

First, we need to obtain a sound cognitive knowledge of the various aspects of embodying Jesus. Christian scholarship cannot be built simply on the expression of personal and subjective convictions. At the same time we cannot reduce Christian scholarship to be a mere academic exercise to obtain objective, theoretical, or theological knowledge that is alienated from any practical applications. A careful study of the Bible through logical and rational analysis can also lead to a spiritual awakening that will enable the knowing subject to see the ways to achieve Christlikeness.

Second, we need to obtain experiential knowledge by internalizing or personifying what we learn from the process of theological training. The predicament of traditional theological education is to dichotomize the subject of learning from the object of study.[15] Experiential knowledge will lead to embodiment of the object of study. Insofar as the dichotomy is not bridged, the experiential knowledge and embodiment of Jesus cannot be achieved. Theological training should help us embody, internalize, and personalize the object of our study (Jesus). We as the subject of learning should strive to achieve a nondualistic unity with the object of study. Our interest does not lie in a mere accumulation of knowledge or cognitive understanding but in an embodiment that the object of study might dwell in the body and mind of the subject of learning.[16]

When I was living in Singapore, I used to explain to my students about winter weather in East Asia. As Singapore is in a tropical region, it is hot all year round. If they had not been exposed to cold winter weather, Singaporeans would not know the rawness in the air that suggests snow on a cold, chilly winter day. They may know cognitively, but without experiencing the rawness of the air in person they cannot say they know experientially. In the Bible there are numerous scenes, episodes, and teachings that require our firsthand experience to claim that we know. Our knowledge of God, Jesus, and the Holy Spirit cannot be limited to a cognitive level; we need to have experiential knowledge of the triune God. Theological training is to lead us into such experiential knowledge of the object of our study.

Third, Christian scholarship should deepen our spiritual knowledge. We can acquire experiential knowledge by putting the biblical teachings into practice. However, there are other things that cannot be experienced or

---

15. Moonjang Lee, "Identifying an Asian Theology: A Methodological Quest," *Asia Journal of Theology* 13 (1999): 270–71.

16. Moonjang Lee, "The Asianisation of Theological Education," *Journal of African Christian Thought* 9, no. 2 (2006): 40.

known through practice but can be known only through spiritual experience. When Jesus came up out of the water after his baptism in the Jordan, he saw the heavens opened. The Holy Spirit descended upon him like a dove, and a voice came from heaven (Mark 1:10). We may explain cognitively or theologically what this particular scene means. But we cannot say we know what these phenomena really are: opening of the heavens, descending of the Holy Spirit, a voice from heaven. Only through spiritual experience that God allows us to have can we know what these spiritual or supernatural phenomena are. The first line in the Gospel of John also goes beyond our cognitive and experiential understanding: "In the beginning was the Word, and the Word was with God, and the Word was God." No one could claim to know what the verse really means unless the actual scene is revealed through an *apocalypsis* to us as it was done to John. We are not able to experience the heavenly reality before the creation and the mode of existence of God and the Word. For such spiritual or supernatural knowing, we have to rely on prayer and meditation on the Word.

Conclusion

As Andrew Walls has shown, the religious environment in the twenty-first century has changed drastically and challenges the global church to realign the way we live our Christianity. Theological education will have to be revised radically to be able to produce holistic spiritual leaders the churches need. The first thing is to revise theological training and to reorient the curriculum to achieve the ultimate goal of embodying Jesus. Future Christian leaders should embody *logos* and *charisma* in a balanced way. That we see this challenge is an integral part of the legacy and ongoing work that Andrew Walls urges us to embrace.

Part III

THEMES IN THE
TRANSMISSION
OF CHRISTIAN FAITH

8

Post-Western Wine,
Post-Christian Wineskins?
The Bible and the Third Wave Awakening

LAMIN SANNEH

The Stage

The happy occasion of our gathering here demands glad and hearty acknowledgment.[1] In a measure, it has brought us from all corners of the world and from a wealth of different backgrounds and disciplines, all of us eager for the opportunity, for one, to honor Andrew Walls for the many gifts he has brought to the study and scholarship on World Christianity and, for another, to inaugurate in his name a new initiative at Liverpool Hope University, itself a unique venture in faith, learning, and engagement. I could not be more pleased to be included in these collective rites of thanksgiving, inauguration, and celebration. I confess to envy that Andrew Walls's legacy is being recognized here rather than at my own institution, but I take consolation in the fact that the Walls institutional legacy at Liverpool Hope will become the heritage of all of us as a beacon of intercollegial endeavor and cooperation.

On that basis I am confident that the new Andrew Walls Center here will bear fruit and form an important link in the rapidly expanding chain of centers and programs that is drawing scholars and organizations right across the world and stimulating the unprecedented development of archival and library materials to provide a solid foundation for historical and religious inquiry and investigation. It is not simply that the records and documents of the Christian movement have been scattered and far-flung but that the organizing principles of research and inquiry have been fragmented and episodic. A center such as the one being established here should go a long

---

1. Paper presented at the launch of the Andrew F. Walls Centre for the Study of African and Asian Christianity at Liverpool Hope University, U.K., on May 24, 2008.

way toward addressing those issues. In my own work at Yale, for example, I have tried to address such issues by rescuing "World Christianity" from its unquestioned Eurocentric domestication and launching for the purpose of the Oxford Studies in World Christianity publication series. The goal is to move beyond the cultural partition of Christianity and to propose a unifying focus for the dynamic and diverse expressions and styles of Christian life and thought. Converging themes of the Christian movement have their roots not so much in a Western-led globalization as in the springs of local renewal. The rubric "World Christianity" in preference to "Global Christianity" is an attempt to recognize and honor the principle of local initiative and agency without the onus of partisan cultural categorization. Variety is proof of vitality and not simply of syncretist deviation.

I daresay much of this way of thinking is congruent with the work of Andrew Walls as well as with his call for a responsive theology of the world Christian movement in its post-Western phase. That is why this occasion stirs personal sentiments of deep admiration, gratitude, affection, and apprecia-tion for Andrew's teaching, scholarship, and service to countless generations of students, friends, and colleagues across the continents, for the unstinting generosity and faithfulness, for their hospitality and graciousness, and for the stewardship of the gifts entrusted to him and Doreen in this cause. Rich in detail and large in sympathy and scope, the biography of Andrew Walls is testament to the truth that in being extravagant with the gifts of God as the apostle enumerates them we receive more — not less — of those gifts, for such is the Kingdom of God. It is right and fitting in that regard that by custom we should address Andrew in the plural. At a personal level, my own family remains grateful beyond words for Andrew and Doreen's friendship and encouragement. I take this opportunity to salute a master, an exemplar, a colleague, and a friend. May the God you uphold in your work continue to uplift you and yours.

Orientation

For my remarks here I want to consider the role of Bible translation as a catalyst in the rise of World Christianity and, by implication, the role of the Bible in Christian life and practice. This is a continuation of the thinking I first developed when I was a colleague of Andrew Walls on the faculty of Aberdeen University. It struck me forcefully then, as it does now, that the specific issue of the Bible in the vernacular, or mother tongue, if you prefer, is an issue about the indigenous scope of Christianity anywhere, with the sharp irony that as foreign experts missionary translators achieved in the religious sphere the preeminence of local languages over European languages.

Allow me for a moment to backtrack. My hitherto unquestioned assumption that because the Arabic of Scripture is reinforced rather than abandoned in successful Muslim mission in Africa and elsewhere, a similar process must occur in Christian mission blinded me to Christianity's vernacular predilection. I assumed that Christianity's bearings in the Roman imperial system survived intact into the modern colonial system, and in both cases provincial and tribal cultures were regarded as barbarian, what the Muslim sources denounce as *'ajamí*. Yet this assumption is no less wrongheaded than its conceptual opposite, namely, because Christian missions produced vernacular Bibles, Muslim mission must similarly have produced vernacular Qur'ans. I knew better, but, confronted with the question, I looked to lower orders of Muslim local adaptation in order to gain the ground lost in conceding the canonical exclusiveness of the Arabic Qur'an. If you don't want to see, no amount of light can make you budge, and that seems an inauspicious way to seek the truth. As the Arab proverb says, you don't talk to the door if you want the walls to hear you. Scholars, too, fall prey easily to classifications of their own devising, and I guess you can consider me to have been in recovery ever since Aberdeen. The Caledonian climate suited this particular tropical specimen very well.

Translation, Incarnation, and Sacrifice

The Bible's special place in the history of post-Western Christianity contrasts rather strikingly with its waning influence in the post-Christian West. According to recent reports, in the United Kingdom, for instance, only 23 percent of people believe in God, and 7 percent that the Bible is the word of God. It is an interesting historical fact that the Bible came to occupy the place it does in the post-Western awakening because of the pioneer work of missionary linguists of the West, something that is particularly evident in the field of Bible translation.

The historical case for Bible translation rests squarely on the primacy of divine encounter rather than on claims of cultural advantage. There was longstanding resistance to the principle of vernacular Bible translation because it was feared that would open the Scripture to corruption, to unauthorized access by the untutored masses, and lead to a diminution of clerical power. Opponents argued that already God had at his disposal numerous

enough languages in which the peoples of the world made their prayers and
performed their worship to need another one, with the suggestion that the
limits had been set. The position adopted seemed unassailable if you grant
the premise that the truth of God would not be diminished by one less translation, by one less national appropriation. After all, critics insisted, had not
God remained content by having his name acknowledged as great in Israel
and in no other place? In those days, the dew lay on Gideon's fleece only,
while the rest of the earth lay dry. Nothing of that partial bestowal detracted
from the omnipotence of God. On the contrary, in spite of the cultural
restriction the singular and generous sovereignty of God was demonstrated
for the world to see.[2]

That issue of restricted access to Scripture dominated Reformation England as it contemplated having the Bible in the national language. Those
appointed to the task wondered whether another translation would be just
a labor of debasement fraught with personal peril, or whether it belonged
with the deeper question about the history and nature of revelation and,
thus, about the future of the church. What kind of merit could another
translation claim? Or, to put it differently, what principle would a fresh
translation promote?

To these questions the translators of what came to be called the King
James Bible gave both a general and a specific answer, and it would repay
us to look closely at their arguments. On the general front, they argued that
translation was not an exercise in linguistic perfection: you do not justify
doing a new translation because of what you consider to be flaws in earlier
translations, for you would then be guilty of the charge of the translator
as traitor (*traduttore traditore*) and be judged to have impugned the faith
of those who came before you. Besides, opinions varied greatly as to what
flaws constituted a good justification for overthrowing a hallowed precedent.[3] "We never thought," the translators declared, "from the beginning

---

2. *The Translators to the Reader: The Original Preface of the King James Version of 1611
Revisited*, ed. Erroll F. Rhodes and Liana Lupas (New York: American Bible Society, 1997), 34.

3. Sir Isaac Newton (1642–1727), in a work entitled *The Philosophical Origins of Gentile
Theology*, argued that the Bible existed in a language of perfect and exact signification — an
orderly universe of meaning — that could be discovered by the rule of mystical interpretation.
"The Rule I have followed has been to compare the several mystical places of scripture where
the same prophetic phrase or type is used, and to fix such a signification to that phrase as
agrees best with all the [other] places... and when I have found the necessary significations,
to reject all others as the offspring of luxuriant fancy, for no more significations are to be
admitted for true ones than can be proved." Only by that procedure might one gain a true and
unvarying understanding of the Bible and remedy the corruptions that have crept into religion.
Thus did Newton set out to remedy the problem of Christianity as a translated, and therefore

that we should need to make a new translation, nor yet to make of a bad one a good one. To that purpose there were many chosen, that were greater in other men's eyes than in their own, and that sought the truth rather than their own praise."[4] Scripture is God's word and not a commodity of national advantage, and so national interest as well as scholarly qualifications should stand in relation to Scripture like the banks to a stream, not to dam but to channel what they encounter. Christianity was a translated religion, and that fact contained at its core the dynamic principle of continuous translatability on account precisely of the imperfection as well as the multiplicity of languages. In the final analysis, translation of religious texts was a theological enterprise, and Bible translation specifically a discourse in truth-seeking. Scripture was God's vigil among us.

It is that impulse of open choice that stirred William Tyndale, "acknowledged as the most formative influence on the text of the King James Bible,"[5] to expand on the theme of popular access in his remarks on the necessity, not just of translation, but of translation in the mother tongue. "If God spare my life," he challenged an opponent in words that eerily smacked of

as a prone-to-be-misunderstood religion. The language of Scripture, Newton maintained, was unlike the languages of the world in its capacity to defy difference and historical contingency, for only such a universal and unifying language was worthy of the one universal God who spoke it. *Theological Manuscripts*, ed. H. McLachlan (Liverpool: Liverpool University Press, 1950), 119ff. See also Michael Holquist, "Local Universes: Myths of a National Language," in *Socio-Cultural Theory and Methods: An Anthology,* ed. Ullabeth Sätterlund Larsson (Udevalla: University of Trollhättan, *Skriftserie,* no. 6, 2001), 66–68. Holquist's incisive examination of the role of language in religion and nationalism leads to what he calls the problem of the contradiction between the moral subject and the psychological personality, between reason and freedom, in the Enlightenment concept of the self. The Kantian subject, Holquist says, is fundamentally at odds with itself by virtue of the doomed arithmetic that requires a divided soul to be one. Bible translation offers a different contrast by taking that dilemma in a positive direction and making the word of the transcendent God transmissible in the historical idioms of the peoples of the world. The universal and particular in Bible translation transcended what Holquist indicates as the contradiction between reason and freedom, or between general truth and unique action. Something of that transcendent confidence is expressed by the translators of the King James Bible, namely, that the one God of Scripture is available to us in the many forms of human communication. Accordingly, they affirmed: "Translation it is that openeth the window, to let in the light...that removeth the cover of the well, that we may come by the water." In the final analysis, translation of Scripture is the god-given channel by which human beings by choice may rise to the status of children of God. Kepler alluded to a similar rule when he declared: "The Bible speaks the language of everyman." Cited in F. E. Manuel, *The Religion of Isaac Newton* (Oxford: Oxford University Press, 1974), 36.

4. The end and reward of Scripture, the translators said, was, among other things, "repentance from dead works, newness of life, holiness, peace, joy in the Holy Ghost, fellowship with the saints." Rhodes and Lupas, *The Translators to the Reader,* 54. Rhodes and Lupas, *The Translators to the Reader,* 32. Michael Holquist argues that "theologies are at root a form of linguistics." "Local Universes," 47–85, 54.

5. Alister McGrath *In the Beginning: The Story of the King James Bible, and How It Changed the Nation, a Language and a Culture* (New York: Anchor Books, 2001), 67; also 78–79.

his imminent tragic fate, "ere many years I will cause a boy that driveth the plough shall know more about the Scriptures than thou doest." The issue for Tyndale was a matter of theological principle, though in the circumstances his views carried social and political implications. He expressed himself with unbounded confidence about opening Scripture to common access.

Tyndale's confidence was remarkable for its unswerving commitment to the people's natural idiom, for what Archbishop Donald Coggan calls Tyndale's "almost uncanny gift of simplicity...a true nobility of homeliness."[6] Tyndale's cause was not alien to Christianity even though he was deemed a heretic for it. The opposition to him proved deadly, but it was not because he was threatening to do a new thing in Christianity altogether but because of the imputation to him of political motives.[7] After all, Tertullian (c. 160–c. 240), who converted to Christianity in 195, expressed similar views about the Gospel in the languages of the peoples of the world, as did Irenaeus (c. 130–c. 200), and numerous others after them, including Otfrid von Weissenburg in the ninth century.[8]

The list of translations was an explicit acknowledgment that Christianity was destined for all peoples and cultures, not just for some people and some

---

6. Donald Coggan, *The English Bible* (London: Longmans, Green, 1963).

7. Tyndale paid with his life for his pains. Escaping to the continent, he was betrayed by a friend and captured near Brussels in 1536. Locked up on the orders of Emperor Charles V in a damp, cold dungeon, he pleaded for items of clothing to stave off the extreme cold, and for a lamp to relieve the icy gloom. Above all, he asked for his Hebrew Bible, Hebrew grammar, and Hebrew dictionary "that I may spend my time with that study." Tyndale was tied to the stake and strangled by the hangman and then "with fire consumed." His ashes were thrown into the river to obliterate all trace of the man. Yet Tyndale's effect on the evolution of English prose and letters was immense. Long after he was gone and several generations had passed, "Tyndale's rhythms had begun to vibrate in the minds of a younger generation, and when at last the final version of the English Bible appeared...the spirit of Tyndale still moved through its majestic cadences...that mighty thing, the power of prose, was at work....The book existed, though the man was dead." Hillaire Belloc, *Cranmer, Archbishop of Canterbury, 1533–1556* (Philadelphia: J. P. Lippincott and Co., 1931). Belloc, otherwise hostile to Tyndale, takes large liberties with his historical facts, though his judgment about Tyndale reflects the general consensus. Ironically, Tyndale's translation was surreptitiously circulated by the prior of an English Augustinian monastery whence it fell into the hands of Miles Coverdale, an Augustinian friar. Coverdale's translation, "best viewed," according to McGrath (90), "as a compilation of other people's translations," was approved by the king even though Coverdale made explicit and extensive use of Tyndale (Olga S. Opfell, *The King James Bible Translators* [Jefferson, N.C.: McFarland, 1982], 17, 20). Thomas Cranmer also lost his life in the cause, being burned at the stake in 1556 on the orders of Mary Tudor. Executed with Cranmer was John Rogers, a Tyndale protégé and author of the Matthew Bible. Rogers's execution was made famous by the encouragement and comfort at the site of the execution afforded him by his wife, Andriana, and the presence of their eleven children, the youngest a suckling infant. See John Foxe, *Acts and Monuments of These Latter and Perilous Days* (Book of Martyrs), 1573.

8. See John Michael Wallace-Hadrill, *The Frankish Church* (Oxford: Clarendon Press, 1983), 386.

cultures. The English — and everyone else — had an open and shut case, who could deny?

It is not merely that the different languages of the world, including English, were an obstacle the church must overcome to establish the faith, but that in its variety language is a God-given asset, allowing Christianity to invest in language, any language, on the basis that God is to be encountered there. The role assigned to language in the Bible makes language deeply theological, deeply sacramental. As Shakespeare put it, "words without thought cannot to heaven go." It is impossible without language to know and to worship God, or even to have personality. And so the translators affirmed their "desire that the Scripture may speak like itself, as in the language of Canaan, that it may be understood even of the very vulgar."[9] Christianity cannot dispense with language as the God-chosen medium of communication.[10] With all its in-built limitation, translation is the imprinting of the divine communication on the rainbow canvas of a rich, diverse humanity. It is that circumstance that emboldened Tyndale, for example, to feel there was nothing new about his wish to translate: God willed it from the beginning. Had God "not made the English tongue? Why forbid ye him to speak in the English tongue then?"[11] It justified instituting English not only in Scripture but also in worship.

As Thomas Cranmer (1489–1556) demonstrated, in the end the case for Scripture in the "vulgar tongue" was inescapable on the general principle that translation is the original language of religion in Christianity. "There are doubtless many different languages in the world," the Apostle Paul observes, "and none is without meaning; but if I do not know the meaning of the language, I shall be a foreigner to the speaker and the speaker a foreigner to me" (1 Cor. 14:10–11). It was that view that Tyndale advanced, and it made him determined to naturalize the Gospel in the common idiom. Having laid

---

9. Rhodes and Lupas, *The Translators to the Reader*, 62.

10. The translators noted that the Roman Catholic Church had never denied the translatability of Christianity and was not in principle opposed to Bible translation: the church only required a written license for it. It was that issue that drew the objections of the translators: the Catholic Church, they felt, ought to play to the script and not interpose artificial barriers between Scripture and its natural milieu of translation. With the gold of Scripture, Christians must not be afraid to come to the touchstone of vernacular validation. In point of fact, Catholics are best fitted to translate the Bible into English. "They have learning, and they know when a thing is well, they can *manum de tabula* ["hands off the tablet," quoting Cicero])."

11. William Tyndale, *The Obedience of a Christian Man* (London: Penguin Books, 2000), 24. Tyndale thrust himself into the political limelight by his determination to wrest religion from political sponsorship, and the clergy from being minions of the state. Religious corruption and political tyranny had for Tyndale a common source in the gelding of the church. Accordingly, Tyndale was a precursor of modern politics.

out the case for the mother tongue, the King James Bible translators for their part carried through with that project of common access as the justification for Anglicanism, saying the Apostle intended to include all languages and to except none.

Sacred Scripture and the Common Idiom

Translation of the Bible was undertaken in the earliest centuries because no one had the idea that the sacredness of the Bible was to be sought in its incomprehensibility. That was how Latin, Syriac, Coptic, and Gothic translations flourished. Both Athanasius and Chrysostom called for the right of the laity to be able to read the Scripture. Chrysostom denied that reading the Bible was only for the clergy and monks, while Athanasius reproached heretics for barring ordinary folk from reading the Scriptures. It was only the lack of interest of the laity that led to Scripture being withdrawn from general use. It resulted in the irony that the habit of lay disinterest was replaced by the habit of clerical monopoly that the lay people caused by their neglect! Ad hoc practice hardened into a doctrinaire rule. In defence of common access to Scripture Milton said it was fitting in view of his work of translating the Vulgate that the devil should whip Jerome in a Lenten dream for reading Cicero.[12]

The Gospel is not a sealed mystery, as the KJV translators made clear when they shifted from the general to the specific case of the task at hand. It was no defect in the ancient prophet that he was raised to public view on the strength only of being handed a sealed book that he could not read, and in that position the prophet was mere emissary of an inaccessible and remote potentate (Isa. 29:11), "since of an hidden treasure, and of a fountain that is sealed, there is no profit."[13] From the point of view of the moral instruction of humanity, however, awareness of God's overbearing, inscrutable will was little better — or worse — than ignorance of God's word; that fault was remedied in the fullness of time when the law regulating faith and worship was not based on race and blood but on God's salvation for all people. James I himself wrote to that effect, saying that "it is one of the golden Sentences, which Christ our Sauiour vttered to his Apostles, that there is nothing so couered, that shall not be reuealed, neither so hidde, that shall

---

12. John Milton, "Aeropagitica," in *Complete Poetry and Selected Prose* (New York: Modern Library, 1950), 688.
13. Rhodes and Lupas, *The Translators to the Reader*, 45.

not be knowen; and whatsouever they haue spoken in darknesse, should be heard in the light."[14]

The fact of Christianity being a translated religion places God right at the center of the universe of cultures, with the effect of all cultures becoming equal in their status as historical bearers of Scripture. For the purposes of Bible translation, all languages have merit and are necessary, yet none is indispensable. As we know from history, many cultures, including ancient Latin, were rescued from inevitable decline — if not from certain death — by the timely intervention of Christian translation and adoption.[15] Similarly, the Christian faith was time and again salvaged from decay by the same cause. St. Augustine describes eloquently that theme of recovery and renewal in his *City of God*. Converts who learn and the agents who taught them were thereby refreshed from a common stream. Thus were Gentile tongues anointed, and, with that, the church's range.

Outcome: Language and Relationality

Having made, then, both the general point that translation is not an exercise in linguistic perfection and the specific point about the rationale for their own translation, the authors of the KJV assured the reader that in no way did they wish to diminish the importance of past achievements or to exaggerate their own effort. On the contrary, in paying tribute to the previous translations, they recognized the failings of their own, saying they were entitled to no higher privilege than to follow in the footsteps of their predecessors by committing their work to the favor of God, and to the judgment of the reader.[16]

The question that has nipped at the heels of Bible translators is whether the act of producing so many different versions of Scripture does not perpetuate divisions among Christians, create a stumbling block for ecumenical solidarity, and undermine the church's authority. In its proliferating translated versions, the Bible has become religious shrapnel, good only for the cause of fragmentation and rebellion. Should we not restrict the Scriptures to

---

14. Cited in Adam Nicolson, *God's Secretaries: The Making of the King James Bible* (New York: HarperCollins Publishers, 2003), 144.

15. W. H. C. Frend, *The Rise of Christianity* (Philadelphia: Fortress Press, 1984), 560.

16. The translators testified: "We are like dwarves sitting on the shoulders of giants. We see more, and things that are more distant, than they did, not because our sight is superior or because we are taller than they, but because they raise us up, and by their great stature add to ours." Cited in McGrath, *In the Beginning*, 176.

those languages that are endowed with cosmopolitan advantage and allow tribal tongues to die a natural death? After all, so the argument goes, not everyone is equipped for life in the age of global responsibility, and Bible translation would serve us all by investing in that global cause rather than invoking the specter of the antagonism that once wracked Christian Europe.

Critics argue that even on the limited ground of nation building Bible translation threatens a major upheaval with its focus on difference rather than on unity. Since most Third World countries are strapped for resources where these are not sucked away by corruption, it is beyond dispute that they cannot provide funds equally for all languages. Better to concentrate the available resources on the languages of social and economic scale than to fritter the resources on remote and marginal tongues. Common sense requires that we do nothing less.

One may briefly respond to these criticisms by pointing out that the multiplicity of languages is not the cause of division and conflict, nor, at the same time, is the promotion of one language the guarantee of unity and harmony. Italy, for example, has many languages without that creating violent fragmentation, while Northern Ireland had bitter intercommunal violence in spite of a common language between the warring Catholics and Protestants. The same can be said about the 1994 genocide in Catholic Rwanda. As for cosmopolitan advantage, Europe's attainment in that respect did not avert Europe's devastating wars of the twentieth century, something equally true, say, of Japan, too.

As for nation building, Somalia's monolingual status, including its adherence to one religion with its untranslated Scripture, has not saved it from chronic wars and strife. Indeed, Somalia is a byword for a failed state, and perhaps, too, for evangelism, which is a classic problem. The view that if we had one language in common we would overcome division and misunderstanding is unwarranted by historical evidence and by theological realism, nor is there much credibility for the idea that multiple language use hinders social harmony. The case for Bible translation, therefore, is unaffected by arguments of political and economic advancement.

Post-Western Christianity is for the most part the religion of multiple language users, in contrast to the post-Christian West, where single language users, it happens, tend to predominate. By adopting languages already in use Christianity makes local comprehension a validation of its mission. The myriad languages of the religion demonstrate the universal scope of God's mission: no one is excluded on account of scale, status, or remoteness. The

Gospel is not marooned in Bethlehem because spiritually Jesus is born in the heart of believers, wherever or whoever they are. Christian translation is about the adoption of multiple idioms and cultural domains, not about preserving an original tongue or place. The affirmation of Kepler (d. 1630) that "the Bible speaks the language of everyman" is a statement about the salvific merit of "everyman's language," because God is like that.

A special word is necessary here about the cultural milieu of language. We cannot help but look at how information technology has changed the role of non-Western languages and idioms in the ferment of accelerating market forces. Yet that is a poor clue about the role of language in primal societies. This writer can recall many a scene of women working in their rice fields, gathering at wells and river banks, convening at markets, festivals, weddings, and naming ceremonies, and cradling their children with lullabies, and on those occasions performing songs, reciting tales and legends, and engaging in verbal displays of the most intricate kind. They passed the time by lively conversation, encounter, and exchange. The relational dimension of language came to the fore in that oral environment, vibrant with the human spirit. We should try to remember this primal background of language when we think of the Bible in the mother tongue. Precisely for this reason, the work of Eugene Nida has been without equal.

This pattern of the correlation between indigenous cultural revitalization and Christian mission is a consistent one in the history of religious development, with evocative traces in the Gentile phase of the primitive church. As they pored over the vernacular Bible, for example, converts saw reflected something of the cultural potential of their own history and experience. The adoption of the vernacular ended the isolation of tribe and language, reversed or slowed the process of neglect and decline. Just as the English of King Alfred was more complicated than modern English, so were vernacular languages before Bible translation. And the simplicity of translation triggered religious currents that inspired comparative inquiry.

In a critical study of the life of Robert Moffat, the outstanding missionary linguist of southern Africa, the observation was made that the vernacular Bible bridged the old and new. It was a living book in the sense of its resonant testimony assuming fresh impetus in homebred tones and accents. It was impossible to ignore. Lifting a vernacular New Testament in his hand, an African convert testified that he and his people once imagined the Bible to be a charm of the white people designed to keep off sickness and to be a trap to catch the people. He knew differently now. "We have never heard of such a thing... but now we not only hear with our ears, we see with our eyes, we read it, our children read it.... We thought it was a thing to be spoken to, but now we know it has a tongue. It speaks and will speak to the whole world."[17] Christian vernacular is in the accent of a universal message, well expressed in the words of Walt Whitman in his *Song of the Open Road:* "I find letters from God dropt in the street, and everyone is sign'd by God's name." In spite of linguistic and cultural difference the capacity of human language to bear the truth of God binds us in the religious life. Being the gifts of God, all tongues and cultures serve a common purpose, so that the parts of our individual idioms share in the sum of united witness and discernment.

A translated Christianity is the natural environment of faith just as the incarnation is the translated form of God's engagement in Jesus who "dwelt among us, full of grace and truth." Translation does not end our brokenness; it simply opens our eyes to the discernment of a different reality. The fact that in the early modern period translators paid the ultimate sacrifice by laying down their lives seems a poignant testament to the mystery of the atonement of the one who is the incarnate word of God. Translation of Scripture was fraught with perils and shadowed by the cross. The whole enterprise of translation seemed like fitting testimony to the God who knew the way of Calvary, and seems a sober, appropriate metaphor of the incarnation, with temporal setbacks an evocation of the deeper divine sacrifice.

Changing Course in the Twenty-First Century

Bible translation into the vernacular confronts us with a key question not only about the mission and vocation of the church (Why and to what end is the church in the world? What tasks define the marks of its true nature?) but also about what form and shape the hopes and yearnings of the present generation take. What are the reigning vernacular idioms translation must engage for the work of God? The church may speak eloquently and rightly of "God's work in history leaving global footprints" in the shape of new communities of faith, which in themselves, incidentally, may be adversely affected by the forces of globalization. We must, however, dig deeper: where and how are these new faith communities coming into being? What circumstances best describe them? What are the hopes and dreams that move them? What can we learn about the meaning of history by the growing evidence of

---

17. Edwin W. Smith, *The Shrine of a People's Soul* (London: Livingstone, 1929), 190.

God's work in the new church communities on the margins of power and privilege? What is the meaning of contemporary history for the church-in-mission in terms of waning old heartlands and emerging new strongholds beyond the West?

Old Contexts and New Horizons

In the centuries since Tyndale and Kepler, Bible translation has revealed in dramatic fashion linguistic difference and diversity as hallmarks of the Christian movement. By playing a necessary and indispensable role as carriers of the Christian Scriptures non-Western languages became channels of discernment and change. In their complex variety languages provided the indispensable channel — and evidence — of God's salvific promise. God *communicated* with the peoples of the world, and translation is testament of that.

The rapid, unprecedented expansion of Christianity from the second half of the twentieth century has thrown into high relief the impact of Bible translation on societies beyond the West and exposed the limitations of post-Christian wineskins in the face of new ferment. The suddenness and scope of the expansion, however, have likely concealed an important theological lesson. Standard theological models of Christianity have presented it as a closed circuit religion whose main pathways of communication and authority have been laid in the trusted channels of the Western canon.

Faced with this imposing system, the task of the theologian consisted in codifying the religion, putting down stakes for its boundary, defining its form and function, predicting and prescribing for changes, holding out against foreign matter entering it, censoring deviations and aberrations, fixing the qualities that alone define the religion, and generalizing about how God works in the world. In this view, translation spawns syncretism, sects, heresy, and apostasy, which are to religion what aberration, mutation, infection, and suicide are to an immutable organism. The system of theology mirrors the neurological design of a living organism: the system has a built-in resonance with the religion's ingrained circuitry. This organic model of Christianity has arguably been the most influential so far and dominates much of the academy and the printed page. Scholars of many different stripes have variously tinkered with it, but few have questioned its central assumption that the science of Christianity is neurological in nature, universal in design, and normative by intention. This approach takes poetry out of religion.

Yet it has become clear that the pace and scale of Bible translation are witness to a far different reality. Translation is evidence that Christianity's neurological center is in flux, that its vocabulary is growing and changing, that historical experience has had cumulative force, that the allotment of "neurons" is continuing because "neurogenesis" is a living process rather than a relic of evolution, that foreign idioms have lodged in the system like oxygen in the bloodstream, and that "localizationism" in the frontal lobe of northern Christianity has shifted to the central cortex of southern Christianity where new, expanded tasks have stimulated tolerance and diversity in the religion. Translation has shifted the "genetic determinism" of the established canon by encrypting the religion with the most diverse cultural chromosomes of other societies. The growing statistics of the resurgence shows the scale of what is afoot. And in this new milieu old school theology has appeared as a relic, which may explain its reported decline in its once hallowed cultural strongholds.

The old theology has stuck to etymological diagnosis and exegetical prescription. By contrast, translation has cultivated idioms in their down-to-earth dynamic concreteness as the crucible of faith, that new idioms are not stray dialects, that God's intervention in the Word made flesh is ground for embracing all flesh — and the words for it — as clean. As the charter of lived Christian experience the translated Scripture is the dynamic pathway of the church's world errand. To tell Christians, for example, that "Europe is the faith," as Hillaire Belloc said, may be true of a phase of history, but, against the background of current developments, it is patently untrue.

Responding to this new situation Andrew Walls has noted that Bible translation aims at releasing the word about Christ so that it can penetrate all aspects and all areas of a concrete linguistic and cultural system. In that way Christ comes to dwell in that concrete setting, and in the lives of the faithful. This is the process, Walls argues, by which new translations carry the word about Christ into new hinterlands of meaning and feeling and thereby "have the potential to reshape and expand the Christian faith."[18] Expansion here has the sense, not just of geographical range, but of cultural scope. The one truth of the Gospel must now embrace the many traditions and experiences of the peoples of the world. Geographical and cultural diversity achieves its coherence in the transformation process that defines conversion. Something

---

18. Andrew F. Walls, *The Missionary Movement in Christian History: Studies in the Transmission of Faith* (Maryknoll, N.Y.: Orbis Books, 1996), 29.

new and different is brought into the language of translation: salvation history breaks into the local medium to transform and expand it. But, Walls argues, that new experience "can only be comprehended by means of, and in terms of, the preexisting language and its conventions."[19]

Translation, and the conversion of its consequence, produces a reciprocal and mutually reinforcing change in the idiom of transmission as well as in that of reception. Vincent Donovan, a Spiritan priest and the apostle to the Maasai of Tanzania, for example, described the willingness of the people to entertain the claims of the Gospel until they realized that it would involve seeking peace and reconciliation with their feuding neighbors, at which point they balked, at least momentarily.[20] Embracing Christianity would expand Maasai horizons of "who is my neighbor?" Uplifted, the vocabulary of kinship must now be taken into new fields of relationship and mutual interdependence. But Christianity itself is not spared in this transformation as the new faith becomes grounded in a new world of unfamiliar landmarks.

While translation submits the Gospel to the terms of local appropriation, it need not result — as it so often is prone to do — either in the isolation of culture or in its fragmentation. The multiethnic New Humanity Walls speaks about is the answer to isolation and fragmentation. National and cultural distinctions, the things that make each segment of human identity and experience unique and recognizable, are united and reconciled in discipleship to Christ. Instead of being condemned to contention and strife, the many members are joined in subjection to the one body, different in their operative functions, but equal in their intrinsic need and, therefore, in their care of one another (1 Cor. 12:25). It is to that fullness and completeness that the act of translation ultimately points. Most observers agree that such fullness and completeness would not happen without the witness of communities of faith emerging in the post-Western world. The Bible translation may be considered intelligent design for the historical human dilemma: given the sin of our existential situation, how can culture and our idioms save us unless God deigns to indwell in them? Theological science cannot discount our idioms as mere accident. In a speech on the occasion of the bicentenary of the British and Foreign Bible Society in 2004 Archbishop Rowan Williams

---

19. Ibid., 28.
20. Vincent J. Donovan, *Christianity Rediscovered,* Twenty-Fifth Anniversary Edition (Maryknoll, N.Y.: Orbis Books, 2003).

summed up the implications of Bible translation for the church. "If scripture can be 're-created' in different languages," he wrote, "the humanity of the saviour who speaks in scripture must be an extraordinary humanity, a unique humanity.... Every language and culture [have in them] a sort of 'homing instinct' for God — deeply buried by the sin and corruption that affects all cultures, yet still there, a sleeping beauty [waiting] to be revived by the word of Christ."[21]

Postlude

To come back to where we are, the city of Liverpool was once the epicenter of the global slave trade, and by virtue of that was a transit point for Africans and others. It profited the city greatly, one of its legacies being the existence of the famous school for the study of tropical medicine and hygiene. Walls's important legacy comprising the documentation and study of developments in African and Asian Christianity at Liverpool Hope University would, all things being equal, be an important rejoinder to that history, and suitable tribute to Walls as a pioneer of the field. As Walls wrote of a mutual colleague at Aberdeen, Abraham lifted his tent pegs and took to the pilgrim trail one more time and, with his sails bulging with the auspicious winds of hope, bore down from the Firth of Forth to the banks of the Mersey. In that new site, the patriarch's gypsy caravan has halted and bivouacked in the welcome and generous space appointed for it. We and future generations will remain in the considerable debt of Gerald Pillay, the vice chancellor of Liverpool Hope University, for his personal commitment that made all this possible. Appropriately, the vocation of itinerancy of which Walls has been a distinguished and tireless exemplar has been secured with the instruments of settlement. All else being equal, the new walls rising at Liverpool Hope — no pun intended — will in due season draw numerous other pilgrims to these halls and offer them a home away from home. Long may these halls echo the notes Walls has sounded so clearly and so faithfully in more than half a century of academic endeavor.

---

21. Archbishop Rowan Williams, sermon at the Service to Celebrate the Bicentenary of the British and Foreign Bible Society, pp. 1–2, St. Paul's Cathedral, London, March 8, 2004.

Appendix:
2001 Scripture Language Report

Continent or Region	Portions	Testaments	Bibles	Bibles, DC*	Total
Africa	213	279	149	(25)	641
Asia	223	228	119	(25)	570
Australia/New Zealand/ Pacific Islands	168	204	33	(5)	405
Europe	110	31	62	(46)	203
North America	40	26	7	(0)	73
Mexico/Caribbean Islands/ Central & South America	127	244	21	(8)	392
Constructed Languages	2	0	1	(0)	3
Total	883	1,012	392	(109)	2,287

*This column is a sub-section of the Bibles column — for example, there is a translation of the Deuterocanon for 46 of the 62 languages of Europe in which the Bible has been translated.

This *2001 Scripture Language Report* provides a statistical summary of Scripture publication in languages of the world as of December 31, 2001. It includes all items registered for the first time by the United Bible Societies during 2001. Languages are registered when copies of printed Scriptures consisting of at least one complete book of the Bible are received in the library of either the American Bible Society or the British and Foreign Bible Society. A few corrections were made to our language databases and are reflected in this statistical summary.

9

Conversion:
Individual and Cultural

WILLIAM R. BURROWS

We are reminded by I. Howard Marshall's essay in this volume that Andrew Walls has been a Methodist "local preacher" (sometimes called a "lay preacher") since 1953. Not to know that about him is to miss something essential about his identity. I have come to believe that the most essential is that the accent that Professor Walls places on "conversion" — as one of two basic hermeneutic keys (along with "translation") to understanding the Christian movement — stems from his Wesleyan background and informs and shapes his work as a historian and crypto-theologian of history. Thus at least passing reference to John Wesley and the reform movement he initiated in eighteenth-century Anglicanism must be made. Those origins are often encapsulated in John Wesley's words in his journal for the date May 24, 1738:

> In the evening I went very unwillingly to a society in Aldersgate Street, where one was reading Luther's preface to the Epistle to the Romans. About a quarter before nine, while the leader was describing the change which God works in the heart through faith in Christ, I felt my heart strangely warmed. I felt I did trust in Christ alone for salvation; and an assurance was given me that He had taken away my sins, even mine, and saved me from the law of sin and death.

Wesley's conversion not only marks the beginning of Methodism but also shapes early modern Christian identity, and is crucial in Professor Walls's interpretation of "world" Christianity and its role in shaping positively today's rapid globalization.

Conversion in Early Modern Christianity

Oceans of ink have been spilt trying to exegete Wesley's words about a heart "strangely warmed." It is sufficient for our purposes to note that this is the language of fundamental conversion or turning in and is emblematic of the regard for an adult form of conversion in early modern Christianity through-out the West. And while the manner in which Wesley expresses conversion to Christ has about it more than a whiff of modernity's concern with the salvation of himself as an individual, the importance of the experience itself is at least as old as the story of Saul's conversion on the road to Damas-cus (Acts 9). That conversion turned Saul's life around and was marked by giving him a new name, Paul.[1]

In Paul's case, conversion conferred on him an intimacy with the Risen Lord and position in the early Jesus movement in no way inferior to that conferred on the eleven apostles at Pentecost (Acts 2; Gal. 1–2). In the life of Anglicanism and Wesley, however, conversion comes — *in actuality* — as a moment of renewal, revitalization, and deeper realization of what had been present — *in principle* — since baptism in a *Christendom* form of Christian life. By "Christendom form of Christian life" I mean a life begun in infancy in a church closely wedded to both British culture and state, a life that the church hoped would blossom fully in adulthood into personal faith. That Christendom model was presumed by sixteenth-century Catholic, Lutheran, Calvinist, and Henrician reform movements. The great persecution wars of religion that racked Europe through the middle of the seventeenth century were waged over *which* family of churches would dominate Christendom in a given area, not over the Christendom principle itself. The exception were reform movements that we lump together under the label "Anabaptist," which did not accept the Christendom principle and were persecuted by virtually everyone with a stake in it.

In his own day, Wesley was the initiator of a revitalization movement that may be regarded as the prototype of renewal movements that sought to rescue Christendom churches from the stultifying effects of being populated by mostly nominal believers. Along with such Catholic contemporaries as

---

1. In Western Christian history, the conferring of a new name on one who has undergone a fundamental conversion became a part of an entry into a monastery or convent as the novice vowed a *conversio morum* ("conversion of manners") in what would later come to be known technically as "religious" life in contradistinction to the "secular" life of ordinary Christians. An essential dimension of the Reformation was to call that distinction into question with the insight that *all* Christians were called to a converted way of life.

St. Alphonsus de Ligouri (1696–1787, founder of the Redemptorist order, which specialized in parish evangelism and revitalization), Wesley knew that Anglicans needed to rediscover their evangelical identity and convert to Christ in the sense expressed in Ephesians, as people "made new in the attitude of [their] minds...to put on the new self, created to be like God in true righteousness and holiness" (Eph. 4:23–24). Similarly, St. Alphonsus's Redemptorists became instigators of a revitalization movement within Catholicism, attempting to accomplish what Wesley was attempting within Anglicanism. Alas, try as he did to remain part of Anglicanism, Wesley suffered the fate of many Protestant[2] revitalization leaders, as his movement was pushed toward the status we today call a "denomination."

Why rehearse all this? Because Andrew Walls has a Wesleyan view that Christianity should be more about renewal and revitalization and less about denominational differences and doctrinal subtlety. And he sought to ignite a *conversion* movement that would attain the momentum of a force for *social* transformation, not just ecclesiastical renewal. His and other such revitalization movements in that period aimed to change individuals from within but they also reveal the activity of the Spirit at a given historical moment in a culture's history just as surely they change the course of an individual's biography. What is *historically* and *socially* noteworthy (as opposed to the *existential* significance of individual religious conversion) are movements that we can legitimately call "cultural conversions."[3]

At another level, one of Professor Walls's most significant contributions is contained in several sentences that are central to his case that proselytes differ from converts. Proselytes takes on the cultural forms of the tradition they join. On the other hand,

> Christian conversion as demonstrated in the New Testament is not about substituting something new for something old. That is in effect to move back to the proselyte model, which New Testament Christianity might have adopted but deliberately rejected. Nor is it a matter of adding something new to something old, a new set of beliefs and values to supplement those that are already in place. *Conversion is about*

---

2. I realize that many Anglicans dislike having the label "Protestant" applied to them. Nonetheless, it is helpful to locate them among the many reform movements of the Christendom variety originating in the sixteenth century.

3. I base this contention on Andrew Walls, "Four Unpublished Lectures," Maryknoll, N.Y., October 1997. Walls has been refining and extending his views for an as yet unpublished book on the "cultural history" of Christian conversion.

the turning of the entire social, cultural, religious inheritance toward Christ, opening them up to him. It's about turning what is already there. Christ is formed by faith among the elements that constitute the preconversion setting. That is the great adventure of Christian faith. It's always taking new shape as Christ enters new territory, as he takes flesh again in cultures where he has not walked in flesh before.[4]

A word about my own perspective on the matters discussed here may be appropriate at this point. In a conversation with Andrew that occurred as I drove him to Kennedy Airport in New York City, Andrew asked me what I meant when he heard me say earlier that day that "I was brought up a theologian but had enjoyed the good fortune in recent years to be reintroduced to the study of history by himself and Lamin Sanneh." I answered that he and Lamin had made me aware that Christian historical studies were profoundly theological when done in the right way. I then observed that in the case of both himself and Sanneh, I detected a *theological* interest at play when they appeared to be doing history. "In what way?" he asked. "As I read Lamin's *Translating the Message* and your essays [that went into the first book that Orbis had just recently published], at a certain point I began to realize that you are articulating a theology of history for the 'cultured despisers of religion' in our age." (I was, of course, using Schleiermacher's subtitle of his famous essays in *Über der Religion* ["On Religion"], "Speeches to Its Cultured Despisers.") I said that I detected in him (i.e., Professor Walls) a distrust of theological systems, but also a conviction that God's footprints were to be found in the events of ongoing history as surely as they were in the history of Israel. He smiled and said, "Ah, you've found me out."

A year or two later, we began a conversation about a book by him, a conversation that's now gone on for at least fourteen years without, unfortunately, the book coming forth. Why? Because it is so difficult to point to God's footprints within all the contingencies of history, if you are — as Andrew Walls is — a man of profoundly "modern" sensibilities of the sort that led Van Harvey to write *The Historian and the Believer: The Morality of Historical Knowledge and Christian Belief*. I said to Andrew, "I'm not quite sure all your missiological readers get it, but I'll be reading you and

---

4. Andrew F. Walls, "Converts and Proselytes: Christianity as a Jewish Religion," first of the four unpublished lectures. Italics represent my effort to indicate the essential element in Christian conversion.

all at once something will grab me and make me say, 'Eureka, he's arguing with Nietzsche here or Hume there.' "

Again he smiled. And I think he agreed with me.

In what follows, I hope to show that understanding the peculiarly inner and public dimensions of conversion in paradigm-changing moments of Christian history unify Professor Walls's work, even when he appears to be explicating something like the importance of the distinction between proselytes and converts, Origen's insights into Christianity and the Greek philosophical ideal, the ambiguity of medieval Christendom, the shifts in emphasis when Franks became Christians amid the ambivalence of Merovingian and Carolingian wars, translating the Scriptures into Yoruba, missions subverting the colonizing intents of their agents, or circuit-riding Methodist evangelists on the American frontier creating something that was not simply an imitation of European Christian life. In all of them — as Andrew tells the tale — there is an inner dimension of conversion occurring alongside an outer and accompanying the work of translating the Gospel. And in key (can one say paradigmatic?) instances, they produce something new and distinct, yet faithful to the Spirit of Christ.

I fear the genetic code of theologian spliced into me at the Gregorian in Rome and the University of Chicago may lead me to make explicit judgments that a cautious historian such as Andrew himself would not. And — as an integral part of my constant attempt to stay aware of my "erroneous zones" — I often recall words that Stephen Toulmin, the eminent British philosopher and historian of science, once addressed to me in a seminar on religion and cosmology in Chicago. I had ventured the opinion that religious intuitions were the basis of most important insights into ethics and cosmology. "You may be right, Bill, but I am rather the tortoise to your hare. That has to be demonstrated and for that we need much more evidence. The problem is: Where are we to get the evidence that religious intuitions on the origin and nature of the cosmos are correct?" That, of course, is the post-Kantian dilemma of every educated person. Where does humanity get evidence that religion's intimations of transcendence and the shape of the Whole are, indeed, "reliable"? Religion since Kant has been forced by its cultured despisers into the realm of opinion while science has donned the garment of knowledge. We will not pursue this issue further in this chapter, but it constitutes one of the key challenges to Christianity translating the Gospel into terms that the contemporary world will find plausible so that conversion can transcend Christendom forms of church that seem incurably passé to today's cultured despisers.

To return to the thread of my argument. . . . If I — a Roman Catholic for whom a 1967 experience with the charismatic movement became the occasion of a significant *individual* conversion — may be permitted a word from that perspective, it is that Andrew Walls helps us to understand the concept of individual and social conversion as a hermeneutic key to identify significant historical moments in Christian life, moments that are as important for understanding that history as the term "translation of the Gospel." The latter, of course, is what Walls and his friend and collaborator Lamin Sanneh — author of the chapter on translation in this book — are better known for. I believe, in other words, that conversion needs to be given equal status with translation.

Two essays and a series of yet unpublished lectures by Professor Walls are important for grasping this point: (1) "Culture and Conversion in Christian History";[5] (2) "The Ephesian Moment: At a Crossroad in Christian History";[6] and (3) "Considerations on the Cultural History of Christian Mission and Conversion."[7] To put these sources in the proper context, I turn to the period from the intertestamental era to the emergence of the Christendom paradigm.

The Entr'acte between the Intertestamental Church and the Carolingian Church

The Greek word for conversion (as in Acts 15:3) is *epistrophê* — "they reported the conversion of the Gentiles." It is derived from the verb *epistrephô*, meaning "to turn around." This turning has deep resonances in texts that use other words that are used more frequently in the New Testament such as Mark 1:4, where John begins his ministry of preparing for the advent of Jesus, "proclaiming a baptism of repentance [*metanoia*] for the forgiveness of sins." The theme of repentance, or *metanoia*, is one of the prime motifs across all four Gospels to characterize the hearer of the Word repenting of past sinfulness, accepting the promise of forgiveness of sin, and beginning the

5. Andrew F. Walls, "Culture and Conversion," in *The Missionary Movement in Christian History: Studies in the Transmission of Faith* (Maryknoll, N.Y.: Orbis Books, 1996), 43–54.

6. Andrew F. Walls, "The Ephesian Moment," in *The Cross-Cultural Process in Christian History* (Maryknoll, N.Y.: Orbis Books, 2002), 72–81.

7. See note 3 above.

transformation of one's self in the Christic pattern realized in the crucifixion and resurrection of Jesus and the bestowal of the Holy Spirit.[8]

One of the key insights of Professor Walls in this area derives from the classical theological teaching that, although Christian salvation depends on Christ suffering under Pontius Pilate, the historical process of redemption was not finished there. Instead, it has run on for another twenty centuries in a still unfinished story. It correlates, according to the letter to the Ephesians, with the realization that the same power that was at work in the life, death, and resurrection of Jesus is now at work in us (Eph. 1:19–23) — in history.[9] And it ramifies to the teaching that we are, according to Pauline doctrine, "parts of a single body of which Christ is the head, the mind, the brain, under whose control the whole body works and is held together" (Eph. 4:15–16).[10] At a present-day, world historical level, Walls reminds us, this body is made up of persons of every nation on earth, and the practical issue becomes "whether or not the church in all its diversity will demonstrate its unity by the interactive participation of all its culture-specific segments ... in a functioning body."[11]

If I may be permitted to raise the issue more concretely than Professor Walls himself does, the relevant question can be posed in other words: Will Christians today — an age when globalization makes us deeply aware of both our common human nature and profound culture and religious divisions and inequalities — convert to realize this challenge from within and draw out the consequences for their work and presence among the nations (*inter gentes*; *entos tôn ethnôn*)? This is, I believe, a fair statement of the challenge of Professor Walls's reading of the crucial issue facing the world Christian movement today.

To answer this question, I first suggest that one of the rare points of convergence between premodern pictures of that mission and modern history of Jesus research resides in the four Gospels' portrayal of what Jesus was about — seeking to bring about a "turning" of Israel from late Second Temple self-understanding to embrace a reality Jesus called the "Kingdom" (*basileia*) of God. As a reformer of Jewish faith and identity, Jesus sought

---

8. Occurring on Easter evening in Johannine theology, at Pentecost in the theology of Luke-Acts.

9. Andrew F. Walls, "The Ephesian Moment," in *The Cross-Cultural Process in Christian History* (Maryknoll, N.Y.: Orbis Books, 2002), 72–74.

10. Ibid., 77.

11. Ibid., 81

the conversion of Israel to on all-inclusive vocation that, as his disciples realized at Antioch (Acts 15), abrogated the requirement that Christians follow
Jewish law in matters such as diet, relativized the ethnic nature of God's chosen people, and substituted the Eucharistic assembly "in memory of Jesus"
and celebrating his continued presence with them in the Spirit for Second
Temple worship. Indeed, both the actions of Jesus and the early Christian
interpretation of his life and work undercut the efforts of Jerusalem-based
royal and sacerdotal power centers, as was recognized when their leaders
had the Romans execute him.

In this view, the historical Jesus sought not to become the founder of
a new religion. Rather he sought to be an instrument for the conversion
of Israel to a self-understanding that embraced a post-ethnic vocation fore-
shadowed in such texts as Genesis 12:1–3 and [Deutero-] Isaiah 55 and 56.
If one finds persuasive the work of Gerhard von Rad, this sort of reinterpretation of tradition was an essential part of Israel's theological growth,
and Jesus is exemplifying an ages-old Jewish tradition.[12] In much the same
way that Luther and Calvin sought the conversion of Roman Catholicism
to a deeper sense of the church's nature and vocation by appealing to biblical tradition and became — against their own desires — the founders of
a separated Protestantism, after his death, Jesus became known not as a
"reformer of Judaism" but as the "founder of Christianity." And the movement he began quickly came to regard itself as having superseded Israel as
the instrument of God's mission.[13] In any case, what Jesus meant by "Kingdom" is not easily grasped, and the early church's sense of mission moved
from ushering in a universal, eschatological kingdom of justice and peace, to
preaching the promise of the forgiveness of sin and eternal life. This shift, in
essence, selected elements deeply consonant with the message of Jesus, but
expressed them in ways that solved a deep set of religio-cultural problems in
traditional Greek and Roman religion. Those religious traditions were losing
credibility for a number of reasons, at least one of which was exacerbated by
the spread of the philosophic ideal proposed by schools such as Stoicism,[14]
which led the educated to see the old religion as an unbelievable, incoherent

---

12. See Gerhard von Rad, *Old Testament Theology: The Theology of Israel's Prophetic
Traditions*, trans. D. M. G. Stalker, 2 vols. (New York: Harper & Row, 1965), vol. 2, chapter
G, "Israel's Ideas about Time and History, and the Prophetic Eschatology," 99–125 and passim.

13. I prescind here from the question of whether Christians believing this in the later centuries
were *correct* in that judgment or fully understood Romans 9–11.

14. On the influence of Stoicism in the Roman world and earliest Christianity, see Ernst
Troeltsch, *Social Teaching of the Christian Churches*, trans. Olive Wyon, 2 vols. (Chicago:
University of Chicago Press, 1976), 1:65–79 and passim.

mass of ritual and myth. More concretely, Professor Walls's lectures on the cultural history of Christian conversion proposes an interpretive framework that yields insights into the manner in which both Justin the Martyr and Origen were able to convert the philosophers' quest for true wisdom into an embrace of Christ as God's word and wisdom personified. In the words of Origen:

> This word, then, and this wisdom, by the imitation of which we are said to be either wise or rational (beings), becomes all things to all men, that it may gain all; and because it is made weak, it is therefore said of it, Though He was crucified through weakness, yet He lives by the power of God. Finally, to the Corinthians who were weak, Paul declares that he knew nothing, save Jesus Christ, and Him crucified.[15]

If one read's Justin's two *Apologies* and his *Dialogue with Trypho the Jew* or Origen's *On First Principles,* the words of Walls in his first lecture come to life: "Discipling a nation includes the turning of a nation's life to Christ." And then, in the words of Andrew Walls in the Fuller lectures:

> In the Christian literature of the second and third and fourth centuries we see the laborious, painful but essential process of Christ entering the mental and moral processes of the Hellenistic world, of Christ being brought into contact with the literary and intellectual past of that whole civilization.

It is common for enthusiasts of the Reformation to see the process of Hellenization as an improper injection of philosophical theory into early Catholicism. On Wallsian principles,[16] however, it is difficult to see how anything else was possible if Greeks were to be converts and not proselytes. And, as Pierre Hadot reminds us in his retrieval of what philosophy was in the ancient world, it was neither purely theoretical nor an exercise in clarifying the meaning of words. Rather it was a way of life replete with spiritual exercises to bring about the conversion of the one who followed that way

---

15. Origen, "On First Principles," IV, 31.

16. In this second lecture, Walls says, "Justin is on the inside of Hellenistic Christianity, a convert, who has found in the Christian Scriptures a source which makes sense in Hellenistic terms, with which to critique his intellectual inheritance and offer criteria by which to test it, both to affirm and to denounce. Origen, born in a Christian home, brought up on the Scriptures and also with the best available education in the whole range of indigenous sources, has the confidence to undertake the rethinking of that whole cultural inheritance in Christian terms. Paul and Justin have both done their work in modern Africa and in modern India. Can Origen be far behind?"

of life from darkness to light.[17] What teachers such as Justin and Origen did was demonstrate that to convert to Christ was to make that passage. And in the words of Professor Walls in his second Fuller lecture, "A Civilization at School with Christ: The Hellenistic Experience of Christianity":

> Those who embrace the philosopher's life do so as a result of enlightenment. Enlightenment is instantaneous, even if preceded by a long preparation. There is no middle point between wisdom and folly. Philosophic enlightenment and subsequent pursuit of the higher life formed one model for Christian conversion in the Hellenistic world, just as the restored, renewed Israel did for the earliest Jerusalem church.

By the fourth century of the Christian era, the reform of Israel was no longer central to the identity of the Jesus movement. Indeed, the divorce of the Jesus movement from both Second Temple Palestinian and Diaspora Judaism was complete by then, and the question was not the relation of Jesus to the Abrahamic, Mosaic, and Davidic "covenants."[18] Instead, it had become that of relationship of Jesus to God (*theos*) in the Septuagint rendering of the Divine Name, as well as in the New Testament (for example in John 1:1, where *theos* / God is called the "Father" [*Pater*] of Jesus, as he is also in Matthew 5:45; 6:6, 9).[19]

The need to answer the question of who this Jesus *is* was necessary to anchor his authority to guarantee what was promised in his name by the church. That exigency led Christians in both the Western Roman Greek- and Latin-speaking Empire — in a series of "Ecumenical Councils" between 325 and 450 — to proclaim it as the belief of the church: (1) that the ones called Father (*pater*), "Son" (*huios*), and Spirit (*pneuma*) in the New Testament were one God in three "persons"; (2) and that through this Triune God and by the ministry of the church, salvation had come to all the world. It would take us far afield to document and justify all this, but my own conviction that it was correct is anchored in the work of Bernard Lonergan, who aims to show that the use of Hellenistic terminology was necessary to clarify in

---

17. Pierre Hadot, Arnold I. Davidson, and Michael Chase, *Philosophy as a Way of Life: Spiritual Exercises from Socrates to Foucault* (Malden, Mass.: Blackwell, 1995), 79–144.

18. I put the word "covenants" in quotation marks to suggest the different meanings of the one word covenant (Hebrew, *berith*). It is taken over into the Septuagint and the Greek New Testament as *diatheke*.

19. For a good theological analysis of this question, see Karl Rahner, "Theos in the New Testament," *Theological Investigations*, vol. 1 (New York: Crossroad, 1961), 79–148

a different culture what the New Testament meant.[20] Suffice it to say that much earlier Jews in both Palestine and the Diaspora decided they could not be part of the Jesus movement. And while the West was holding its councils, Christians in Nubia, Syria, and Persia found other language with which to express the same point. In one way or another, though, Christians had moved to believe that Jesus had instituted a new covenant that renewed the universalism of the call of Abraham to be the Father of a nation that would be a blessing to all nations (Gen. 12:1–3). Forever after Christians and Jews would disagree over the question of whether Jesus was indeed God's unique son and instrument for the salvation of the whole world and whether the fulfillment of texts such as Ezekiel 36:22–28 (promising a new covenant instilling a new heart capable of obeying God's commands) had been realized in him. Any Christian who fails to consider carefully Jewish objections (for example, that war, injustice, poverty, and the disunity of humankind are still rampant, so Jesus could not have been the Messiah promised by the prophets in texts like Ezekiel 36:24–37:14) has not grasped their seriousness.

As I observed above, what the "Kingdom" preached by Jesus was *in the mind of Jesus* is not easy to discern, as anyone who has tried to work through the paradoxical "parables of the Kingdom" with their abundance of reversal and irony can attest. But as we consider the sixth century, it is clear that the church had taken on a self-understanding of itself as the Kingdom of Christ, who was himself God. But the new Christian movement saw the promises of Ezekiel and Isaiah realized in Jesus and themselves as a new people of God — a new *qahal Yahweh* or *ekklesia* superseding the people of the first covenant — this despite Pauline texts such as Romans 11:1 on the continuing validity of the Abrahamic covenant with Israel. The point I am moving toward, however, is not an argument for or against Christian supersession. Rather, I seek to draw attention to the fact that as the peoples of the Roman Empire began to convert to the new religion, it was the natural for them to seek in both Jewish and Christian texts for ways to convert their cultural belief that the gods authorized and protected the social order to conviction that Jesus had ushered in an age in which the church was the Kingdom of Christ on earth. Already in the work of Justin Martyr (c. 103–65), the case was made that Jewish texts were now the possession of Christians, who had the right to interpret them in light of the Christ-event. In time it became

---

20. See Bernard J. F. Lonergan, *The Road to Nicea: The Dialectical Development of Trinitarian Theology* (Philadelphia: Westminster Press, 1976).

plausible to apply to Christ and the church the protective role of the gods to the needs of a new social order as Rome responded to the weakening of the empire, confronted its moral rottenness, and adjusted to the flood of Germanic peoples forced into the empire by Mongolians moving off the Asian steppes.

In the first major cultural conversion of the faith in the West, Jesus was portrayed as the wisdom sought by the philosophers. Those who understood what this meant became the cultural mediators between a faith expressed in Jewish terminology and Hellenistic culture, providing Christianity the intellectual underpinning it needed to be taken seriously by cultural leaders in the Hellenistic world.[21] The passage to membership in the Jesus movement is by *epistrophê* ("conversion"), which carried the connotation of *metanoia* ("change" of heart, and "repentance" for sin). This dynamic meaning cluster is translated into Latin as *conversio* (noun) and *convertere* (transitive verb) and becomes important in the West, where it is the term used for the conversion of the Frankish ("Barbarian") nations to Christianity. In Richard Fletcher's reading of the history of the "conversion" of the barbarians from the fourth through the fourteenth centuries of the Christian era, conversion and mission become synonymous, and an escaped slave, St. Patrick (c. 387–493), a Romanized Briton, is midwife to the insight that even barbarians are fit subjects for undergoing it. In Fletcher's words, "[Patrick] was the first person in [Western] Christian history to take the scriptural injunctions literally; to grasp that teaching all nations meant teaching even barbarians who lived beyond the frontiers of the Roman empire."[22] Although Patrick himself sought to convert Celts to Christ *within* their own culture and not to supplant it with Roman culture, the contamination of conversion and mission with concepts of cultural superiority and the right to use force to make sure that the "right" culture wins is poignantly illustrated by the Italian and the German words for the events that surrounded the next chapter in mission and conversion. In German the events are called the great *Völkerbewanderung*. In Italian they are *l'invasione dei barbari:* the "Migration of the Nations," as opposed to "The Barbarian Invasion." There is

---

21. Meanwhile, at another level, the sort of witness Christians gave during periods of famine and pestilence were giving the new faith the *moral* heft it required to be taken seriously by both the leaders and masses of people. This is one of the key insights of Rodney Stark's *The Rise of Christianity: A Sociologist Reconsiders History* (Princeton, N.J.: Princeton University Press, 1996).

22. Richard Fletcher, *Barbarian Conversion: From Paganism to Christianity* (New York: Henry Holt, 1997), 86.

also a paradox in the fact that, as James Russell contends, when the Germanic nations had been converted to the Latin form of Christianity, they translated Christianity into Germanic language and culture.[23] The triumph of Germanization is symbolized in Charlemagne's coronation, the direction of the church he assumed, and the authenticity of his theological conviction of his and his empire's *Christian* vocation.[24] German "Christendom" converted the ideals of *pax Romana* into forms that were relevant to the Franks and provided the socio-cultural-ethical framework of an age that ran from the eighth through at least the eighteenth century in the West. In Alessandro Barbero's reading of the events and personages from the Merovingian to Carolingian eras that gave birth to the Middle Ages, although there were profound differences of opinion on how imperial and church authority interacted, there is no question that what today we call and often condemn as Christendom represents both a translation of the Gospel into terms the Germanic people could understand and served as a medium to lead these people to a Christ who was relevant to their world.

What has this to do with Walls? In his essay "Culture and Conversion in Human History," Walls enunciates two principles that bear on what was happening in the drama of Christianity in intertestamental times, the Hellenistic period, and moving into the formation of Christendom. In his account of the drama, "the Jesus Act" is "not a voice from heaven separate from the rest of reality." Rather,

> The Jesus Act, the Gospel, is *in the play* [the drama of human life in history as a whole]. That is the implication of the incarnation. It has to be received, therefore, under the same conditions as we receive other communication, through the same faculties and capacities. We hear and respond to the Gospel, we read and listen to Scriptures, in terms of our accumulated perceptions of the world.[25]

In the West, Walls says, we are accustomed to think of ourselves responding to the Word *as individuals,* and to judging the authenticity of faith as being a matter of individual conviction and authenticity. In other ages and cultures, however, an individual's primary sense of identity comes from

---

23. James C. Russell, *The Germanization of Early Medieval Christianity: A Sociohistorical Approach to Religious Transformation* (New York: Oxford University Press, 1994), 183–208.

24. See Alessandra Barbero, *Charlemagne: Father of a Continent,* trans. Allan Cameron (Berkeley: University of California Press, 2004), 142–44 for a fine summary of Charlemagne's understanding of himself as both king and priest.

25. Walls, "Culture and Conversion," 44.

incorporation into a tribe, a people, or a nation. The challenge for us in "modern" Western cultures is:

1. The need to overcome the notion that all these other ways of conceiving identity have been superseded, on the one hand, and to overcome the notion that our own culture is superior.

2. The need to imagine that the authentic Word of God can be translated into other languages — with their own inner logics — and that authentic conversion to Christ can occur in different ways.

Implications of the Walls View of Conversion

In this final section, I reflect on several implications of Professor Walls's view of conversion for the understanding, study, and practice of World Christianity. First, though, I need to do a bit of etymological reflection on the adjective "world" when used with Christianity.

"World" can be and is used in an *empirical* sense to point to the fact that Christianity is no longer the religion of the West but a world religion. The implications of that insight are immense in their own way. At one level, Walls uses the term in exactly this way. On the one hand it is a strategy to avoid calling the reality "global" Christianity. But he also uses it in ways that allude to a more theological dimension that is too-little attended to and the ecclesiological implications that are virtually ignored. In what follows I seek to draw attention to that second dimension of the word "world" and to link it to an ancient criterion for the authenticity of a church — its *catholicity*.

"Catholic," we are told, comes from the Greek word *katholikos* ("universal") and connotes an "extensive" or "geographic" dimension, as is denoted in the term "the church everywhere or universal." At an etymological level, lie the words *kata* ("according to") *holon* (whence the English word "whole"). But the elided version of the two words *kat' holon* also has an important "theological" or "intensive" meaning. A good way to phrase that dimension of catholicity is found in the phrase, "according to the whole [Gospel of Christ]." In the extensive sense of the word, the catholic church is the term favored for speaking of the "universal church" as it spread from Jerusalem and Antioch to Lyons to Baghdad to Alexandria, to Rome, and eventually to Lima, Beijing, and Cincinnati. The intensive sense of the word denotes as "catholic" a church recognized by other churches in the nascent communion of churches as one that preserved the whole Gospel as the message *of* Jesus and *about* Jesus as the Christ, the universal savior. As such, intensive catholicity is closely related to "apostolicity," which denotes both a historical link to the twelve original apostles (i.e., the "eleven" plus Paul) and a church that can trace its roots back to and preserves the integral teaching of those apostles.

In Wallsian terms, the challenge of *translating* the Gospel is one of faithfully translating the original text into terms understandable in another linguistic-cultural setting. That challenge is complemented by a second act or *conversion,* the process in which an individual and a church appropriate (i.e., make their own) the translated Word in such a way that both the individual and the church as a body turn their cultural history into the drama of Christ becoming incarnate.

Studies of "world" Christianity are spreading throughout the academy, and I applaud that. Nevertheless, if these studies do not go deeper into an examination of the catholicity of these churches and promote communion among the world's churches, they are historical and sociological *religious* studies, not *theological* or *missiological* studies properly so called. And to the extent that catholicity and apostolicity of the church are important, world Christian churches need to be in a dialogical process that revolves around the authenticity of church life, for theology and ecclesiology cannot avoid the responsibility of judging what is genuine and what is spurious. As I see matters, this is the implicit challenge of Professor Walls's retrieval of the conversion trope.

Christianity is about the transformation of individuals and communities as they embrace Christ and direct their lives and cultures toward God. Christian mission is not simply, as Rahner describes it at its worst, the overseas marketing arm of European and American churches seeking "to impose the bourgeois morality of the West on people of different cultures" or "in the rejection of religious experiences of other cultures."[26] Mission deserves any bad press it gets, if it is carried out as a mere expansion of a given church's franchise to another place. It rises to the level of a truly catholic member of the world Christian movement and attains the stature of fullness of church only when conversion leads to an authentic dynamic of incarnating the spirit and person of Christ. And in the context of our own day, that incarnation

---

26. Karl Rahner, "Toward a Fundamental Theological Interpretation of Vatican II," *Theological Studies* 40 (1979): 724.

must entail what I am going to call a form of "mysticism" — that is to say, a realization of being part of a body of Christ comprised of peoples of every culture, race, and tongue, a sense that this identity, indeed, reaches maturity when the member of Christ has a sense of his or her personhood as rooted in that self-transcending dimension.

Fanciful? Perhaps, but another of Karl Rahner's most quoted lines runs, "The Christian of the future will be a mystic or will not exist at all."[27] What did he mean? That a passive form of Christian identity conferred by membership in a certain clan, nation, or tribe would wither. He uses the word "Mystic"(once a major turn-off word for Protestants) as the functional equivalent of being "born again" in the Protestant language (which is itself a turn-off for many Catholics). Beyond the terminological chasm, however, what being a mystic or born again means is nothing less than the experience of Pentecost that breathes Spirit into the heart and animates conversion.

Conversion in a world Christian perspective informed by Professor Walls's acute awareness of cultural and historical particularity is not a step toward becoming a proselyte into the fine points of Roman Catholic canon law, nor is it the replication of the pattern of life that an American Evangelical converted in California brings to Indonesia. And neither is it becoming a proselyte in the mold of, say, an Indonesian Catholic priest working in Memphis nor conforming to the dictates of a Korean mission board sending missionaries to Kenya. That said, the Korean, the Californian, and the Indonesian — if they are authentic human beings — are bringing a tradition of responding to Jesus and the witness of turning their own selves to Christ in a situation where they seek to live on other people's terms. Essential to world Christian identity today, in other words, is precisely the kind of enrichment and cross-fertilization that contemporary migration patterns make possible. In cities like New York, where institutions like City Seminary and New York Theological Seminary help men and women reflect on the kaleidoscopic nature of Christian identity today, theology is giving rise to more adequate ways of articulating the post-Christendom shape of the church.

Theology grounded in a Wallsian understanding must go deeper than reflecting on the external phenomena of this reality. Bernard Lonergan's work is almost unique in the centrality he gives to inner conversion as an

---

27. Karl Rahner, "The Spirituality of the Church of the Future," in *Theological Investigations* 20 (New York: Crossroad, 1981), 149.

area for theological reflection. He begins with the insight that morality in the truest sense is not about following rules, as if there were a Christian or Confucianist recipe book for producing virtue. It is, instead, about being converted to a new, disorienting, and reorienting level of consciousness. For Christians that breakthrough occurs when one recognizes in one's inmost being that Jesus is God's self-revelation and allows his Spirit to begin transforming oneself (see Eph. 1:18, a prayer for inner, converted understanding of the theological doctrines Paul propounds in verses 3–13). In Lonergan's view of the process, for the converted person, ethics transcends law and becomes the creative act of making good things happen that would not have happened if this transformation of consciousness had not occurred.[28] (I said "transcends" law in the previous sentence. I did not say that faith-knowledge makes law superfluous.) Law reflects wisdom and is important. Luther interprets the New Testament to teach several "uses" of the law: (1) to curb evil doers from harming others; (2) to lead sinners to know their disordered state; and (3) to provide a guide for the direction of believers' lives. The transcendence of law by the Gospel that I am talking of is contained in these words in a sermon of Luther:

> When the consolation of the Gospel has once been received and it has wrested the heart from death and the terrors of hell, the Spirit's influence is felt. By its power God's Law begins to live in man's heart; he loves it, delights in it and enters upon its fulfillment. Thus eternal life begins here, being continued forever and perfected in the life to come.[29]

What does this mean in today's "world" Christian context? For example, is something like homosexual activity immoral for Christians in Nigeria and moral in the United States? Is the "prosperity Gospel" an authentic concretization of God's promise to bless those who convert? Alas, down the trail of such questions lie in wait dragons that wiser people than I must

---

28. For Bernard J. F. Lonergan on conversion, see *Insight: A Study of Human Understanding* (New York: Philosophical Library, 1957), 595–633 (esp. 627–33), where he deals philosophically with the higher integration of the self needed to recognize what is truly of "value" and then to make good things happen on a sustained basis. Lonergan explicates conversion more theologically in *Method in Theology,* 101–24, where he deals with religion as a "being in love with God" made possible by God's bestowal of grace. That bestowal enables a form of consciousness of one who has "undergone a conversion, as possessing a basis that may be broadened and deepened and heightened and enriched but not superseded....So the gift of God's love occupies the ground and root of the fourth and highest level of man's intentional consciousness. It takes over the peak of the soul, the *apex animae*" (105, 107).

29. See Martin Luther, *Sermons of Martin Luther* (Grand Rapids: Baker Books, 2000), 8:224.

grapple with. More modestly, what I want to suggest on Lonerganian and Wallsian principles is that the existential nature of conversion means that the converted person will be creative in making good things happen in Lagos that might not be appropriate in San Francisco. Are there then no universal standards? That is not my position. For a starter, I suggest that Paul on the fruits of the Spirit in Galatians 5:13 is helpful, "For you were called to freedom, brothers and sisters; only do not use your freedom as an opportunity for self-indulgence, but through love become slaves to one another [in love]." Paul goes on in 5:16–25 to contrast life in the spirit of the Spirit who engenders freedom and the spirit of the "flesh" that engenders negativity. The Pauline text is basically a gloss on Matthew 19:37 ("You shall love the Lord your God with all your heart, and with all your soul, and with all your mind."), which is itself a gloss on Deuteronomy 6:5.

While questions of sexual ethics are vital for practical guidance of Christians who seek to live out their lives and for cultures that seek to inculcate values that will lead to respect for others and guide women and men in experiencing the gift of sex, it seems to me that reflection on how Christians will implement the Deuteronomic injunctions in issues like overcoming poverty, human rights violations, and environmental degradation are equally important. In similar fashion, the most lively forms of Christian life today seem to spread in areas where the charismatic or Pentecostal movements are most present. Does ecclesiology need to broaden itself to entertain questions about ecclesial authenticity in relation to charismatic renewal? World Christian studies that move beyond empirical realities and take their cue on what conversion means in the Christian life will be driven to reflect more deeply on such matters, as well as on how Christians in their present state as the world's most truly world religion can deepen their communion and become a blessing for all the world's peoples. This is the challenge of the lifework of Professor Andrew Walls.

10

Ecclesiology, Andrew F. Walls, and the Fortunate Subversion of the Church

STEPHEN B. BEVANS

Introduction

The invitation to contribute a chapter in this volume in honor of Andrew F. Walls was to write on his "historical and missiological understanding of the church," or, in other words, on his ecclesiology. The challenge has been that, at one level, Professor Walls has no clear, articulated ecclesiology. While he has written much about the church, he has written very little sustained reflection on the church's nature, work, and structure. On another, more implicit level, however, one can find in Walls's work a very rich and profound ecclesiology, one that is not systematic or complete, but one that is thoroughly missionary and, in the widest sense, ecumenical. It is this ecclesiology that this essay will attempt to bring to light.

As the title of the chapter indicates, Walls's implicit ecclesiology is subversive. This is so, first, because it is a *missionary* ecclesiology, and missionary societies and movements, as Professor Walls argues in the essay to which my title alludes, have always functioned as "God's theological jokes, whereby he makes tender mockery of his people when they take themselves too seriously,"[1] focusing too much on their own concerns and not on the already-but-not-yet Reign of God. Walls's ecclesiology, however, is fortunately subversive as well in that it challenges a church still captured by the illusion that its center, future, and deepest identity is in the West. Andrew Walls calls the church today to a new "Ephesian Moment," in which its cultural diversity can display the real identity of Christ in ways never experienced before. Such subversion will lead the church to new expressions of theology, new commitment to its mission, and a new embrace of its vulnerability.

---

1. Andrew F. Walls, "Missionary Societies and the Fortunate Subversion of the Church," in *The Missionary Movement in Christian History: Studies in the Transmission of Faith* (Maryknoll, N.Y.: Orbis Books, 1997), 247.

The Serial Nature of the Church

"The rhetoric of some of our hymns and many of our sermons about the triumphant host streaming out to conquer the world is more Islamic than Christian."[2] As the great historian of the expansion of Christianity Kenneth Scott Latourette had said years before, Christian history is not one of "steady progress, let alone resistless triumph."[3] There have been times when Christianity flourished in one place, and then was stamped out or withered, only to spring up in another place with the same vigor but with new questions and insights. Indeed, "Islam can make a much better claim than Christianity for progressive expansion, for steady numerical increase and geographical growth."[4] In contrast, the Christian Church possesses a serial nature. No one place or people or culture owns it. This is a subversive idea, because it shatters the complacency of Christians who think that the history of the church is one great triumphal procession toward where we are today. Walls's idea of the serial nature of the church calls for humility on the part of some and courage on the part of others.

Walls outlines six serial ages that the church has experienced so far in history. The first age was that of the Jewish identity of the church, when the Jesus community still had no idea (as Walls wrote in 2004) that they "had taken on a new religion. Rather, these beliefs gave them deep insight into, and deeper understanding of, the religion they had always had."[5] Soon, however, with the destruction of Jerusalem in A.D. 70, the church had passed into its second age, thanks to its ability to translate Christian faith into the Hellenistic culture of the Roman Empire. With the collapse of the Roman Empire, however, the heartland of the church moved to the north of Europe, thanks to the missionary work of Christian monks who had slowly, painfully, and imperfectly spread Christianity among the migrating tribal peoples.[6] In a fourth age, a Christian Europe emerged as Eastern Christianity separated from the West and continued to be threatened and eventually conquered by a powerful Muslim presence, only to begin receding there a

---

2. Andrew F. Walls, "The Mission of the Church Today in the Light of Global History," *Word and World* 20, no.1 (2000): 19.

3. Ibid., 18.

4. Ibid.

5. Andrew F. Walls, "Converts or Proselytes? The Crisis over Conversion in the Early Church," *International Bulletin of Missionary Research* 28, no. 1 (2004): 3.

6. Andres F. Walls, "Culture and Coherence in Christian History," in *The Missionary Movement in Christian History: Studies in the Transmission of Faith* (Maryknoll, N.Y.: Orbis Books, 1997), 19.

few centuries later as Western Christianity began to succumb to the secularism brought on by the Enlightenment.[7] It was in these two periods, however, which Walls in later writings calls the "Great European Migration,"[8] that Western missionaries, first Catholic and then Protestant, engaged in the missionary movement, which planted the seeds for the sixth age of the Christian church. Now, in a sixth age, the heartland of the church is in the "non-Western" world of Africa, Asia, Latin America, and Oceania. We do not know, writes Walls, "whether we are living in the very last days or in the days of the early church."[9] What we do know, however, is that in the immediate future the shape of the church will be determined by the peoples and cultures of the new heartland of Christianity as they wrestle with problems never experienced in Christian faith before, as they discover in their cultures new ways to organize the church, worship, and reflect on their Christian identity, and as they recover truths and values once vital but then eclipsed in Christian tradition. A new church is coming into being.

The Missionary Nature of the Church

Andrew Walls would resonate with the Second Vatican Council's affirmation that "the pilgrim church is missionary by its very nature."[10] "Christian faith is missionary both in its essence and in its history." Faith is not a personal possession, but something to be shared, because "both the faith of Christians and the nature of the church are missionary in a much deeper sense, more closely related to the 'sending' idea from which the word 'missionary' came. 'As the Father has sent me,' said Jesus to his first apostles, 'so I send you.' "[11] Walls would agree with Alexander Duff's idea that "the study of mission lies at the center of the theological curriculum, not at its margin, for mission is the reason for the existence of the church."[12]

---

7. Ibid., 20–22.

8. Andrew F. Walls, "Afterword: Christian Mission in a Five-Hundred-Year Context," in *Mission in the Twenty-First Century: Exploring the Five Marks of Global Mission,* ed. Andrew F. Walls and Cathy Ross (London: Darton, Longman and Todd, 2008), 195.

9. Andrew F. Walls, "Globalization and the Study of Christian History," in *Globalizing Theology: Belief and Practice in an Era of World Christianity,* ed. Craig Ott and Harold A. Netland (Grand Rapids: Baker Academic, 2006), 71.

10. Vatican Council II, Decree on the Church's Missionary Activity (*Ad Gentes*), 2.

11. Andrew F. Walls, "The Old Age of the Missionary Movement," in *The Missionary Movement in Christian History: Studies in the Transmission of Faith* (Maryknoll, N.Y.: Orbis Books, 1997), 255.

12. Andrew F. Walls, "Missiological Education in Historical Perspective," in *Missiological Education for the Twenty-First Century,* ed. J. Dudley Woodbury, Charles van Engen, and Edgar J. Elliston (Maryknoll, N.Y.: Orbis Books, 1996), 14.

Should the church take its missionary nature seriously its whole existence would be radically changed, and so such a conviction is already quite subversive. However, Walls understands the missionary nature of the church in an even more subversive sense. He makes a crucial distinction between extending Christian faith in a *crusading mode* as opposed to a *missionary mode*.[13] Around 1500, Christianity could be totally identified with the West, with the fall of the Byzantine Empire and the defeat of the Muslims in Spain. Christendom, as Europe had come to be called, had developed a way either to extend itself into new territories or reclaim territories lost to it, and thus extend the faith or recover it. This was the crusade — "first developed with the idea of reclaiming formerly Christian territory lost to Islam, but subsequent crusades had been fought against northern pagans and Christian heretics."[14] It was this mode of spreading the faith that was used in the evangelization of the new world. "Whole populations were baptized, and were compelled to take Christian instruction. Thus Mexico and Peru entered Christendom, through the gate of crusade."[15]

But in Africa and especially Asia, the crusading mode could not work. First of all, there was no way that the European powers could defeat powerful Asian empires like China or Japan. Secondly, as Europe began to be secularized, colonial nations like the Netherlands and Britain were not that much interested in spreading the faith at all. It was in this context that the missionary movement was born. A number of radical Christians, both Protestant and Catholic, eschewed the idea that to extend the faith was to extend Christendom and opted for another way of proclaiming Christ. While crusaders were "prepared to compel," missionaries opted against compulsion and attempted to "demonstrate, invite, explain, entreat, and leave the result with God."[16] Further, since they could be heard only by communicating, women and men using the missionary mode needed to learn local languages, immerse themselves in a culture, find a place in the local society. While the crusader relied on power to bring people into Christendom, missionaries had to learn "to live on terms set by other people."[17] Taking on the

---

13. See Walls, "Afterword," 196; "Christianity in the Non-Western World: A Study in the Serial Nature of Christian Expansion," in *The Cross-Cultural Process in Christian History* (Maryknoll, N.Y.: Orbis Books, 2002), 38–41.

14. Walls, "Afterword," 196.

15. Ibid.

16. Ibid.

17. Ibid., 197.

missionary mode is to take an "Abrahamic journey"[18] out of Christendom into the risk-filled promised land of faith.

"Living on someone else's terms" is a definition of missionary existence that occurs regularly in Walls's writings.[19] This is the only valid way of spreading the Christian message, the only valid way of being a missionary church. Walls connects such a mode of mission with the mode of the Divine Word as such: "Mission involves moving out of one's self and one's accustomed terrain, and taking the risk of entering another world. It means living on someone else's terms, as the Gospel itself is about God living on someone else's terms, the Word becoming flesh, divinity being expressed in terms of humanity. And the transmission of the Gospel requires a process analogous, however distantly, to that great act on which Christian faith depends."[20] A missionary church is in every sense a church that does mission according to the pattern of the incarnate Word.

The Missionary Task of the Church

How might the church, in imitation of its incarnate Lord, live out its mission on others' terms? Foremost in Walls's mind is the work of *translation* on the one hand and *conversion* on the other.

"Christian mission is not simply about the multiplication of the church; it is about the discipling of the nations. It is about the penetration of cultures and ways of thought by the word about Christ. It is about translation — one might almost say the translation of the word into the flesh, since its starting point is the incarnation."[21] The Gospel, Walls insists, is infinitely translatable,[22] and so it would seem that one of the main tasks of the church is to work to make such translation possible.

---

18. Walls, "Christianity in the Non-Western World," 43.
19. For example, in "Christian Scholarship and the Demographic Transformation of the Church," in *Theological Literacy for the Twenty-First Century*, ed. Rodney L. Peterson with Nancy M. Rourke (Grand Rapids: Eerdmans, 2002), 170; "Commission One and the Church's Transforming Century," in *Edinburgh 2010: Mission Then and Now*, ed. David A. Kerr and Kenneth R. Ross (Oxford: Regnum, 2009), 27; "Christianity in the Non-Western World," 42.
20. Walls, "Christian Scholarship and the Demographic Transformation of the Church," 170–71.
21. Andrew F. Walls, "The Evangelical Revival, the Missionary Movement, and Africa," in *The Missionary Movement in Christian History: Studies in the Transmission of Faith* (Maryknoll, N.Y.: Orbis Books, 1997), 85.
22. Walls, "Culture and Coherence," 22.

Translation has sometimes been characterized as a rather superficial "putting the Gospel into," or clothing a "supracultural" Gospel in a specific cultural garb.[23] Such superficiality, however, seems not to be Walls's intention in his use of the concept. He speaks of "*deep* translation, the appropriation of the Christian Gospel in terms of that culture, down to the very roots of identity."[24] Such translation is necessary to deep mission, for it aids not only in the communication of the Gospel ("putting the Gospel into"), but it acts in the transformation of the church itself, giving the entire church a new and fresh understanding of the Gospel that it works at translating and preaching.[25] This is what happened in the first moment of translation, when those unnamed evangelists began preaching to Greeks in Antioch and daringly began to use the term *kyrios* to refer to Jesus. It is what happened with Origen as he tried to rethink the content of Christian faith in terms of Hellenistic culture,[26] and what happened at the Council of Nicea with the risky choice of *homoousios* to express the Savior's identity.[27] It is what happened in northern Europe when Christian ideas were restated in terms of tribal and legal thought forms, when Matteo Ricci encountered Confucian thought, when Africans told other Africans of the benefits of Christian life. It is what needs to happen today as African, Asian, Latin American, and Oceanian scholars and ministers reach deep into their cultures to find ways that God has always been present in them.

"There is no 'safe' theology,"[28] Walls insists. He might say as well that there is no "safe" mission. It is always risky, certainly subversive to the status quo, for it takes the church places it has never been. But it is a road that leads ultimately to the New Jerusalem.[29]

The work of translation is for the sake of conversion, but such conversion is not the mere act of a person joining the church. For Walls, as he says over and over again in his writings, *conversion* must be distinguished from

---

23. This is how I have characterized the "translation model" in *Models of Contextual Theology* (Maryknoll, N.Y.: Orbis Books, 2002), 37–53. The term "putting the Gospel into" is from Bruce Fleming, *Contextualization of Theology: An Evangelical Assessment* (Pasadena, Calif.: William Carey Library, 1980), 66.
24. Walls, "Christian Scholarship," 171.
25. See ibid.
26. See Walls, "Christianity in the Non-Western World," 30–31; "In Quest of the Father of Mission Studies," *International Bulletin of Missionary Research* 23, no. 3 (1999): 98–105.
27. See Walls, "Commission One," 37.
28. Ibid.
29. See Andrew F. Walls, "Old Athens and New Jerusalem: Some Signposts for Christian Scholarship in the Early History of Mission Studies," *International Bulletin of Missionary Research* 21, no. 4 (1997): 153.

proselytism.[30] Jewish religion before Jesus was a missionary religion. Non-Jews could become Jews if they became proselytes — that is, if they left their native culture behind and took on Jewish culture and practices, namely, circumcision for males, and dedication to the Torah. The rite receiving such women and men into the community even included baptism as a symbolic washing away of their past lives and total dedication to the God of Israel. The earliest followers of Jesus were Jews, and their mission was to preach to fellow Jews that, indeed, the Reign of God had come in the person of Jesus of Nazareth. A Jew who accepted Jesus as Messiah and was baptized remained a Jew, but it was a "Jewish life and thought converted," a "life lived, and thinking done, in terms of the messianic age.... Jewish life and thought turned toward Messiah Jesus."[31]

The problem came when non-Jews, Gentiles, were invited by those unnamed evangelists in Antioch to become members of the community. It is clear from Acts 15 that they had not become proselytes, and that was the objection of the visitors from Jerusalem and the question discussed when Paul and Barnabas went up to Jerusalem. The outcome of that "Apostolic Council" was revolutionary: "the apostles and elders at Jerusalem... agreed that followers of Jesus the Messiah, even if not ethnic Jews, had indeed entered Israel. They did not need the traditional signs of Jewish religious culture, circumcision and Torah-keeping."[32]

The decision at Jerusalem set a pattern for the church's mission. The church is not about proselytism. It does not call people away from their culture or past or ancestry. The church is rather an instrument of conversion. When a person converts to Christ, she or he does not merely add beliefs or values to what is already there. "Conversion," says Walls, "requires something much more radical. It is less about content than about *direction*. It involves turning the whole personality with its social, cultural, and religious inheritance toward Christ, opening it up to him. It is about turning *what is already there*."[33] The church calls people not out of their cultures, but to

---

30. See Andrew F. Walls, "Culture and Conversion in Christian History," in *The Missionary Movement in Christian History: Studies in the Transmission of Faith* (Maryknoll, N.Y.: Orbis Books, 1997), 51–53; "The Mission of the Church Today in the Light of Global History," 20–21; "Eusebius Tries Again," 20–21; "The Ephesian Moment in Worldwide Worship," in *Christian Worship Worldwide: Expanding Horizons, Deepening Practices*, ed. Charles E. Farhadian (Grand Rapids: Eerdmans, 2007), 33; "Old Athens and New Jerusalem," 146–48; "Converts or Proselytes?" 1–6.
31. Walls, "Converts or Proselytes? " 4.
32. Ibid.
33. Ibid., 6.

them. Becoming Christian means losing nothing of real value in one's deepest identity. And yet at the same time it means a radical turning to Christ, living one's life and participating in one's culture entirely in his light, discovering and sharing new aspects of Christ that such turning will unearth and uncover.

The process of conversion takes place in three stages or steps. The first stage is that of the *missionary*, who attempts to translate the Christian message in ways that his hearers can understand. Thus Paul seizes on the Greek idea of *pleroma*, and this takes the Christian message beyond Jewish concepts of messiahship and already extends the understanding of the meaning of Christ. Then there is the stage of the *convert*, embodied, says Walls, in the example of Justin. Justin struggles to maintain his identity, which has been shaped by Hellenistic culture, and brings the Hebrew and Christian Scriptures to bear on his understanding of philosophy. This is a process, Walls says, that Kwame Bediako has identified as operative in today's African theologians. The third stage is embodied in the work of Origen (whom Walls argues is the father of mission studies), who uses all the wealth of Greek philosophy to construct a system of theology. His method is akin, Origen says, to the Hebrews fashioning the gold cherubims of the Ark of the Covenant from Egyptian gold, and the tabernacle curtains from Egyptian cloth.[34]

Once again, Walls's discussion of conversion reveals a church that is about risky, subversive business. "The way of proselytes is safe," he writes. "They give up their old customs and beliefs and take up those of someone else. There is a sacrifice involved — they give up their national heritage and social affiliations. But once this is done, the guideposts are clear. There is a precedent for every eventuality, every situation has been met before."[35] But if proselytes walk by sight, converts walk by faith. This is because "in a very profound sense conversion is the work of the Holy Spirit in the church."[36] Perhaps the greatest and most persistent heresy in the history of the church is the earliest — the heresy of Judaizing. This is because, in all its various forms throughout history, often out of a sincere motive to preserve orthodoxy or order, Christians have tried to turn converts into proselytes, encouraging

---

34. Walls, "Old Athens and New Jerusalem," 148–49. See also "In Quest of the Father of Mission Studies."
35. Walls, "Converts or Proselytes?"
36. Ibid.

them to copy "the lifestyle of others rather than turning their own existing life to Christ."[37]

True, the task of the church is both to make people "feel at home" by means of the "indigenizing principle" and to challenge people by means of the "pilgrim principle."[38] The work of the church, nevertheless, as translator of faith, by its very nature is to encourage true conversion.

Images of the Church

In contemporary ecclesiology it is common to reflect on the three great Pauline images of the church: People of God, Body of Christ, and Temple or Creation of the Spirit. Andrew Walls's implicit ecclesiology deals with the latter two images, and often together, with special emphasis on the church as Christ's body.

Like other aspects of his ecclesiology, Walls roots his understanding of the Body of Christ in the doctrine of the incarnation: "The incarnation of the Divine Word does not conclude on the cross or with the opening of the tomb or with the ascent to glory. It continues wherever Christ is received by faith in another segment of social reality."[39] Such continuing incarnation takes place in two dimensions: time and space.

"Time," writes Walls, "is valorized by the incarnation," and sacred time is not only the time when Jesus of Nazareth walked the earth, but throughout the whole of history. The church at every period demonstrates Christ's presence, even though at times "the community's actual representation of Christ may sometimes be a misrepresentation. Nevertheless, genuine manifestations of Christ cannot be separated from specific segments of social reality that occur in time."[40]

This kind of understanding of the church is quite different from other religions' conceptions of time. For Muslims, for example, "obedience to Allah lies in faithful reproduction of conditions that obtained at the time the

---

37. Walls, "The Ephesians Moment in Worldwide Worship," 33.

38. Andrew F. Walls, "The Gospel as Prisoner and Liberator of Culture," in *The Missionary Movement in Christian History: Studies in the Transmission of Faith* (Maryknoll, N.Y.: Orbis Books, 1997), 3–15.

39. Andrew F. Walls, "Evangelical and Ecumenical: The Rise and Fall of the Early Church Model," in *Evangelical, Ecumenical, and Anabaptist Missiologies in Conversation*, ed. James R. Krabill, Walter Sawatsky, and Charles E. van Engen (Maryknoll, N.Y.: Orbis Books, 2006), 34.

40. Andrew F. Walls, "The Ephesian Moment," in *The Cross-Cultural Process in Christian History: Studies in the Transmission and Appropriation of Faith*, ed. Andrew F. Walls (Maryknoll, N.Y.: Orbis Books, 2002), 74.

Qur'an was revealed."[41] Christian faith, in contrast, is "ancestor conscious," and all Christians "are parts of a single body, and that body needs them all."[42] As Christians of every generation and culture come to faith, "it is as though Christ himself actually grows."[43]

But there is also a spatial dimension to the image of the church as the Body of Christ. This is the theme of the Letter to the Ephesians. In the Ephesian community — for one brief moment — two cultural communities, Jewish and Greek, struggled to live together. Paul says that it is Christ's cross that has broken down the wall between them (Eph. 2:13–18), so now Jews and Greeks are like "different bricks being used for the construction of a single building — a temple where the One God would live" (Eph. 2:19–22).[44] This temple, manifesting the continuing presence of God in the world, can also be understood as the very body of Christ, "of which Christ is the head, the mind, the brain, under whose control the whole body works and is held together" (Eph. 4:15–16).[45] And, even more, it is the fact that the two cultures have come together to form one that brings the church to its full maturity and Christ to his full stature (Eph. 4:13). Only together — Jew and Greek — can the church become fully the church, and can Christ become fully who he is and is meant to be.

The Ephesian church existed for one brief moment in time. Soon Jerusalem was destroyed and Jewish Christianity faded. For all practical purposes the church became monocultural again — this time captured by Hellenistic and then European culture. But, Walls proclaims, the "Ephesian Moment" has come again as in our day the church for the first time in centuries has become once again a non-Western religion, and its center of gravity has moved to Africa, Asia, Latin America, and Oceania. Now it is not just two cultures that Christ has reconciled, but many, and now — in ways not even dreamed of by the Ephesians — Christ can come to his full stature. Walls's subversive challenge is to embrace this new diversity, because the church, as Christ's body, can now give witness to the unity that lies beneath such diversity. Each culture, gender, generation, social location "is a building block belonging to a new temple still in process of construction. Like them, each is an organ necessary to the proper functioning of a body under Christ's

41. Ibid.

42. Ibid., 75.

43. Andrew F. Walls, "Introduction," in *The Missionary Movement in Christian History,* xvii.

44. Walls, "The Ephesian Moment," 77.

45. Ibid.

direction. Only together will they reach the fullness of Christ which is the completion and perfection of humanity."[46]

Marks of the Church

Through the centuries, a number of "marks," "notes," or "dimensions" of the church have been distinguished. Usually we speak of four — unity, catholicity, holiness, and apostolicity, but some Catholic theologians have found as many as one hundred. Luther speaks of seven.[47] Walls identifies unity and especially catholicity as particular marks of the church, but speaks also in several places of several more, namely vulnerability, suffering, witness, renewal, persecution, and faithful wrestling with impossible situations.[48] Here we will reflect on the marks of unity and catholicity, and vulnerability and suffering.

Perhaps for Walls the chief mark of the church today is its catholicity, as the great "Ephesian Moment" has come again. In one of his essays on this, Walls reflects on Revelation 21 as a picture of the church as it is in essence now and will be in the future. The church of the New Jerusalem is different from the Old in that it is "perfectly square, with three gates in each wall, so that it is opened equally to the north, south, east, and west. The gates are never shut in any direction. The church, that is, has no front door, no privileged point of entry.... The doors of the church are perpetually open, equally in each direction, to receive the best of the wealth of all the nations."[49] The church, in all its diversity, is a witness to the growing stature of Christ.

But the church is also radically one. Its unity, however, is also its diversity. The church needs diversity because of the diversity of humanity, but "it must be one because Christ is one."[50] Unity and catholicity offer two dangers, however. One danger is to err in favor of too much unity and seek a normative standard for all. The other, perhaps the more dangerous in today's postmodern relativity, is to proclaim the validity of any and all expressions and for Christians then to live in uncritical isolation from one another.[51]

---

46. Walls, "Afterword," 204.
47. See Hans Küng, *The Church* (New York: Sheed and Ward, 1967), 266–67.
48. Walls, "The Mission of the Church Today," 19; "The Cost of Discipleship: The Witness of the African Church," *Word and World* 25, no. 4 (2005): 441; "Commission One," 36–37.
49. Walls, "The Ephesian Moment in Worldwide Worship," 27.
50. Walls, "The Ephesian Moment," 77.
51. Ibid., 78–79.

Unity and catholicity will always demand dialogue, with the conviction that "only together are we complete in Christ."[52]

In an eloquent article on the costly witness of the African church through the ages, Walls points to the mark of suffering as the way that the church in Africa has been shaped. The martyrs of Scilli, Antony, Takla Haymanot, the Ugandan Martyrs, and the suffering Christians in the Sudan today are examples of "Christian disciples who refused the easy option and took up the Master's cross."[53] Such suffering is also seen in the church's vulnerability. It is because of such vulnerability that the church does indeed have a serial nature. "Christian history reveals the faith often withering in its heartlands, in its centers of seeming strength and importance, to establish itself on or beyond the margins. It has a vulnerability, a certain fragility, at its heart — the vulnerability of the cross, the fragility of the earthen vessel."[54] It is particularly in these marks of suffering and vulnerability that we glimpse Walls's subversive ecclesiology once again, although the embrace of the "Ephesian Moment" is certainly equally so.

Conclusion

Anyone who knows or who has met Andrew Walls knows what a gentle, kind man he is. He hardly seems subversive. And yet if people would fully accept his ideas of history, of Christianity, and of church, they would soon realize how radical his thinking is. If the church would truly embrace its vulnerability, its missionary nature; if it would give over its resources to a deep translation of the Gospel and renounce the heresy of proselytism; if they would commit themselves to unity in diversity — then the church would truly bear witness to what it is: the many-splendored Body of Christ. That would indeed be a fortunate subversion.

---

52. Ibid., 79.
53. Walls, "The Cost of Discipleship," 440.
54. Walls, "From Christendom to World Christianity," 67.

Part IV

TRANSFORMATIONS IN UNDERSTANDING CHRISTIAN HISTORY

11

Historiographic Foundations
from Latourette and Van Dusen
to Andrew F. Walls

DANA L. ROBERT

If I have seen further,
it is only by standing on the shoulders of giants.[1]

This quotation by Sir Isaac Newton is a favorite of scholars, who are acutely conscious that their ideas owe much to the giant intellects who preceded them.

All those contributing to this volume, myself included, are standing on the shoulders of Andrew Walls. I remember when I first saw him in the reading room at Yale Divinity School. I was a graduate student working on my dissertation in the early 1980s. My professor, Charles Forman, pointed him out as probably the greatest living mission historian of the late twentieth century. In the early 1980s, mission history was intellectually unpopular and my dream of teaching what I called "comparative Christianity" a mere fantasy. I needed all the intellectual guidance I could get. So I mustered my courage, introduced myself, and invited Andrew Walls to his first encounter with a bagel and cream cheese. Although the meal was filled with awkward silences, it was the beginning of a friendship and intellectual relationship that has lasted over a quarter century.

Andrew Walls is clearly a giant in the contemporary scholarly consciousness of twenty-first century "World Christianity." But who are the giants upon whose shoulders he stands? There are many answers to this question, including the teachers who mentored him, the students who challenged him, and the colleagues with whom he exchanged ideas. There are also the forgotten scholars of yesteryear, men whose ideas were echoed and extended —

---

1. Sir Isaac Newton, Letter to Robert Hooke, February 15, 1676.

both consciously and unconsciously — in Andrew Walls's own thoughts. Standing on the shoulders of these mid-twentieth-century giants, Andrew was able to see the outlines of the emerging world Christian movement better than they. In expanding their ideas, Walls has pushed a new generation of scholars toward a fruitful interplay among mission, history, and the growing self-consciousness of Christianity as a worldwide religion.

In this essay, I will discuss the work of Andrew Walls in reference to that of Kenneth Scott Latourette and Henry P. Van Dusen. I have chosen these men based on their contributions to the mid-twentieth-century creation of "World Christianity" as a historical construct. Other mid-century "giants" could be referenced, notably Stephen Neill or Max Warren. But I have selected Latourette and Van Dusen because of their visible roles as advocates of "World Christianity" during the 1940s, and the fruitfulness of comparing their ideas to those of Andrew Walls. By examining the wells from which they drew their inspiration, I propose to show how Walls's work links contemporary scholarship to the preceding generation of ecumenists and Christian public intellectuals.

Kenneth Scott Latourette (1884–1968) and Mission History

The first giant who shaped the idea of "World Christianity" was "Uncle Ken" Latourette, former missionary to China and the "father" of twentieth-century mission history. As professor at Yale Divinity School from 1921 to 1953, Latourette trained doctoral students and built up the Day Missions Collection. He never married, and his substantial bequest to the Divinity School Library has been used over the years to purchase missions-related materials. The Latourette legacy pushed the mission collection of YDS to a preeminent place in the documentation of mission history and World Christianity. According to head librarian Paul Stuehrenberg, Latourette "was instrumental in changing the focus of the Day Missions Collection at Yale from a resource for training missionaries to a collection documenting the history of Christian missions."[2]

In more than one sense, therefore, Kenneth Scott Latourette was the father of the historical study of Christian missions. His seven-volume *History of the*

---

2. Paul Stuehrenberg, "The Latourette Initiative for the Documentation of World Christianity," *www.library.yale.edu/div/latourette.html* (accessed February 13, 2009).

Expansion of Christianity (1937–45) was a masterful survey of the cross-cultural spread of Christianity from the time of Jesus. Three volumes focused on what he called "The Great Century." By using the nineteenth century as the focal point of Christian missions, Latourette privileged the western European trajectory in its period of colonial expansion. Blurbs for the book shared the bias that all roads led through European Christendom. Said the *New York Times,* "A majestic panorama of world-wide progress toward the more abundant life of man." And from the *Saturday Review of Literature,* "It will stand as a monument to exhaustive scholarship, as a source for all future studies of the first nineteen centuries of Christendom's spread." Latourette's stature as a pioneer historian of both East Asia and of Christian expansion was cemented by his election as president of the American Historical Association. His presidential address, delivered in 1962, was entitled "The Christian Understanding of History."[3]

While historians of the World War II era praised his seven-volume masterpiece as "the most ambitious one-man multiple-volume historical projects of our generation,"[4] the end of European colonialism in the 1960s — including the collapse of Christendom as an intellectual and political construct — gave rise to a historiography that exploded with critical theory and failed narratives. Anti-colonial, nationalist, and Marxist historians jettisoned consensus history as a tool of elitism and castigated Christian missions as an expression of European colonialism. With the rise of postmodernism, the overarching historical synthesis fell into disrepute.

After a quarter century of historiographic neglect, sympathy for mission history began to revive with the publication of Lamin Sanneh's masterful *Translating the Message* in 1989. But Latourette remained the "whipping boy" of the failed "Christendom" synthesis of mission history. As Sanneh accused in his essay "World Christianity and the New Historiography," "Latourette has applied a cultural and civilizational test to the undisputed success of Christianity, not the plurality of idioms and epicenters of impact around the world."[5] The enduring significance of Latourette, according to

---

3. See *www.historians.org/info/AHA_history/kslatourette.htm* (accessed August 2, 2009) for Latourette's presidential address.

4. Blurb from *American Historical Review.* All blurbs are found on the first edition book jacket of *History of the Expansion of Christianity* (New York: Harper, 1937).

5. Lamin Sanneh, "World Christianity and the New Historiography: History and Global Interconnections," in *Enlarging the Story: Perspectives on Writing World Christian History,* ed. Wilbert Shenk (Maryknoll, N.Y.: Orbis Books, 1989) 96–97.

Sanneh, lay not in his voluminous writings, but in his historical method as imitated by others.[6]

Latourette was clearly a man of his generation in interpreting Christian missions as the greatest achievement of the West. As he invented mission history, he unintentionally and unavoidably imprisoned it in a Christendom narrative. Or did he? If we go beyond the "expansion" motif that caricatures his oeuvre, we see that his historical consciousness was shaped during the 1920s, the postwar period of disillusionment with European Christianity. The 1920s saw creative thinking about and early experiments with inculturation.[7] Like Andrew Walls many years later, Latourette's passion for mission history grew from his experience as a missionary.[8] His first two major books were on East Asia. He worked as a teacher in China for two years before being invalided home and beginning his career as historian.

An article he published in 1925, "The Study of the History of Missions," shows that Latourette's core achievement lay in charting a path for the history of Christianity as a series of social movements. In the questions he asked, he was decades ahead of his time. The historiographic questions he raised in the article, written only a few years after he became professor at Yale, were the same ones that came to preoccupy Andrew Walls and other historians of mission and World Christianity in the late twentieth century. The article began by rehearsing the kinds of approaches commonly taken toward the history of Christianity — institutional histories, biographies, and histories of doctrine. Lacking, argued Latourette, was study of how Christianity became a popular religion of the "great and usually uncomprehending majority" at the end of the early period, its spread among the Germanic Goths and other northern peoples, and an evaluation of the spread of Christianity from Europe since the 1400s.[9]

Latourette identified six key issues that needed exploration in the context of researching the history of Christianity as a cross-cultural movement. First was the question "What has been the Christianity that has been propagated?"[10] With his missionary's instinctive understanding of inculturation —

---

6. Ibid., 98.

7. Dana L. Robert, "The First Globalization: The Internationalization of the Protestant Missionary Movement between the World Wars," *International Bulletin of Missionary Research* 26, no. 2 (2002): 51–66.

8. His diligence in building up a library collection for mission history is also echoed by Walls's efforts to build collections documenting Christianity in the non-Western world.

9. Kenneth Scott Latourette, "The Study of the History of Missions," *International Review of Mission* 14 (1925): 108–9.

10. Ibid., 109.

even though that term was not yet in use — Latourette eschewed Eurocentric dogmatic formulations. Christianity, he wrote, has "changed from age to age and from people to people in its emphasis on doctrines and its organization, so that we must know not only what it was in the days of Jesus and the Apostles, but what it was at each of the various times when it was newly carried to a new country."[11] Latourette assumed that Christianity differed across peoples and cultures, denominations, and generations. "Difficult though it may be to determine the main features of Christianity as it enters a country," he stated, "the attempt must be made."[12]

The second theme to pursue in mission history, according to Latourette, was "the process, the agents and the methods by which Christianity was introduced."[13] Missionary methods, including the motives of those who accepted the faith, shaped the character of the church that resulted in each time and place. The third theme was the relationship between "the missionary enterprise" and associated social and political movements, including commerce, national expansionism, and industrialization. Said Latourette, "The prominence of Protestant missions in the past hundred and twenty-five years seems to owe to the commercial and industrial expansion of England and America only a little less than it does to the religious awakening in these countries."[14]

Latourette's fourth scholarly theme for the history of the "expansion" of Christianity was: "What effect has Christianity had upon each of the peoples to which it has gone? In how far and in what ways has Christianity altered its environment?"[15] What was Christianity's impact on social issues like slavery, on science and legal systems, politics and geography and economics? In the context of the Western impact on Japan, China, India, and the Near East, how has Christianity influenced diverse cultures and regions?[16]

The reverse of the question was Latourette's fifth query, "In how far has Christianity been altered by its environment?"[17] For example, suggested Latourette, "No one yet has carefully examined the interesting suggestion that Protestantism is the reaction of the Teutonic mind upon Christianity."[18]

---

11. Ibid.
12. Ibid., 110.
13. Ibid.
14. Ibid., 111.
15. Ibid., 112.
16. Ibid., 113.
17. Ibid.
18. Ibid.

It is premature to examine the impact of non-Western cultures on Christianity, Latourette wrote cheerfully, "but it is not too early to begin the attempt."[19]

Apologizing that the latter two questions might seem "remote" from mission history, he nevertheless summarized their connection in his sixth question, "In how far have the conditions under which Christianity spread, and particularly the missionary methods employed, affected both the influence of Christianity upon its environment and of the environment upon Christianity?"[20] Latourette's interest in this final question was not only historical, but missiological. For historical research could help to guide future mission policy through examining such things as the relationship between mission methods and church structures, the nature of mass conversion movements, and the connection between colonialism and missionary paternalism.

Kenneth Scott Latourette knew it was impossible to answer these questions in one lifetime. Just one important topic, like the "narrative of Nestorian missions," could fill the entire career of one scholar and still not be complete.[21] Projecting his own life task, he remarked, "It is, however, not too early for some scholar to attempt to summarize what is already fairly well known of the entire story. He should approach the task modestly, with frank recognition of the fact that all he can hope to do is to ask some intelligent questions, suggest possible answers and state such few conclusions as seem well established."[22] Thus Latourette began his encyclopedic seven volumes with a sense of humility and in hopes of putting together in one convenient set the known facts of mission history. He sat patiently in his office at Yale, with students bringing him volume after volume, which he synthesized into a coherent narrative. He did not expect his own work to be the final word or to present the definitive portrait of the great movement to which he devoted his life. He sought rather to build a platform upon which other historians would stand. As Andrew Walls did years later, Latourette placed his scholarship at the service of Christian missions.

Latourette raised the foundational questions for Andrew Walls and succeeding mission historians. He refused to confine the history of Christianity to "church history," or the study of doctrines and institutions. He assumed

---

19. Ibid.
20. Ibid.
21. Ibid., 115.
22. Ibid.

that broader historical contexts shaped Christianity as a movement, and that Christianity itself shaped cultures and politics. He was undoubtedly one of the first historians to ask whether Protestantism itself was a product of its cultural milieu. Latourette's original questions are ones that have guided Andrew Walls in his many essays on mission history and World Christianity. Both historians simultaneously put historical methodologies at the service of mission practice and drew upon insights gained from mission experience to shape the historian's craft. The creative symbiosis between mission and history has not only shaped the scholarly understanding of Christianity as a social movement of "lived religion," but has provided the intellectual framework for the conceptualization of "World Christianity."

Despite their shared emphases, Latourette and Walls remain scholars of different generations. Latourette called the nineteenth century the "Great Century" of Christian expansion. He was a product of "Christendom," a pre–World War II "internationalist," and an activist for the interdenominational ecumenical movement. Although both scholars used a periodization of expansion and recession, Latourette assumed an overall narrative of progress, while Walls emphasized that today's center might be tomorrow's periphery because of decline in the Christian heartland. From his vantage point in Africa in the late twentieth century, Walls could see that twentieth-century Christianity was even "greater" than that of the nineteenth, but not as a Western or ecumenical Protestant story.[23]

The contrast in their literary oeuvres reflects their changing contexts. While Latourette devoted his life to the task of drawing together a great synthesis of mission history, Walls has largely confined himself to pungent essays that grasp particular moments or concepts in the history of Christian movement across cultures. By the time Walls began to write, the complexities of the historical moment meant that the comfortable days of synthetic, Western consensus history had vanished.

Both scholars recognized the multicultural diversity of World Christianity. But Latourette emphasized the centrality of the European migrations of the fifteenth through the twentieth century, while Walls concentrated on the cultural diversity of the post-colonial era. Latourette was interested in Asia in general and China in particular. Walls's strength lay in Africa in general and Sierra Leone in particular. Their differences notwithstanding, Andrew

---

23. Andrew F. Walls, "Eusebius Tries Again: Reconceiving the Study of Christian History," *International Bulletin of Missionary Research* 24, no. 3 (2000): 105.

Walls stands on Latourette's shoulders in interpreting history through the lens of mission and in using mission to advance the study of church history beyond its Eurocentric frame of reference.

Henry Pitney Van Dusen (1897–1975) and World Christianity

A second historiographic moment that prepared the way for Walls's work was the formal articulation of the concept "World Christianity." In the mid 1940s Archbishop William Temple famously referred to the growing ecumenical movement as "a great world-fellowship," the "great new fact of our era."[24] But it was following the Second World War that the euphoria of "World Christianity" inflamed the imaginations of ecumenical theologians. One of its most prolific advocates was the "evangelical liberal" Henry P. Van Dusen, systematic theologian, president of Union Theological Seminary in New York City from 1945 to 1963, and author of twenty-five books.

To Van Dusen, the encounters of American soldiers with Christians in the Pacific Islands, who fed them and hid them from the Japanese, revealed the potential of Christianity as a worldwide religion. Even though he recognized that based on population statistics Christianity was largely a Western faith, the wartime stories of Christian witness across ethnic and national divisions showed that "only a world church is effective amid planetary war.... To an age destined to survive, or to expire, as 'one *world*,' we bring a *world church*. We have seen that in the past century Christianity has become, for the first time, a *world* reality."[25] To support his commitment to a common world fellowship, Van Dusen launched the Henry W. Luce Visiting Professorship in World Christianity at Union Seminary in 1945. Chinese university president and Christian intellectual Francis Wei was its first incumbent.

In his writings, Van Dusen extended Latourette's idea of the Great Century and argued that the previous 150 years — from roughly 1800 to 1950 — saw the largest achievements in two thousand years of Christianity. That period experienced unprecedented numerical and geographic expansion,

---

24. "As though in preparation for such a time as this, God has been building up a Christian fellowship which now extends into almost every nation, and binds citizens of them all together in true unity and mutual love.... Almost incidentally the great world-fellowship has arisen; it is the great new fact of our era." Archbishop William Temple, *The Church Looks Forward* (New York: Macmillan, 1944), 2.

25. Henry P. Van Dusen, *World Christianity: Yesterday, Today, Tomorrow* (New York: Abingdon-Cokesbury, 1947), 248–51, quoted in Dana L. Robert, *Christian Mission: How Christianity Became a World Religion* (Oxford: Wiley-Blackwell, 2009), 67.

with one-third of the world becoming Christian, and widespread influence on humanity in such areas as advocacy for human rights. The centrifugal movement of missions gave birth to the centripetal movement of church unity, which together characterized the world church of the twentieth century. Van Dusen not only used missions and ecumenism as the two poles of his historical analysis, but he worked to unite them in his role as chairman of the joint commission for the integration of the International Missionary Council and the World Council of Churches in 1961.

"Pit" Van Dusen's vision of "World Christianity" was not so much that of multiculturalism, but of organic unity. While he predicted that by the year 2000, all churches would be united except for "sects" and Roman Catholics, he noted the "countervailing trends" of the largely Western demographic base of Christianity, the twin threats of secularism and communism as alternative global visions, and anti-Christian nationalist revolutionary movements.[26] Nevertheless, Van Dusen argued, Latourette's analysis of church history as a series of advances followed by periods of retreat was correct. Because each recession was less than before, the totality created a cumulative record of Christian progress to its present condition of encompassing one-third of the world. The 1948 founding of the World Council of Churches represented both the culmination and the end of the historic expansion of Europe.

Clearly Van Dusen's mid-century optimism about the inevitable victory of Christian unity was unwarranted. As Andrew Walls would popularize decades later, Van Dusen recognized that the mid-twentieth century marked the end of the era of European expansion. But his fixation with primarily mainline Protestant unity and the prevailing European ethnic dominance of mid-century Christianity meant that his definition of World Christianity lacked the multicultural and ecclesial diversity that Andrew Walls was promoting by the 1980s. The emerging independent movements that Van Dusen dismissed as "sects" Andrew Walls would later celebrate as key to the fulfillment of the Revelation vision: "Never before has the Church looked so much like the great multitude whom no man can number out of every nation and tribe and people and tongue. Never before, therefore, has there been so

---

26. Van Dusen, *World Christianity,* 95. The global unity expressed by the term "World Christianity" was also used by other mission scholars during the early Cold War as a counterweight to the equally global vision of communist revolution. See, for example, M. Richard Shaull, *Encounter with Revolution* (New York: Association Press, 1955).

much potentiality for mutual enrichment and self-criticism, as God causes yet more light and truth to break forth from his word."[27]

Van Dusen's 1947 volume, *World Christianity: Yesterday, Today, Tomorrow*, contained the fullest expression of his vision and provides the most striking comparison with the ideas of Andrew Walls. Chapter 2 follows Latourette's analysis of the history of Christianity as four major epochs of advance and decline. One difference with Walls's idea of "serial progression" is Van Dusen's use of only western European markers for the periodization.[28] Because he used political rather than cultural categories to denote the periods, Van Dusen did not mark early Jewish Christianity as a period in its own right. But as Walls did later, Van Dusen recognized that decline occurred at the heartland of Christianity, while revival occurred from the margins. Speaking of the decline of early Mediterranean Christianity, Van Dusen noted, "It was on the frontiers of culture and the Church, in Gaul and western Europe, that Christianity continued robust. And it was from these unpromising outposts that the vital impulses for recovery mainly came."[29] Thus Walls's description of the "donut effect" in the serial progression of Christianity was consistent with Van Dusen's rendering of Latourette's basic historical framework.

In an imaginative effort to gain a bird's-eye view of this historical process, Van Dusen postulated the arrival of a "visitor from Mars" to observe the state of World Christianity at different points in history.[30] Van Dusen's Martian appears in the early nineteenth century to observe a Christianity apparently in decline, only to return at the end of the "Great Century" to experience its remarkable resurgence. Says Van Dusen of 1914,

> Christianity had become at last, for the first time in the nineteen centuries of its life, a world religion. More than that. It had validated its claim to be a universal faith, embracing men and women of every race and culture and stage of civilization, from the crudest tribesmen just wrested from cannibalism to the most cultured and sophisticated descendants of sages who had achieved civilization centuries before

---

27. Andrew F. Walls, "The Gospel as Prisoner and Liberator of Culture," in *The Missionary Movement in Christian History: Studies in the Transmission of Faith* (Maryknoll, N.Y.: Orbis Books), 15

28. For Andrew F. Walls's periodization, see "Culture and Coherence in Christian History," in *The Missionary Movement in Christian History: Studies in the Transmission of Faith* (Maryknoll, N.Y.: Orbis Books, 1997).

29. Van Dusen, *World Christianity*, 65.

30. Ibid., 46.

Christ and millenniums before our ancestors left their tree huts and their savage ways.[31]

While Andrew Walls used the "Professor of Comparative Inter-Planetary Religions" as an analogous heuristic device, his space visitor arrives to experience the great variety of Christian movements from the Jewish followers of Jesus, through the Council of Nicea and medieval Irish monasticism, all the way to the Aladura churches of Nigeria.[32] Van Dusen's "man from Mars" illustrates the cycle of decline and advance that culminates in worldwide Christian unity. Walls's space professor observes obvious differences in culture and practices throughout the history of Christianity but nevertheless finds the unity of inherited biblical tradition, sacraments, and mission energy. Van Dusen's "Martian" and Walls's "space professor" are both concerned with the identity of "World Christianity." The Martian finds it in the self-conscious interconnectedness of a worldwide movement toward Christian unity. The space professor sees lines of historical continuity amid cultural diversity. In both cases, Christian mission is the mother of worldwide Christianity.

The writings of Henry Van Dusen foreshadow in significant ways some of the ideas for which Andrew Walls is known, but their differences reveal much about the divergent historical contexts in which they wrote. Van Dusen was an administrator and stateside theologian, not a missionary. More attuned to the world church than most North American theologians of the 1950s, Van Dusen nevertheless wrote from within the cozy club of mainline ecumenism, not from the missionary frontiers of struggles over devolution and revolution. Speaking as a public intellectual at the apex of mainline Protestant power, Van Dusen graced the cover of *Time* Magazine in 1954 in connection with the second World Council of Churches General Assembly in Evanston, Illinois. Yet with prescience, he meditated on the probability that the postwar era was also the beginning of a great recession in the spread of Christianity — by implication, the recession of European Christianity. He asked, "If ours be the beginning of the fourth recession, where shall we most hopefully expect the impulses of vitality for the next advance?"[33]

---

31. Ibid., 51–52.
32. Walls, "The Gospel as Prisoner and Liberator of Culture," 3–7.
33. Van Dusen, *World Christianity*, 65.

Early in his career, Andrew Walls experienced the massive decline and repudiation of missions by intellectuals and by Western mainline Christians that occurred from the late 1960s onward. As the old mainline vision of an organically united World Christianity fell away, even Van Dusen's language of "World Christianity" disappeared from view, lost in debates over liberation versus evangelization and the radical localism of "contextualization." But from his outpost as a teacher of early church history in Sierra Leone, Walls experienced the grassroots resurgence of what he called "second century Christianity."[34] Because he lived on the margins of the old empire, away from its declining center, Walls was able to recognize and to name the resurgence that Van Dusen hoped for but did not live to see. The resurrection of the concept "World Christianity" occurred bottom up, through its growth and diversity at the grassroots.

By the 1990s, the margins were becoming the center. Walls used his experiential knowledge to reread all of church history as the diverse stories of conversion and cultural translation. He concluded that "the most urgent reason for the study of the religious traditions of Africa and Asia, of the Amerindian and the Pacific peoples, is their significance for Christian theology; they are the substratum of the Christian faith and life of the greater number of the Christians of the world."[35] For Andrew Walls, the story of World Christianity is that of Christianity as a non-Western religion with multiple local manifestations — neither Latourette's expansive Christendom, nor Van Dusen's dream of Christian cooperation and organic unity.

Conclusion: The Giants of Hopeful Humility

As we remember those who first recognized and articulated the captivating vision of Christianity as a worldwide religion, I am struck by what they have in common. Latourette, Van Dusen, and Walls were each acutely aware of the limitations of his own reason, yet bold in analysis because each anchored his scholarship in Christian hope. Despite definitions of the subject that reflected the human limitations of their own eras, they shared a faith in the existence of worldwide Christian community. This essentially

---

34. Walls, "Eusebius Tries Again," 106.
35. Andrew F. Walls, "Old Athens and New Jerusalem: Some Signposts for Christian Scholarship in the Early History of Mission Studies," *International Bulletin of Missionary Research* 21, no. 4 (1997): 146–53.

eschatological conviction undergirded their work, regardless of the obstacles stacked against them.

When Kenneth Scott Latourette died in 1968, he had lived long enough to see his field of study stripped from the approved doctoral subjects at Yale University, and his style of history pilloried as "colonialist."[36] When Henry Van Dusen ended his life in 1975, he thought that Christianity had entered a major recession.[37] His postwar ideas about "World Christianity" had disappeared in a cloud of acrimony and institutional power politics. In significant ways, they realized their predictions had been wrong. Such is often the sad fate of bold academics who live long enough to see their work rejected or even vilified by the next generation.

Informed by his missionary experience and the lessons of history, Andrew Walls is acutely aware that his own scholarly formulations are as contextually bound as those of his predecessors. And yet the Revelation vision of Jesus' followers, called out from every tribe and nation, sustains his commitment to the existence of Christianity as a worldwide faith. Mission influences the historian's task, and history shapes mission. Like Latourette and Van Dusen, historian Andrew Walls is a humble giant of Christian hope.

---

36. The Religious Studies Department separated from Yale Divinity School in 1963. After that time, mission studies (including the history of non-Western Christianity) were stricken from Ph.D. subjects by being ghettoized in the Divinity School. Thus the secularization trends of the 1960s effectively ended the scholarly tradition of Kenneth Scott Latourette, and Yale stopped producing historians of mission and World Christianity. Latourette's successor as Willis James Professor, my own teacher Charles Forman, was not allowed to direct Ph.D. students in the Department of Religious Studies. He was permitted to become my major professor at my request upon the death of my advisor, Sydney Ahlstrom. The current Willis James Professor of Missions and World Christianity, distinguished scholar Lamin Sanneh, is not even listed in the faculty roster for Yale's Department of Religious Studies. Despite Yale's distinguished history of scholarship in this field, the history of Christianity is not an approved field of study in its Department of Religious Studies.

37. Van Dusen and his wife believed in euthanasia and died in a suicide pact.

12

Andrew F. Walls for Americans?

MARK NOLL

Andrew Walls's path-breaking contributions to the reconceptualization of "World Christianity" and his profound theological reflections on the missionary enterprise might seem to offer only a little for those who study the history of Christianity in North America. To be sure, Walls has written perceptively about a few individual Americans like the historian Kenneth Scott Latourette.[1] He has also written perceptively about subjects with an obvious bearing on the experience of Americans — like his analysis of how missionary involvement in colonizing ventures almost inevitably turns back to shape the perceptions of the missionaries.[2] Or how evangelical assumptions about "revival" presuppose a Christian background for Americans as well as Europeans that usually does not exist in the newer regions of Christian expansion.[3] Yet with the exception of only one essay in *The Missionary Movement in Christian History* and *The Cross-Cultural Process in Christian History,* and a few scattered treatments elsewhere, North America has not bulked large in Walls's work.

The suggestion of this chapter, however, is that guidance from Andrew Walls offers a powerful framework for understanding the history of Christianity in America. In addition, this guidance helps explain why Christianity in the American experience is now more generally relevant to the world at large than Christianity in the European experience. For American history, it may be that what Andrew Walls has written is just as pertinent as for the missionary regions of the world.

---

1. Andrew F. Walls, *A History of the Expansion of Christianity Reconsidered,* Day Missionary Library pamphlet (New Haven: Yale Divinity School Library, 1996); and Andrew F. Walls, "Kenneth Scott Latourette," *Christian History* 20, no. 4 (2001): 44.

2. Andrew F. Walls, "Christianity in the Non-Christian World," in *The Cross-Cultural Process in Christian History* (Maryknoll, N.Y.: Orbis Books, 2002), 44.

3. Andrew F. Walls, "The Evangelical Revival, the Missionary Movement, and Africa," in *The Missionary Movement in Christian History: Studies in the Transmission of Faith* (Maryknoll, N.Y.: Orbis Books, 1997), 79–84.

The place to begin is his essay "The American Dimension of the Missionary Movement" from *The Missionary Movement in Christian History*. I was privileged to be present when the lecture that became this essay was first delivered in June 1986 at a Wheaton College conference organized by Joel Carpenter and Wilbert Shenk. Before this event I am not sure if I had heard of Andrew or his work. At the event I came away very much impressed with the speaker (diffident yet insightful, witty yet spiritually serious), but what he had said left only a slight impression. The chance to read a fuller version of the essay when it appeared in book form began to turn on the lights.[4] Reading it once more in Walls's own collection of essays completed my conversion.[5] From that time the whole history of Christianity in North America has for me been refracted through the compelling prism provided by Andrew Walls. In what follows, I first explore this seminal essay and then outline how the Walls perspective can orient the place of American Christianity in the world as well as define the character of developments in America.

The American Dimension of the Missionary Movement

It might be expected that Andrew Walls's focused attention on African Christian history would stimulate general reflections on missiological themes. It was a surprise to me that the missionary insights that Walls drew from linking African Christian history to ancient and medieval Christian history could yield so many compelling insights for writing the history of Christianity in North America.[6]

Walls began his essay with a telling quotation from Kanzo Uchimura, a Japanese Christian who in 1926 was writing about what Americans could — and could not — teach the Japanese about religion:

---

4. Andrew F. Walls, "The American Dimension of the Missionary Movement," in *Earthen Vessels: American Evangelicals and Foreign Missions, 1880–1980*, ed. Joel A. Carpenter and Wilbert R. Shenk (Grand Rapids: Eerdmans, 1990), 1–25.

5. Andrew F. Walls, "The American Dimension of the Missionary Movement," in *The Missionary Movement in Christian History: Studies in the Transmission of Faith* (Maryknoll, N.Y.: Orbis Books, 1997), 221–40.

6. This account of "The American Dimension of the Missionary Movement" draws on Mark A. Noll, "Translating Christianity," *Books and Culture* (November/December 1996): 6–7, 35–37.

Americans are great people; there is no doubt about that. They are great in building cities and railroads.... Americans have a wonderful genius for improving breeds of horses, cattle, sheep and swine.... Americans too are great inventors.... Needless to say, they are great in money.... Americans are great in all these things and much else; but *not in Religion*.... Americans must *count religion* in order to see or show its value.... To them big churches are successful churches.... To win the greatest number of converts with the least expense is their constant endeavor. Statistics is their way of showing success or failure in their religion as in their commerce and politics. Numbers, numbers, oh, how they value numbers![7]

Uchimura might stand accused of hyperbole, but not Andrew Walls as he undertook a careful effort to define "a specifically American Christianity, an expression of Christian faith formed within and by American culture."[8] For Walls, mission insights were crucial both for understanding the shape that Christianity had assumed in America and for evaluating that faith with critical sympathy.

Walls moved quickly to indicate how important the subject of America's missionary history was for the history of Christianity as a whole. In his picture, the shape that Christianity took in winning America dictated its expression when American missionaries carried the Gospel overseas: "The Christianity displayed in American missions was determined by the nineteenth-century Christian movement along the frontier and the evangelization of new cities. The whole climate of American Christian thinking was conditioned by expansion."[9] In other words, after the United States succeeded Britain as the greatest source of missionary volunteers at the time of World War I, and after it became the overwhelmingly dominant force in world missionary effort after World War II, American Christian expression took on world-historical significance.

To be sure, Walls recognized that Christianity in America grew from the stock of Christian Europe. But the special circumstances of new-world settlement — which mingled immigrants of many religious traditions and many ethnicities and which was accompanied by a growing attachment to democratic liberalism — meant that Christianity in North America would also

---

7. Walls, "The American Dimension of the Missionary Movement," in *The Missionary Movement,* 221–22.
8. Ibid., 234.
9. Ibid., 227.

differ significantly from what it had been in Europe. Thus, American dispositions were not theoretical but activist, not traditional but self-starting, not dependent on the state but voluntary, not institutional but individual. In Walls's terms, Christian believers in America came to be characterized by "vigorous expansionism; readiness of invention; a willingness to make the fullest use of contemporary technology; finance, organization, and business methods; a mental separation of the spiritual and the political realms combined with a conviction of the superlative excellence, if not the universal relevance, of the historic constitution and values of the nation; and an approach to theology, evangelism, and church life in terms of addressing problems and finding solutions."[10]

With his ability to see local culture as shaping much that American believers have often regarded as simply an unadorned expression of the faith, Walls was prepared to find fault. He concluded, for example, that Americans, and especially American missionaries, have been politically naive. The naiveté lies in thinking that the American practice of separating church and state somehow represents a cessation of politics. But Walls pointed out that most Americans have embraced a separation of church and state for practical rather than theoretical reasons. There were simply too many different representatives of competing European churches to reestablish any one of them as the established religion. As a result, when Americans treated their practical solution as a theological principle, "the effects," according to Walls, "have been paradoxical. American missions have tended to think of themselves as nonpolitical: how can it be otherwise if [as an assumption of American life] church and state live in different spheres? Non-Americans have seen continual political implications in their activities: how can it be otherwise if [as an assumption of life in most of the rest of the world] church and state inhabit the same sphere, or at least overlapping spheres?"[11]

Similarly, Walls suggested that the habit of perpetually writing new statements of faith for an ever growing number of freshly minted denominations and institutions was as much a product of distinctly American circumstances as were American instincts on church and state. To Walls, it was evident that this practice of continual self-definition in theology reflected "the characteristically American problem-solving approach at work," in which the common procedure was to "identify the problem [in this case doctrine],

---

10. Ibid., 235.
11. Ibid., 232.

apply the right tools, and a solution will appear. Then move on to the next problem."[12] Equally characteristic of American mental habits was the tendency to use such statements of faith as "tests for fellowship and a basis of separation." Walls was not surprised to see fragmentation by formula flourish in America, for "the principle of separation is the converse of the principle of free association." Nor was he shocked that "the inevitable result" of this process was "the atomization of the church."[13] Rather, that result was only what one might expect, once the distinctives of Christianity in America were compared with what usually did not occur in other venues.

Yet in this important essay, Walls was not like many other critics who have decried the dismaying self-delusions of the American churches. Since it was always central in his understanding of World Christianity that all vigorous forms of Christianity needed to be incarnated in their own cultures, his question for the United States (as for all other regions) was not *if* a cultural form of the faith had developed, but *what kind of* cultural Christianity emerged. Walls, despite his criticisms, was a critic with genuine sympathy. As he has labored to explain at length in other places, the whole history of Christianity has been a series of successive adaptations of the faith to local situations. If this adaptation has occurred in America, of course it yields skewings, distortions, and disfigurements of the faith, but it also yields a genuine incarnation. "None of these marks, and none of their effects, is nearly as important as the universal Christianity, the Gospel of the risen Christ, to which historic American Christianity witnesses." In missiological terms, the only serious problem with American Christianity is forgetfulness. "There is nothing wrong with having local forms of Christianity — provided that we remember that they *are* local."[14]

Walls's conclusion — "American missions are thus both products and purveyors of American culture"[15] — was much more admiring than critical. But admiration came specifically from his perspective as a historian of Christian mission. Although he was much taken by the importance of American missionary work in the twentieth century, he was even more impressed by the conversion of Americans in the nineteenth century.

Walls did not provide extensive historical background for his assertion, following Latourette, that "in no part of the world did that century see

---

12. Ibid., 234.
13. Ibid.
14. Ibid., 235.
15. Ibid., 226.

such a striking outcome [resulting from missionary activity] as in North America."[16] But he was on solid ground. At the time of the formation of the United States, and the continuation of Canada in loyalty to Great Britain, the condition of Christianity in both countries resembled more the current European picture of recession than the current African picture of expansion. Not only were churches and denominations disrupted by the Revolutionary War, impoverished by economic dislocations, and suffering under the strains of uprooting (Canadian Loyalists), starting over again (United States patriots), or both (settlers moving westward into frontier regions in both Canada and the United States). Believers also found themselves in societies where, along with significant influence from the European Christian past, non- or at best quasi-Christian values were increasing their cultural power. The broader culture in post-Revolutionary North America — guided by leaders wed to non-Christian versions of the Enlightenment, imperiled by the barbarism of the frontier or (in Canada) the clash of ethnicities, and eagerly internalizing principles of all-out market capitalism — was moving speedily away from the traditional faith.

In this unpropitious setting, marvels occurred in both the United States and Canada. Evangelization and the expansion of recognizably Christian civilization advanced with extraordinary speed. Walls was especially taken with American success in exploiting the voluntary society (or parachurch agency) as a means of promoting mission at home and abroad. If Protestant voluntary societies resembled Catholic precedents in the history of monasticism more than either Protestants or Catholics recognized at the time; if they had begun with German Lutherans in the late-seventeenth century and High Church Anglicans in the early eighteenth century; and if they were used with telling effect by John Wesley and other British awakeners — still, they had come into their own in America.

Walls devoted most of one other essay in *The Missionary Movement in Christian History* to the importance of the mission-generated voluntary societies that flourished in Britain and, even more, in America.[17] He called them "one of God's theological jokes"[18] since they developed with almost no forethought, they received almost no attention from church leaders and

---

16. Ibid., 227.
17. Andrew F. Walls, "Missionary Societies and the Fortunate Subversion of the Church," in *The Missionary Movement in Christian History: Studies in the Transmission of Faith* (Maryknoll, N.Y.: Orbis Books, 1997), 241–54.
18. Ibid., 246.

theologians, and they worked their leaven for change almost before they were recognized. Yet immense consequences flowed from the organization of voluntary societies for missionary service: for example, the relativizing of denominational barriers by people who were actively cooperating to spread the Gospel, a door for service and leadership opened wide to the laity (especially women), and the development of new worlds of knowledge and spiritual partnership through the distribution of missionary periodicals.

Walls has had much more to say about the critical role of voluntary societies in recent Christian history. But for North America, a missiological perspective resulted in his generally positive assessment of the kind of Christianity that developed on this continent. In a word, without an American form of Christianity, warts and all, the world would have experienced far less revitalization from voluntary mission association.

Thus, in one short essay Walls expanded his missiological purview to take in North America. In so doing, he pointed the way to a richer understanding of Christian developments in America and also of American connections to the rest of the world.

Christianity in North America as a Missiological Narrative

Following the trajectory of that essay and drawing on several of Walls's other insights about mission history, it is possible to reconceive the history of Christianity in North America as a missiological narrative. In this picture, theological and ecclesiastical development in early American history represented an indigenization of forms inherited from Europe but adjusting to the new conditions of the new world.[19] Differences between Christian experience in the United States and parallel experience in Canada resulted from variations in the Christianities imported from Europe and variations in the environments where these faiths took root.[20] The relevance of American Christianity for the rest of the world includes not only acknowledging direct influence, but also recognizing that the pattern of Christian indigenization in North America anticipated the patterns that are now being witnessed in

---

19. See Mark A. Noll, *America's God: From Jonathan Edwards to Abraham Lincoln* (New York: Oxford University Press, 2002), especially 3–18; 53–113.

20. See Noll, *The Old Religion in a New World: The History of North American Christianity* (Grand Rapids: Eerdmans, 2002), chap. 10, "In the Shadow of the United States — Canada and Mexico"; and "What Happened to Christian Canada?" *Church History* 15 (2006): 245–73 (reprinted as a separate pamphlet, Vancouver: Regent College Press, 2007).

many other parts of the world.[21] An outline history — divided into seven segments — shows how fruitful it can be to think about the American history of Christianity along these lines.

1. The missionary settlement of America involved the cross-cultural transmission of several subvarieties of Christian faith: state-church Catholicism (Quebec), state-church Protestantism (Anglicans and Presbyterians), and a variety of dissenting Protestants (Baptists, Anabaptists, Moravians, eventually Methodists). Yet in no case did the transplanting lead to duplicates of what had existed in Europe.

2. The special circumstances of early American settlement worked their effects on all the faiths coming from the old world. These circumstances included denominational pluralism, huge expanses of lightly inhabited space, frontier conditions that put a premium on small-group initiative, and eventually the separation of church and state.

3. In these conditions, all expressions of Christian faith began to reflect new-world realities. In particular, American environments favored religion that was biblicistic (rather than traditional or historical), commonsensical and pragmatic (rather than self-consciously doctrinaire), entrepreneurial (rather than hierarchical), informally personal (rather than formally ecclesiastical), communal through self-selection (alongside communal through inheritance), and oriented toward the middle and lower-middle classes (rather than the highest and lowest classes). Over time, the awareness of change-through-indigenization would be lost, and Americans would come to regard these new-world adjustments as natural expressions of the faith.

4. Vigorous voluntary organization became especially important for Christian developments in the United States and quite important for parallel developments in Protestant Canada because the voluntary mind-set fit perfectly with American circumstances. In particular, it was a mind-set keyed to innovative leadership, proactive public advocacy, and entrepreneurial goal-setting.

Increasingly, American believers practiced the faith by forming their own churches and religious agencies, generating their own financial support, and taking responsibility themselves for guiding the faith. For the most part, voluntarism became the pattern for all churches in America — first for Europe's Dissenting traditions (Baptists) and the newer Christian movements of the

---

21. This argument, which is indebted to Andrew Walls throughout, is developed in Mark Noll, *The New Shape of World Christianity: How American Experience Reflects Global Faith* (Downers Grove, Ill.: InterVarsity Press, 2009).

modern period (Methodists, Disciples, independents of many varieties), but then also for the older European state-churches (Catholics, Episcopalians, Presbyterians, Lutherans, English Puritans). Although this pattern of self-starting, self-financing, and self-spreading Christianity was not entirely new, it came into its own when American believers used the powerful resources of a liberal democracy to establish and support their churches.

Voluntarism began with church organization, but then mushroomed to inspire local and national mobilization on behalf of myriad social and political causes. Local civilization would be built as local groups and individuals enlisted to address local needs. Not government, not an inherited church, not the dictates of Big Business, but enterprising connections forged voluntarily built American civilization in the decades before the Civil War.

As self-created vehicles for preaching the Christian message, distributing Christian literature, encouraging Christian civilization, and networking philanthropic activity, the voluntary societies were flourishing by the second decade of the nineteenth century. Many of the new societies were formed within denominations, and a few were organized outside evangelical boundaries, like the American Unitarian Association of 1825. But the most important were founded by interdenominational networks of evangelicals for evangelical purposes. The best-funded and most dynamic societies — like the American Board of Commissioners for Foreign Missions (1810), the American Bible Society (1816), or the American Education Society (1816) — were rivaled only by the Methodist church in their shaping effects on national culture.

5. Inherited forms of Christianity adjusted with varying degrees of enthusiasm to this new environment: wholeheartedly in the case of dissenting and African American Protestants, cautiously in the case of magisterial Protestant movements and Catholics in what became the United States, and least of all in the French-speaking enclave that the British empire and later Canada provided for Catholicism in Quebec.[22]

Historically, Eastern Orthodox, Catholic, and the major European Protestant denominations had differed substantially among themselves, but almost all assumed that Christianity required Christendom — which meant taking for granted formal cooperation between church and state as well as a prominent place for the churches in the formal legal life of a society. It also meant

---

22. On varieties of adjustment, see Mark Noll, " 'Christian America' and 'Christian Canada,' " in *The Cambridge History of Christianity,* vol. 8: *World Christianities, c. 1815–c. 1914,* ed. Sheridan Gilley and Brian Stanley (Cambridge: Cambridge University Press, 2006), 359–80.

that great weight was given to historical precedents — how things should be done depended as much on previous patterns as upon assessments of current opportunities. In short, Christendom meant that society was intended to function as an organic whole, with comprehensive public acknowledgment of God and comprehensive religious support for the nation.

The new American pattern did not abandon the Christendom ideal entirely, but it nonetheless developed a much more informal Christianity and pushed consistently for ever more flexible institutions and ever newer innovations in responding to spiritual and temporal challenges. A great deal of traditional European faith survived, especially among the Lutherans, Episcopalians, Roman Catholics, Eastern Orthodox, and some of the Calvinistic denominations that continued to value their European roots. But even in these groups, the voluntary principle worked with unprecedented effects. In other Christian traditions — among African Americans, for holiness and Pentecostal movements, in contemporary megachurches — it became completely dominant.

6. The marvel of the Christian world in the nineteenth century was the rapid Christianization that took place in the United States and Canada, which was driven by groups that adjusted most thoroughly to the circumstances of new-world civilization. Along with denominations organized by voluntary principles, revivalistic energy and voluntary agencies transformed the shape of American religion in the first half of the nineteenth century. A period of tumultuous, energetic, contentious innovation first reversed the downward slide of Protestantism and then began, as an almost inevitable process, to shape all of American society by the standards of voluntaristic evangelical religion. Most remarkably, evangelicals even conquered the South, where an honor-driven culture of manly self-assertion had presented a far less propitious field for labor than regions to the North where the Puritan leaven survived.

To the intimidating challenges posed by disestablishment and the vigorous competition of a rapidly expanding market economy, the combination of anti-formalist denominational mobilization, revival, and the voluntary society offered a compelling response. Observers at the time took note of the innovation. Rufus Anderson, an early organizer of the American missions movement, wrote in 1837 that "the Protestant form of association — free, open, responsible, embracing all classes, both sexes, all ages, the masses of the people — is peculiar to modern times, and almost to our age."[23]

---

23. Rufus Anderson, "The Time for the World's Conversion Come" (1837–38), reprinted in *To Advance the Gospel: Selections from the Writings of Rufus Anderson,* ed. R. Pierce Beaver (Grand Rapids: Eerdmans, 1967), 65.

As these adjustments of old-world Christianity to the voluntary democracy of the new world took place, the results were dramatic. From 1815 to 1914, the U.S. population grew very rapidly (from 8.4 million to 99.1 million). Yet over the same century Christian adherence grew even faster, from under one-fourth of the population to over two-fifths of the population, that is, from something around two million to something around forty million. This American expansion may have been the most rapid in the entire history of Christianity — until, that is, the even more rapid expansion on the continent of Africa over the last century and (perhaps) in China over the last half century. To notice where, and under what circumstances, these later expansions have taken place is to see the missiological connections between American and world experience.

The antebellum period's dynamic voluntary evangelicalism established an enduring template for the nation. Later religious movements would move well beyond the boundaries of evangelical Protestant belief and practice. But religions that have flourished in the United States have done so by adopting, to at least some degree, many of the free-form, populist, and voluntaristic traits that evangelical Protestants pioneered. Elsewhere in the world, Catholics until the Second Vatican Council looked for establishmentarian arrangements with local regimes. But not in the flourishing American Catholic Church. To this day, some Muslims elsewhere in the world demand the privileges of Sharia law for themselves and its imposition on those under their jurisdiction. But not, for the most part, in the flourishing U.S. Muslim communities. American religious groups have maintained all manner of traditional practices and beliefs in their own institutions and families. For the most part, however, almost all have accommodated themselves to the public practice that defined the nation's social forces in the early decades of the nineteenth century. In the lead for maintaining these practices have been the evangelical denominations and parachurch agencies for whom voluntary Christianity became simply second nature.

7. The expansion of voluntary, disestablished religious organization became important for the whole world when the United States and Canada became more important in the world. The shape that Christianity took in winning Canada and the United States defined the missionary message that North Americans took to other parts of the world when they became leaders in world missionary effort.

Yet the relevance of this American history goes well beyond the issue of direct missionary influence. It extends also to a broader understanding of recent world history. That is, the flourishing of lay-led, voluntaristic, and disestablished forms of Christianity in a North America that had mostly moved beyond Christendom helps explain why lay-led, voluntaristic, and disestablished forms of Christianity have recently flourished in other parts of the world that never knew Christendom. For world comparison, the most important reality has been the affinity between voluntaristic Christianity and the American setting, between conversionistic, voluntaristic forms of faith and fluid, rapidly changing, commerce-driven, insecure, and ethnically pluralistic social settings.

It has become a truism to note that Christianity in various forms is now advancing rapidly in parts of the world where the instincts of ancient Christendom are largely absent. Not coincidentally, such expansion often takes place where societies are marked by at least some characteristics similar to what developed in the nineteenth-century United States. These characteristics are especially obvious in the burgeoning cities of the global South and in the rural areas worldwide that are being reshaped by global economic forces. These newer societies tend to be competitive and not deferential, open to Christian witness but not officially Christian, allowing space for entrepreneurial activity while not restricting religious expression too drastically. To the extent these conditions have developed, it is not surprising that styles of Christianity that flourished in North America's competitive, market-oriented, rapidly changing, and initiative-rewarding environment would also flourish in other environments that look more like nineteenth-century America than fifteenth-century Europe.[24]

Examples multiply from around the world. Catholic charismatics flourish in the chaotic social systems of Nigeria and the somewhat more controlled social flux of Brazil. Protestant mega-churches blossom in South Korea alongside the fruits of aggressive entrepreneurial capitalism. Lay-led base communities and lay-led Bible study fellowships have expanded throughout Latin America, among both Catholics and Protestants, especially in regions where natural disasters, urbanization, or Protestant missionary efforts have undercut the once-hegemonic character of Latin Catholicism. Most remarkable has been the dramatic rise of a great variety of Christian movements in China, which has taken place *after* the expulsion of Western missionaries,

---

24. Especially useful for seeing these connections are the works of David Martin, Dana Robert, and Lamin Sanneh.

despite a full generation of intense persecution, and *alongside* the turn to commercial and industrial development.

In a word, forms of conversionistic and voluntaristic Christianity seem to be flourishing where something like nineteenth-century American social conditions have come to prevail — where, that is, the Christian message is active in situations marked by social fluidity, personal choice, the need for innovation, and a search for anchorage in the face of vanishing traditions. In such circumstances, it is still possible to observe much that is different from the United States, where wealth, local traditions, political connections, and forms of religious pluralism remain untypical. But viewed from a long historical perspective, similarities are just as striking as differences.

Conclusion

It would be possible to extend this historical sketch into an elaborate evaluations of American Christianity and much recent World Christianity. Many of the strengths and the weaknesses apparent in North American forms of lay-led, voluntaristic, and disestablished Christianity have also become apparent in new and rapidly expanding Christian populations elsewhere in the world. For example, in both North America and many of the new Christian regions of the world, one strength of strongly voluntaristic Christianity has been the ability to enlist, empower, and motivate lay believers. But this strength has a complementary weakness, as illustrated by the course of the American Civil War. In the clash between Northern Bible-believers and Southern Bible-believers, which fueled the war's intensity and extended its longevity, there was no authority able to deflect the antagonistic energy generated by the societies that had been so strongly shaped by the forces of Christian voluntarism. Whatever judgments need to be made about questions of quality, this chapter has perhaps shown enough to justify the conclusion that the missiological vision of Andrew Walls is as relevant for the American "home front" as it has proven to be for "the regions beyond."

13

Andrew F. Walls and
Documenting World Christianity
in the Twenty-First Century

MICHAEL POON

My aim is to explore Professor Andrew Walls's legacy in documenting World Christianity. Andrew Walls is not only a leading mission historian in the post-1945 world. His influence reaches well beyond his writings. Walls has devoted himself as well to a lifelong task in collecting present-day Christian source materials and in making them available for church and academic use. The fruits of his ministry are written in the hearts of his students from the late 1950s to the present (2 Cor. 3:3): at Freetown, Nsukka, Aberdeen, Edinburgh, Princeton, New Haven, Akropong-Akuapem, and beyond. Where Christians apply their hearts and minds to historical scholarship, there Andrew Walls *is*. He is a supreme network builder. Walls's lasting contribution lies in creating a community of missiologists and mission historians worldwide for advancing solid historical scholarship in post-Christendom times.

I shall begin with a sketch of Walls and his time, and then discuss Walls's contribution to documenting World Christianity. I shall end by engaging his underlying ecclesial and missional vision and set out the importance of Walls's contribution for the future of World Christianity.

Fundamental Shifts in the Study
of World Christianity

Walls's fifty years of global ministry from the late 1950s to the present span across deep shifts in the study of World Christianity.

The Community

First, social scientists, historians, and political analysts have replaced Western missionaries to be the main interpreters of global realities in the post-1945 years. This coincides with the close of an age of intense and confident Western missionary expansion in Asia and in Africa. Take the China mission for instance. Robert Morrison and Elijah Bridgman's *The Chinese Repository* (1832–51), Samuel Wells Williams's *The Middle Kingdom* (1848), and Henry Latourette's *The Chinese: Their History and Culture* (1934) once stood as standard references for interpretation of China. John Fairbank, Paul Cohen, Jonathan Spence, and others from the social sciences and history disciplines have now supplanted the roles of Western missionaries. They now interpret Christianity on a wider religious and cultural canvas — at least with few Christian interests in mind. The reasons for this shift are complex. Retreat of Western missionaries from the newly independent nation-states is one of the reasons. The growing secularization in the West — at least in Europe — is another. Governments would provide funding for research in critical areas around the world for national security purposes, and naturally enlist academics in social science disciplines for help. There is also a growing dissatisfaction with Western-centered approaches to interpreting global realities. Social science disciplines, so this argument runs, can give a more balanced understanding of the complex forces that are shaping the present-day world.

All of which means there is a marked shift in the variety of records that are collected. Clearly, documentation does not take place in the abstract. Records are gathered for specific purposes and audiences; such considerations govern the ways that they are classified. The minutes, reports, and correspondences of missionary archives inevitably reflected the institutional interest of parent organizations. Present-day social scientists and historians, however, approach Christianity with different sets of questions, and therefore with different suppositions and methodologies. Oral interviews, ephemeral material, personal papers, and "born-digital" material yield important information that official records and publications cannot give. They all add up to enable researchers to gain a better understanding of the complex interplays in real life.

The multiple ways that Christianity is studied raise important questions on how Christian records should be organized. Classification systems and word lists that had served well for missionary societies are no longer adequate for multidisciplinary settings. The forms and content of Christianity are also undergoing radical changes. It is no longer helpful to classify Christian activities along the previously standard categories: evangelism, medical services, education. It would also be misleading to analyze present-day Christianity in terms of Western denominational presences. It seems that Christian studies needs to rediscover its place in the wider disciplines of religious and social studies.

The shift from missionaries to academics poses another set of problems. Missionary societies and churches pay long-term and systematic attention to records; academics in today's grant-driven world work within much shorter time-frames. Their interests often end on completion of their research projects. Churches outside the West rarely have documentation programs in place. The end of Western missionary enterprise may well spell the end of the systematic documentation of World Christianity.

Geographical Focus

Missiological reflections in the post-1945 years have been mainly guided by African experiences. The Communist victory in China in 1949 was a watershed. China with its largest unitary people group and the oldest continuous history has been the main focus of missionary activities and studies. The forced departure of Western missionaries from China at the beginning of the Korean War brought an abrupt end to all that. Clearly, China still captures the popular imagination as the last frontier and crowning prize for missionary activity. But academic missiological reflections for the past five decades have shifted to sub-Saharan Africa, which has not experienced wide-scale and organized anti-Western movements to the same extent that China has undergone. So Africa enjoys a greater sense of continuity in mission scholarship. The most influential exponents of World Christianity today are all African specialists. To list: Max Warren and John V. Taylor; Adrian Hastings, Harold Turner and Andrew Walls; Kwame Bediako, Lamin Sanneh, and Jonathan Bonk — their mission outlooks are all shaped by African experiences.

This shift has much more than geopolitical significance. Western missionaries had largely devoted their intellectual energy to engage Confucian and Buddhist thought-forms in China. Matteo Ricci and James Legge's lifelong studies in Chinese classics are cases in point. The shift to Africa opened new intellectual horizons. The religious worlds of peoples outside the influences of axial religions and "high cultures" took center stage. The realities they revealed opened new questions on forms and content of the Christian faith, as well as on sources and methodologies in Christian theology.

The Reality

Above all, deep geopolitical and ecclesiastical changes are taking place since 1945. The world has developed in multiple ways. There are new forms of growth and new centers of authority and, with that, new forms of knowledge and of information. Globalization has realigned historical boundaries, makes them fluid, and opens new ways of social identity formation. The terms "post-colonial," "post-missionary," "post-denominational," "post-Christendom," and "post-modern" only underscore the vast transitions that are still unfolding in Christianity and in the wider world. Generally speaking, identities have become more localized. Martin Marty rightly pointed out that the ecumenical movement has lost most of its energy and vision by the close of the 1960s. By the close of the twentieth century centrifugal forces are breaking up traditional forms of Christianity; transnational and local forces are refiguring relationships in multiple ways.[1] All of which means the world today can no longer be understood by rote. The need for fresh source materials to piece together this emerging world becomes all the more important.

Christianity and Primal Religious Traditions

Andrew Walls's contribution to historical mission scholarship is set against these fundamental shifts. Frank Whaling's *Religion in Today's World: The Religious Situation of the World from 1945 to the Present Day*, published in 1987, featured two essays by Walls.[2] These two essays "The Christian Tradition in Today's World" and "Primal Religious Traditions in Today's World" provide a convenient point to assess his legacy.

The date was important. Walls moved from Aberdeen to Edinburgh that year; and with him, the Centre for the Study of Christianity in the Non-Western World (CSCNWW) he founded in Aberdeen in 1982. Clearly then, the two essays were Walls's summary statements in a time of personal transition.

---

1. Martin Marty, "The Global Context of Ecumenism 1968–2000," in *A History of the Ecumenical Movement*, vol. 3, 1968–2000, ed. J. H. Y. Briggs, M. A. Oduyoye, and G. Tsetses (Geneva: World Council of Churches, 2004), 3–26.

2. Andrew F. Walls, "The Christian Tradition in Today's World," in *Religion in Today's World: The Religious Situation of the World from 1945 to the Present Day*, ed. Frank Whaling (Edinburgh: T. & T. Clark, 1987), 74–107; "Primal Religious Traditions in Today's World," in *Religion in Today's World*, 250–78.

Walls began his essay "The Christian Tradition in Today's World" with an observation of the "fundamental shift" in Christianity since 1945.

Today over half the Christians in the world live in the southern continents of Africa, Asia, Latin American, and Oceania. The change has much more than demographic significance. Within a very short period of time the conditions which have produced the phenomena characteristic of Christianity for almost a millennium have largely disappeared....The conditions [in the southern continents] increasingly provide the context within which the Christian mind is being formed. The process is already beginning to produce changes in Christian priorities, and in the structure of Christian thought, practice and government.[3]

Walls went on to argue "the end of Christendom": "In the continuing Christian histories of Africa, Asia, and the Pacific, the missionary period is already an episode."[4] He proceeded with a survey of present-day Christianity in Africa, Latin America, Asia, and the Pacific, and summed it up with an optimistic note: "The diversification of Christianity [that he had just described] has not yet produced fragmentation." He underscored the new "conciliarism" in the post-1945 world: "This is the re-emergence of a process of consultation and consensus involving Christians of different areas."[5] He ended his essay, however, with a pointed observation on the Christianity outside the West that he did not develop in the essay:

The Christianity expressed in the southern continents has shown no special desire to abandon or even revise the creedal and confessional statements which have been the landmarks of Western Christian history. It is simply that *these statements have little direct to say about the matters that most concern the Christians of the new heartlands.* (emphasis added)[6]

What are the matters that most concern the Christians of the new heartlands? His other essay pointed the way. "Primal Religious Traditions" showed the fruits of his long-time partnership with Harold Turner. Turner

---

3. Walls, "The Christian Tradition in Today's World," 80.
4. Ibid., 85.
5. Ibid., 105.
6. Ibid., 108.

joined Walls in Aberdeen in the early 1970s, and went on to found the Centre for New Religious Movements at Selly Oak Colleges, Birmingham, in 1981. In the essay Walls discussed the content and structure in "primal religions" in conversation with his contemporaries Aylward Shorter, Geoffrey Parrinder and Harold Turner. "Primal Religious Tradition" was in fact a phrase that Walls and Turner finally settled with, after earlier experiments with the terms "living tribal religions" and "traditional religions."[7]

Walls began his treatment by underscoring that:

> Primal religions underlie all the other faiths, and often exist in symbiosis with them.... The influence of primal world views thus continues long after adhesion takes place to Christianity or Islam...; but this is not the same as saying that the "conversion" is superficial or negligible. The major symbolic change may be highly significant, and making a turning point in the religious development of a primal society. And thus, in one sense, in "primal" religion itself.[8]

He went on to explain in length why primal religions should not be treated as if they are static, timeless entities:

> Like all other faiths, the primal religions have always known adjustments and alterations, fossilizations and revivals, prophets and reformers, new directions and new institutions.[9]

The second half of Walls's essay consisted of a penetrating exposition on the situation of primal religions in the post-1945 years. The rise of new nation-states and economic developments posed "threats to primal religions." They created "disturbance of values," "disturbance of hierarchy" and "disturbance of focus and perceptions":

> None of these forms of disturbance is new in itself: the basis of life, and thus of perception, of primal peoples has constantly changed through war, conquest, migration, intermarriage, adaptation from neighbors, epidemic, environmental change. What is new is the extent, intensity and universality of the forces of change.[10]

---

7. Edward Geoffrey Parrinder, *African Traditional Religion* (London: Hutchinson's University Library, 1954); Harold W. Turner, *Living Tribal Religions* (London: Ward Lock Educational, 1971).

8. Walls, "Primal Religious Traditions in Today's World," 250–51.

9. Ibid., 253.

10. Ibid., 266–67.

He then identified eight forms of responses to these forces of change:[11]

1. *Recession:* Large numbers of primal peoples have moved toward Christianity or Islam since 1945.

2. *Absorption:* The configuration of primal religions is absorbed into Christian and Islamic communities.

3. *Restatement.* Contact with the world faiths forces primal religious believers to take on some of the language of the outside faith.

4. *Reduction.* A primal religion can become reduced or confined in its scope, either by the removal of major institutions or, conversely, by the institutions being cut from the complex of tradition affecting the whole of life. Reduction is a mark of secularization.

5. *Invention.* From within the primal religions sometimes come bursts of new creative activity that transpose them into new settings, freely absorbing and adopting elements from other cultures, reinventing themselves as "universal" religion and alternatives to Christianity or Islam.

6. *Adjustment.* Attempts to adjust and expand world views to take account of new phenomena continue to be a feature of primal religions.

7. *Revitalization.* Non-Western peoples sometimes would revitalize primal religions in order to assert their cultural identity against encroachment of Western standards.

8. *Appropriation.* Primal religions are being adopted or recommended by those who historically belong to another tradition.

Is there any schema for interpreting the religious situations today? Walls did not offer a ready solution. He suggested, however, that any such model should both allow for the "permanent interconnexion of cultures in this century, and for some fluidity between the categories." It needs to recognize the principal change in primal religions since 1945: "The search for a universal, not a purely local or ethnic field of reference, a new focus suited to a village all now know to be global."[12]

The 1987 expositions of present-day Christianity and of primal religions in the same volume arguably gave a succinct summary of Walls's work and vision shortly before his move to Edinburgh. His 1987 expositions at the

---

11. Ibid., 267–77.
12. Ibid., 278.

same time pointed to further tasks. He did not at that time carry through his own penetrating assessments of the post-1945 religious situations (in his essay on primal religions) to his analysis on present-day Christianity. Clearly, the analyses on the disturbances on primal religions and the eight types of responses have important ramifications for the structure and content of Christianity as well. The southward movements of Christian demography do not only have implications for mission practice. But as Walls underscored, the conditions of Christianity in the southern continents "produce changes in Christian priorities, and in the structure of Christian thought, practice and government." The southern continents have in fact become the arena of lively engagements between Christianity and primal religions. This means that they form the material basis for the realization of a truly "World Christianity," which so far has centered on the Roman-Orthodox axis. The shifts to the "Third" World hold the promise of a "third" partner in theological engagement and development.

Walls ended both essays on a high note. Amid the huge changes that are taking place in World Christianity and in the wider religious worlds, Walls was confident that peoples of different areas would become more connected to one another in the same global village. The prospects of civilization clashes and of intense ideological wars between rival carriers of similar religious traditions, all of which would increasingly dominate religious landscapes in the 1990s, had not yet surfaced.

The character of World Christianity in post-Christendom times would become a main theme in Walls's writings since 1987.[13] To him, the end of Christendom holds historic significance; it opens the prospect for genuine international partnership. He looks forward to a renaissance in mission studies:

> It must be international, because the gifts of the church belong to the whole church. And as students of mission worldwide our histories are interdependent, our materials and our methods cross-cultural. We are all — Northern continents and Southern, American and European — dependent on one another.[14]

---

13. Andrew F. Walls, *The Missionary Movement in Christian History: Studies in the Transmission of Faith* (Maryknoll, N.Y.: Orbis Books, 1996); *The Cross-Cultural Process in Christian History: Studies in the Transmission and Appropriation of Faith* (Maryknoll, N.Y.: Orbis Books, 2002).

14. Andrew F. Walls, "Structural Problems in Mission Studies," *International Bulletin of Missionary Research* 15, no. 4 (1991): 154.

He elaborated this insight in his famous lecture "The Ephesian Moment." For him, Christians across the divides need to grasp the Ephesian moment and calling:

> We need each other's vision to correct, enlarge, and focus our own; only together are we complete in Christ.... The Ephesian moment, then, brings a church more culturally diverse than it has ever been before; potentially, therefore, nearer to that "full stature of Christ" that belongs to his summing up of humanity.... The Ephesian question at the Ephesian moment is whether or not the church in all its diversity will demonstrate its unity by the interactive participation of all its culture-specific segments, the interactive participation that is to be expected in a functioning body.[15]

Sadly, Walls's observations on World Christianity have not attracted much attention from church leaders and Christian theologians. Mission practitioners, especially those involved in world evangelization projects, greeted his comments on demographic shifts with much interest. Statistical tabulations of people and groups became a central research activity. That is, source materials of present-day Christianity are now mainly expressed in numerical data sets, and with this a narrowing of realities. The *World Christian Encyclopedia* and the recently published *Atlas of Global Christianity* fulfill such needs.[16] Strikingly, such literature adopts traditional categories, without explanation, in interpreting present-day religious worlds. Little attention is paid to the huge changes in the structure and content in religions that Walls underlined.

Building to Last

Walls's vision for World Christianity underpinned his infrastructural undertakings. He recognized that long-term institutional commitment, coordination, and collaboration are crucial to building solid scholarship. In other words, he was clear that he needed to create an international community of

---

15. Walls, *The Cross-Cultural Process in Christian History*, 79, 81.

16. David B. Barrett, *World Christian Encyclopedia: A Comparative Study of Churches and Religions in the Modern World, AD 1900–2000* (New York: Oxford University Press, 1982); David B. Barrett, George Thomas Kurian, and Todd M. Johnson, *World Christian Encyclopedia: A Comparative Survey of Churches and Religions in the Modern World*, 2nd ed., 2 vols. (Oxford: Oxford University Press, 2001); Todd M. Johnson and Kenneth R. Ross, *Atlas of Global Christianity 1910–2010* (Edinburgh: Edinburgh University Press, 2009).

missiologists, mission historians, and practitioners from different parts of the world. And clearly as well, source documents are indispensable for the study of present-day Christianity in its multiple settings. So new *repositories* and libraries need to be established, and new *instruments* need to be developed, to gather the hard evidence of Christianity around the world. And if World Christianity is central to the theological formation of future pastors, the discipline must then become an integral part of mainstream ministerial formation programs.

Walls embarked on three infrastructural projects. To list:

1. Walls set up the Standing Committee on Bibliography, Documentation and Archives at the 1978 International Association for Mission Studies (IAMS) Meeting, Maryknoll, New York. Arthur Glasser recalled: "One unresolved matter of business [in the 1978 IAMS Meeting] was the need to set up a *Standing Committee on Bibliography, Documentation and Archives*. This was hastily accomplished in the closing minutes of that memorable gathering."[17] It was a bold move that he carried out with his characteristic flair. He remembered it in these words: "There was a desire to secure the place of historical scholarship in mission studies, and a fear that without some 'hard' scholarly activity on its agenda, the Association [founded in 1972] might drift into becoming just another succession of ecumenical conferences." Walls included "documentation" of gray literature alongside the more established interests in archives and bibliography. That is, he underscored the importance of relevant material (like "mission magazines, street posters or hymn sheets from Africa or Asia") that are not held traditionally in archives, or that are not confined to the activities of narrow constituencies.[18] IAMS leadership then in fact did not realize the significance of their decision. Glasser did not refer to it in his editorial to the special issue of *Missiology* dedicated to the 1978 proceedings. Strikingly, Johannes Aagaard, IAMS president, did not even mention it in his Letter in the same issue of the journal.[19] Perhaps it was not clear to Walls as well. The ordering of Bibliography, Documentation and Archives underwent several changes in those early years until it settled with the name Documentation, Archives and Bibliography (DAB)

---

17. Arthur F. Glasser, "Archival Alert — Rome 1980," *Missiology* 8, no. 4 (1980): 389–90.
18. Andrew F. Walls, e-mail message to author, March 19, 2010.
19. Johannes Aagaard, "Letter from the President of IAMS," *Missiology* 7, no. 1 (1979): 4; Arthur F. Glasser, "The Report of a Happening!," *Missiology* 7, no. 1 (1979): 2–3.

Network in the late 1980s — it certainly cannot be in reverse order (BAD!), Walls recalled.

2. Walls founded the Centre for the Study of Christianity in the Non-Western World in Aberdeen in 1982. It moved with Walls to Edinburgh. The Andrew F. Walls Centre for the Study of African and Asian Christianity, founded in Liverpool Hope University in 2008, to a great extent continues Walls's vision to develop repositories for present-day Christianity.

3. Walls founded the M. Litt. program in Religion in Primal Societies in Aberdeen, and later the undergraduate Primal Religions studies in Edinburgh. His two essays "Eusebius Tries Again: Reconceiving the Study of Christian History" and "Structural Problems in Mission Studies" to some extent were reflections on the successes and setbacks in realizing his vision amid present-day realties.[20]

A Discussion of These Three Institutional Undertakings

Creating an International Community for Documenting World Christianity

The Standing Commission on Documentation, Bibliography and Archives held its first meeting at the Urban University in Rome from July 24 to 30, 1980, under the title "Mission Studies and Information Management."[21] It took place at the beginning of a global communication and information revolution. Andrew Walls and Willi Henkel (head librarian of the Urban University and secretary of the standing committee) explained in the preface to the report:

> [It] sought to consider the implications for mission studies world wide of the communications revolution, ... and to do so in the recognition that tools for mission studies are still by no means well-developed and that access to higher technology is very unequally distributed.[22]

---

20. Walls, "Structural Problems in Mission Studies," 146–55; Andrew F. Walls, "Eusebius Tries Again: Reconceiving the Study of Christian History," *International Bulletin of Missionary Research* 24, no. 3 (2000): 105–11.

21. The report of this important meeting, ironically, was intentionally not published in print. An electronic copy is available at the Centre for the Study of Christianity in Asia Web site, *www.ttc.edu.sg/csca/arch-pres/dab1980.pdf.*

22. Andrew F. Walls and Willi Henkel, "Preface," in *Mission Studies and Information Management: Report of a Working Party Organized by the Committee on Documentation,*

Looking back, the 1980 meeting set the directions that would be remain remarkably consistent throughout the next three decades. Walls highlighted three key concerns in his closing address:[23]

1. *Accessibility.* A liberal policy of access for bona fide users is needed. The fundamental problem is less established policy than lack of resources. But for Walls,

   > There is another dimension to the accessibility question... of the possibility of creating a colonialism of information potentially more oppressive than either political or economic colonialism. ...We saw how the development of technology permits those who have it to amass, hold, release and manipulate information; shutting out those who do not have that technology from information which vitally affects them,... or forcing them to a choice between accepting a controlled flow... or to the immense waste of that most precious of human resources, time.

2. *Compatibility.* The theme of the conference underscored the participants' enthusiasm for technological advances. Microfilms offered great prospects for document preservation and access. Walls predicted: "The day is fast approaching when the microfiche reader will be a standard piece of equipment for libraries and indeed for the individual scholar." Issues on standards, media, and formats therefore receive much attention. He cautioned at the same time:

   > We have to find ways of using the new technology, and using it in noncolonial ways; to find appropriate technologies, technologies which do not leave the Third World out of the reckoning or in perpetual dependence.

3. *Responsibility.* Above all, Walls was most concerned about accountability in the postcolonial world. He pleaded:

   + We have a responsibility to the *whole Christian church*, for it needs information for the proper fulfillment of its mission on earth.

Bibliography and Archives of the International Association for Mission Studies, ed. Andrew F. Walls and Willi Henkel (Urban University, Rome: IAMS, 1980), i.

23. Andrew F. Walls, "Mission Studies and Information Management: The End of the Beginning," in *Mission Studies and Information Management: Report of a Working Party Organized by the Committee on Documentation, Bibliography and Archives of the International Association for Mission Studies,* ed. Andrew F. Walls and Willi Henkel (Urban University, Rome: IAMS, 1980), 137–39.

◆ We have a responsibility to the *churches and people of Africa, of Asia, Latin America, and the Pacific:* for it is their history, their documents, the expression of their faith and life over which we in differing degrees hold power.

◆ We have a responsibility to the *mission agencies* of the West.

◆ We have a responsibility to our colleagues in scholarship in other disciplines.

◆ And we have a responsibility to *each other.*

To be sure, the Committee on Bibliography, Documentation and Archives that Walls founded underwent several changes in leadership and in emphasis. Near the end of 1980s, it became the Documentation, Archives and Bibliography (DAB) Network. It took the name Project for Archives, Documentation and Oral History (PADOH) in the early 2000s. From 2005 it became the Documentation, Archives, Bibliography, and Oral History Study Group (DABOH). But Rome 1980 set the course for future directions. The successive meetings at Paris (1987), Rome (1988) and Basel (1990) followed up the work that Rome 1980 began. DAB was at the center of worldwide coordination in documentation under Norman Thomas and Paul Jenkins. DAB discussions centered on publishing missiological bibliography, building up missiological databases, as well as producing an agreed computer format (hardware and software) and common thesaurus of descriptors for computer searches and indexing.[24] The Mundus Gateway to Missionary Collections in the United Kingdom and Norman Thomas's *International Mission Bibliography, 1960–2000* typified the fruits of that period.[25] Rome 1980 had hoped to produce in microform an International Association of Missionary Archives.[26] The on-line Mundus Gateway was in fact part of that wider project. In Rome in 2002, PADOH held a conference titled "Rescuing the

24. Paul Jenkins and Willi Henkel, "DAB Workshop in Paris, 5th–9th January, 1987," *Mission Studies* 3, no. 3 (1986): 100–36; Joseph Lévesque, Norman E. Thomas, and Paul Jenkins, "Reports on IAMS Projects and Activities: Documentation, Archives and Bibliography Network (DAB)," *Mission Studies* 5, no. 2 (1988): 137–45; Norman E. Thomas, "Documentation, Archives and Bibliography (DAB) Progress Report," *Mission Studies* 7, no. 2 (1990): 237–43.

25. Mundus: Gateway to Missionary Collections in the United Kingdom. *www.mundus .ac.uk/*; Norman E. Thomas, *International Mission Bibliography, 1960–2000,* ATLA Bibliography Series; no. 48 (Lanham, Md.: Scarecrow Press, 2003).

26. Stephen Peterson and Paul Jenkins, "Future Steps in Church and Mission Archives," in *Mission Studies and Information Management: Report of a Working Party Organized by the Committee on Documentation, Bibliography and Archives of the International Association for Mission Studies,* ed. Andrew F. Walls and Willi Henkel (Urban University, Rome: IAMS, 1980), 132–33.

Memory of our Peoples." This led to the on-line publication of Martha Smalley and Rosemary Seton's *Archives Manual* into English, Chinese, French, Portuguese, Spanish, Korean, and Swahili.[27] The DABOH Balaton 2008 Conference, "Mission and Memory: Documenting World Christianity in the Twenty-First Century," in fact revisited similar issues that Rome 1980 had identified nearly thirty years before.[28]

Over the years, DABOH had invested much energy in technical issues. To some extent, rapid advances in information technology have made many of the earlier decisions on computer hardware and software formats obsolete. It would be misleading, however, to think that documenting World Christianity has become a technical enterprise. Walls's three-point summary in Rome 1980 rested on a deep concern to underpin international partnership with Christian foundations and commitments. An undisciplined use of information and communication technology could become tools of exclusion that further alienate the Third World from genuine partnership in mission studies. Equally funding practices, with the best aims, could perpetuate a culture of dependence, to the end that local programs stop when grants dry up.

Building Structures for Documenting World Christianity

Walls's tribute to his friend and colleague Harold Turner in fact reflects his own journeys in documenting Christianity. The title of his essay is telling: "Building to Last: Harold Turner and the Study of Religion."[29] It underlined the challenges in documentation. Building up source documents is a systematic and collaborative undertaking. The scale of the work makes it a daunting prospect for individual scholars and entrepreneurial enthusiasts. The task becomes even more difficult because "World Christianity" is not yet recognized as a mainstream academic discipline in Western scholarship. To some, it is a clerical undertaking for librarians and archivists — and not for academics. Furthermore, preserving historical documents is often not a priority for churches on the southern continents. Documenting World Christianity, then, is a ground-breaking enterprise. The challenge is "building *to last.*"

---

27. DABOH, "DABOH Study Group: Milestones," International Association for Mission Studies. *http://missionstudies.org/index.php/study-groups/daboh/daboh-milestones/.*

28. DABOH, "Mission and Memory: Documenting World Christianity in the Twenty-First Century," International Association for Mission Studies. *http://missionstudies.org/archive/4groups/DABOH/balaton2008/dabohbalaton2008.htm.*

29. Andrew F. Walls, "Building to Last: Harold Turner and the Study of Religion," in *Exploring New Religious Movements: Essays in Honor of Harold W. Turner,* ed. Andrew F. Walls and Wilbert R. Shenk (Elkhart, Ind.: Mission Focus, 1990), 1–17.

Walls began his tribute by recalling Turner's first engagements with African Christianity. Turner had to adopt new modes of investigation to understand these "newer forms" of "independent" movements. It became clear to him that these churches were "of different types but had in common that they were African independent churches, over against the older churches of Christendom."[30] Historical trajectories and Western missionary models were then inadequate to explain these new realities. So Turner devoted himself to detailed work in clarifying and fixing terminology, as well as in charting the forms and flux of multilayered interactions between mission-organized Christianity and African traditional society. Turner eventually defined the field of "new religious movements," surveyed it worldwide, identified the materials, and established the area as having a distinctive place in the study of religion.[31]

For Walls, a conventional scholar would have been satisfied with academic publications and speaking tours. Harold Turner's brilliance lay in building infrastructures for continuing research in the new field of studies. The Centre for New Religious Movements at Selly Oak Colleges, Birmingham, eventually became the repository for the body of material that Turner collected "in every continent, in a multitude of languages, and in every conceivable genre." More than that, he made his whole collection accessible for researchers worldwide, rather than keeping it for his own current research.

> In the first instance it was to be available in a center specifically dedicated to the study of the movements. But he also wished to it to be available throughout the world, available above all to those in Africa, and Asia and Latin America and Oceania whose religious history the materials reflect.... [He made] the corpus available in modest microfiche form and [distributed] it worldwide.... The most invidious colonialism of our day is the colonialism of information, the establishment by large Western agencies of proprietary rights over it, the

---

30. Ibid., 8.
31. Harold W. Turner, "New Religious Movements in Primal Societies," in *Australian Essays in World Religions,* ed. Victor C. Hayes (Bedford Park: Australian Association for the Study of Religions, 1977), 38–48; "The Primal Religions of the World and Their Study," in *Australian Essays in World Religions,* 27–37; "The Way Forward in the Religious Study of African Primal Religions," *Journal of Religion in Africa* 12, no. 1 (1981): 1–15; Harold W. Turner, "New Religious Movements in Primal Societies," in *The New Penguin Handbook of Living Religions,* ed. John R. Hinnells (London: Penguin, 1998), 581–93.

fencing of it round with logistical or financial barriers. In this matter
Harold Turner has always been a pugnacious anti-colonialist.[32]

Walls's portrayal of Turner also testified to his own ideals and perhaps
to the difficulties he faced in translating visions to realities. For Walls and
Turner, the study of present-day Christianity must rest on solid historical
research. Therefore, systematic collection of source materials is indispensable to building up this field of studies. This demands lifelong sacrificial
commitment and institutional support that perhaps few are willing to
undertake.

Establishing World Christianity as an Academic Discipline

James Cox took over the study program that Walls started in Edinburgh.
He transformed it into "a full-blown study of what the School of Divinity accepted as 'Indigenous Religions,' which students could take singly as
part of their overall Honours program or study alongside other religious
traditions." To Cox, the term "primal religions" is loaded with Christian assumptions. Changes were then necessary "to avoid theologizing the
subject."[33]

To be sure, the changes in Edinburgh represented a broad shift away from
Christian foundations in religious studies programs in Western academic
institutions. But why was Walls keen to go against the current? Unlike Cox,
Walls did not think that Christian suppositions would undermine academic
integrity. He has in mind that the study of present-day Christianity would
lead to a renaissance — both in Christian theology proper and the wider
intellectual world. That is, the study of present-day World Christianity is a
mission.

Walls developed this argument on two fronts. First, for Walls, mission
studies demands theological integration. Walls argued that the mainstream
theological fraternity has not yet grasped the historic changes that are taking
place. For him, the southward shifts in Christianity are of the same extent
as the Copernican Revolution and the European discovery of America. The
theological discipline needs to be overhauled:

> New discoveries were intellectually threatening, requiring the aban-
> donment of too many certainties, the acquisition of too many new

---

32. Walls, "Building to Last: Harold Turner and the Study of Religion," 13–14.
33. James L. Cox, *From Primitive to Indigenous: The Academic Study of Indigenous Religions*, Vitality of Indigenous Religions (Aldershot: Ashgate, 2007), 27, 29.

ideas and skills, the modification of too many maxims, the sudden irrelevance of too many accepted authorities. It was easier to ignore them and carry on with the old intellectual maps.... The shape of the church as it is today [needs to be inserted] onto intellectual and theological maps that were drawn according to the canons of what it used to be.[34]

The study of independent Christian movements in the southern continents is especially important. Turner explained:

It is a commonplace in the West to acknowledge that both the fact and the theology of the Holy Spirit have been neglected through many centuries.... Theology as a science depends upon access to its appropriate data in their most authentic and vital forms.... Here at the growing edges of Christianity in its most dynamic forms, the theologian is encouraged to do scientific theology again, because he has a whole living range of contemporary data on which to work. It is not that these dynamic areas of the Christian world are free from imperfection; but being full of old and new heresies they need theology to offer it an important task.[35]

Second, Walls argued that mission studies are important not only for "the church throughout the *oecumene.*" "The whole world of scholarship, sacred and profane" needs such scholarship. Walls noted that Western missionary movements had played an indispensable role in advances in modern scholarship. The present secularization of knowledge, therefore, represents a rejection of Christian heritage. Walls noted:

[The nineteenth century] saw scholarship immensely enriched by the missionary movement.... The legacy passed to the learned world in various ways; it helped to create new sciences (linguistics), helped to shape or was absorbed into new ways of organizing knowledge (anthropology), contributed to new clusters of subjects that brought the non-Western world within the parameters of Western learning (Oriental and African studies). But the other great modern religious

---

34. Walls, "Structural Problems in Mission Studies," 149–50.
35. Harold W. Turner, "The Contribution of Studies on Religion in Africa to Western Religious Studies," in *New Testament Christianity for Africa and the World: Essays in Honour of Harry Sawyerr,* ed. Harry Sawyerr, Mark E. Glasswell, and Edward W. Fasholé-Luke (London: SPCK, 1974), 177–78.

development — the recession from the Christian faith in Western lands and the consequent marginalization of theology — has intervened. The secularization of thought has submerged the missionary connection of learning with the missionary movement.[36]

Mission studies today, then, must be pursued with rigor and depth.[37] Walls insisted that the world of learning needs Christian scholarship; and so Christianity cannot retreat into a ghetto despite the growing secularizing tendencies in the post-Christendom world. For him, Lightfoot and Westcott provided an exemplary model for present-day Christian scholarship:

> To abandon the labour of integrating old and new learning would have been simply destructive. The nineteenth century saw plenty of wild theorizing, plenty of unbalanced sloganizing. But the agents of revitalization, the abiding influences for good, were those with depth of scholarship, who sought its integrity with the ongoing faith and life of the church.... Mission studies must interact with ongoing work in the history, languages, political, economic and social organization, cultures, and literature of the Southern continents (not to mention many aspects of the Northern). It is necessary therefore to realize that the world of learning is a mission field too. Quality, depth, and range of scholarship are the marks of a vocation — and a collegial and demanding vocation, needing all the traditional missionary attributes of devotion, perseverance, and sacrifice.[38]

Inheriting the Tasks

How then should we inherit Walls's tasks? Despite the southward shift in Christian demography, the end of the Western colonial and mission-ary period has not in fact brought about a new spring of theological developments worldwide. The opposite is the case. Mission studies and interpretation of World Christianity are firmly rooted in the West. Amer-ican professional bodies — for example, the American Society of Missiology (ASM) — continue to set the directions and standards of mission scholarship. The Yale-Edinburgh Group on the History of the Missionary Movement and Non-Western Christianity — which Walls and Lamin Sanneh started

---

36. Walls, "Structural Problems in Mission Studies," 150.
37. Ibid.
38. Ibid.

in 1992 — is perhaps the most credible forum for mission historians, with annual meetings alternately in Edinburgh and New Haven. Those who live outside the West, though they are on the list of the informal study group, are often excluded from such fraternity for practical reasons.

Western academic institutions too have mature infrastructures in place; so they can offer far more conducive settings for focused academic work. So the West continues to attract able scholars worldwide. The unstable socio-economic and ecclesiastical situations in the southern continents also contribute to this relentless brain drain to the West. And so mission scholarship is still mainly built on cross-Atlantic conversations. To be sure, such "international community" embraces the present-day ethnic and linguistic mix in Western societies. However, the worldwide collaboration that Walls hopes for is still a distant dream. The participant composition of the 1980 Rome Conference in fact underlined this. The fifty-six participants came mainly from Europe (thirty-six) and North America (thirteen). Two of the three African participants were from South Africa. Only four came from Asia, Latin America, and Oceania.[39]

More sobering still, real programs to survey, identify, collect, preserve, and make accessible present-day records are rare. The reasons are complex. Present-day Christianity is still a controlled field of studies in many geopolitical settings. China is case in point. Mainland Chinese scholars still approach Christianity as part of Western civilization. However, the relevant questions — where Christianity in China is today, what forms it takes, and how it came to be so — are still not open to public inquiry within China.

Churches too might also put their resources into more practical tasks. While many see mission outreach to be a top priority; few would put resources in academic studies in mission and history. To build up source materials to enable "hard" historical scholarship is even a more remote consideration. Academics would rather devote their time to publication than to what is often seen as "library work" that has little to advance their own credentials in a competitive academic world.

Indeed, the West also faces its own set of challenges. Few institutions are willing to support long-term studies on present-day World Christianity. Those that have source materials programs are even rarer. The successive

---

39. "Registered Participants," *Mission Studies and Information Management: Report of a Working Party Organized by the Committee on Documentation, Bibliography and Archives of the International Association for Mission Studies,* ed. Andrew F. Walls and Willi Henkel (Urban University, Rome: IAMS, 1980), 143–48.

relocation of the archives at the Centre for the Study of Christianity in the non-Western World is a case in point. The Christianity in Asia Project and the M.Phil. in World Christianity program at Cambridge University came to an end with recent faculty movements. It is clear the study of World Christianity is still at infant stages. Developing a body of source materials is important to establishing the discipline; but so far this has not gained real grounds.

How then to inherit Walls's vision? Roman Catholics might well suggest the way forward. In the 1988 IAMS Conference at Rome, Heinz Hunke (executive director of the International Documentation on the Contemporary Church [IDOC]) spoke on "Documentation for a New Millennium of Mission" in his opening address to the DAB Network. Strikingly different from the task-oriented DAB approaches then, he set out an ecclesiological understanding of documentation.[40] His paper in fact can be regarded as a Roman Catholic theological response to the Rome 1980 recommendations.

Hunke insisted from the outset that documentation is not a neutral and noncommittal undertaking. It is a communication process: "Information in order to be meaningful must be relevant, that means situational, it must be coherent, that means contextual, it must be operational, that means purposeful."[41] Documentation is integral to the Gospel; for the incarnation (and communication) of the Word stands at the heart of the Gospel. He explained:

The word "document" has its roots in the Greek *deignumi:* to signify. A document, in this etymological sense, is an instrument to lay bare significant processes for the Word-to-become-Flesh: the local emergences of incarnation. Documentation for mission must give access to the contents in which modernity becomes transparent for the Word, the Word of the Cross and the assurance of Humankind's Resurrection.[42]

That is, documentation is a deeply Christian undertaking. Thus documentation stands in sharp contrast with information-technological processes. For him, telecommunication in today's world privileged "image" and the "spectacular" over the "Word." It delocalized information, making information irrelevant, incoherent, and impotent. Information was then turned

---

40. Heinz Hunke, "Documentation for a New Millennium of Mission," *Mission Studies* 6, no. 1 (1989): 73–86.
41. Ibid., 75.
42. Ibid., 77.

into a noncommittal flow of infotainment. In other words, information technology can strip words of their truth-revealing quality.

Set against the information technology culture stands the church — the "contextual result of the history of the Word." The reception of faith does not take place in the abstract. Communication of the Word consists of a "dialogue between a Christian community and its local environment."[43] The "local," then, is of primary importance in Christian documentation:

> Documentation for mission . . . would concentrate on contexts of mission in action, i.e., on the local processes, experiences, efforts, movements of Christians, the new patterns in which it becomes evident (documented!).[44]

So documentation carries a deep apologetic edge in the technological age. Hunke insisted:

> Documentation is thus cultivation of the context, the multidimensional and multifaceted reality behind information, cultivation of the dialogical structure of human reality and information. It calls for critical assessment, selection, choice, and commitment. Without this cultivation of the context, illiteracy will grow enormously, and to get informed will simply mean to conform to somebody else's whim and fancies when they produce their piece of "infotainment."[45]

Documentation enables the Christian community to interpret its settings with purpose and hope. Hunke underlined the connection-making power of documentation in these words:

> The Church of the 3rd millennium will have a tremendous need to assimilate the input of life experiences and patterns of even the smallest local communities in the global diaspora . . . and aggregate them to the life substance of the Una Oecumenica catholica. Thus documentation entails a strong commitment for communion, in order to strengthen witness and service, always in regard to the local contexts.[46]

---

43. Ibid., 75, 78.
44. Ibid., 79.
45. Ibid., 76.
46. Ibid., 80.

With this powerful incarnational understanding of documentation, Hunke approached the question of access and control that Walls alerted in the 1980 Rome Meeting:

> Documentation for mission (= communion, witness, commitment) is very different from the "normal" build-up of databases which pretend to provide neutral, noncommittal information and data on a commercial basis in the modern decontextualization of "transnational" corporations.[47]

The Roman Catholics in the 1990s produced three directives on documentation that have important bearings on pastoral formation.[48] In contrast, Protestants in the main devoted their energy in more technical aspects in documentation and have not thought through the theology of documentation to the same extent the Roman Catholics have done.

To connect documentation with the central Christian drama of the incarnation of the Word offers an imaginative way forward. It exposes at the same time the theological (and ecclesial) deficit in Protestant documentation enterprises. Roman Catholics helpfully reconnect documentation with the central principles of the Christian faith, and in doing so give it a sharp apologetic edge. Documentation becomes a distinctively *Christian* undertaking in a technological world.

Protestants could ill afford to ignore documentation. The traditional suspicion of centralized and institutional authorities — in Roman Catholic forms — has often veered Protestants toward individualism. Protestants see churches in congregational and voluntarist terms. Catholicity is then more an object of hope than something that can be concretized in institutional forms in time and in space. So the formal confession in "the one holy catholic church" finds little expression in real life, for fear that such a worldwide church would become a centralized and overbearing structure that would impede the freedom of local communities. Christians then are in danger of becoming parochial in what they see and in how they interpret, with disastrous results in the present-day world that requires fresh and sensitive reading.

---

47. Ibid., 81.
48. *The Circular Letter regarding the Cultural and Pastoral Training of Future Priests in Their Upcoming Responsibilities concerning the Artistic and Historic Heritage of the Church* (October 15, 1992); *The Ecclesiastical Libraries in the Mission of the Church* (March 19, 1994); and *The Pastoral Function of Church Archives* (February 2, 1997).

This problem shows up in theological education. Fresh seminarians in Protestant theological colleges often begin their theological formation with little understanding of the great traditions of their forebears. More strikingly they are unaware of the theological and spiritual traditions of their own churches. Source document studies — so much part of the staple diet in classical traditions — has almost disappeared in theological formation. Curricula may expose students to the history and theologies of Western Christianity; but students are often ill-informed of the Christian pilgrimage of their own localities. Still less have they been equipped with interpretative lenses to understand the forms of present-day Christianity in the new heartlands of Christianity in today's world. Again Western seminaries face similar problems, though perhaps in different forms. To some, the end of Western missionary expansion in fact may mean the end of "Western experience and interest" in the wider world. Therefore, within the Christian church, studies in World Christianity have become a largely irrelevant subject. A casual stroll through the Special Collections divisions in Yale Divinity School Library and the School of Oriental and African Studies Library would show that present-day users of missionary records are more likely academic researchers from different parts rather than seminarians and church pastors. Except for resourceful institutions like Yale Divinity School Library, seminaries in the West have stopped collecting Christian literature outside their own cultural and geographical confines. The reason is clear: World Christianity is not in the core program for ministerial formation. Clearly, this raises serious questions about the theological competence of future generation of Christian ministers. Source documents from the diverse situations in World Christianity would have helped them to challenge their "localized" categories and assumptions. Pastors that have little knowledge of the wider realities cannot put their own situations into context. They then cannot challenge their own suppositions and ask the right questions. Without an informed understanding of World Christianity, future church leaders are in danger of becoming theologically illiterate. Christianity then is in danger of becoming a culturally and socially determined phenomenon.

Documenting World Christianity is crucial to reconnecting Christians to one another and to the wider world. It is a human task. Information technology has to a great extent succeeded in making the world impatient with uncertainties and eager for fame. Walls, however, invites us to reimagine another way of being a scholar and missionary. With tireless stamina, humble spirit, and inquisitive mind, he is constantly "on the move" (cf.

2 Cor. 11:26). Are not these the much-needed qualities that present-day Christianity needs most? We live in uncertain times at the beginning of the third millennium. The settings are complex and fast-changing; the social goals are multiple and conflicting. If Christianity has indeed become "post-Christendom," we are still unclear what "post-Christendom" actually is. Our understanding is at best imperfect and provisional in today's polyphonic settings. What Christianity will become depends on whether Christians from different settings can work with common purposes. Here Walls has shown us the way. His capacity to improvise, to accept setbacks and move on, above all his capacity for friendship and his commitment to rigorous and sturdy scholarship challenges the superficialities of the technological culture. Walls bequeaths to future generations of church leaders and Christian academics a vision for World Christianity: it is to be a life-giving force that can rejuvenate the world of learning. Such a vision, if fulfilled, would depend largely on cultivating a connection-building community of scholars with the virtues that Walls has displayed. Walls would remind us, as he did in the 1980 Rome meeting, that we owe this to one another.

Part V

AFRICA'S PLACE IN CHRISTIAN HISTORY

14

"Turning That Which Is Already There toward Christ": The Contribution of Andrew F. Walls to Understanding African Christianity

J. KWABENA ASAMOAH-GYADU

In fact, nowadays, if you want to study Africa, you have to know something about Christianity. But it is equally true that if you want to know something about Christianity, you must know something about Africa.[1]

The epigraph of this essay, which appears in an article written by Andrew Walls at the beginning of the twenty-first century, aptly captures his thoughts on the relationship between Christianity and Africa. That at the dawn of the twenty-first century Africa could be described as one of the major heartlands of Christianity is now an indisputable fact. References to this shift in the demographic center of gravity of the Christian faith from the northern to the southern continents, as Andrew F. Walls often describes the development, can be found in the writings of leading scholars in the field of African Christianity. Notable among these are John S. Mbiti, Lamin O. Sanneh, Kwame Bediako, and Ogbu U. Kalu. More recently Jehu H. Hanciles and Philip Jenkins have also written about the increasingly dominant role of Africa in global Christianity, a fact that is most notably discussed in Jenkins's book *The Next Christendom*.[2] The writings of these and other like-minded scholars demonstrate the extent to which the Christian tradition has over the past century, in particular, become part of Africa, and indicate some

---

1. Andrew F. Walls, "Of Ivory Towers and Ashrams: Some Reflections on Theological Scholarship in Africa," *Journal of African Christian Thought* 3, no. 1 (2000): 1.
2. Philip Jenkins, *The Next Christendom: The Coming of Global Christianity*, rev. and expanded (Oxford: Oxford University Press, 2008).

of the distinctively African shapes that it is taking following the translation of the Bible into African languages and cultural forms.[3] Among the lot Andrew F. Walls, who lived through the twentieth century and is still soldiering on into the twenty-first could without doubt be described as one of the leading interpreters of Christianity in Africa in our time. He is one of two people to whom we dedicated our work *African Christianity: It's an African Story*. The editor-in-chief, the late Ogbu Kalu, aptly summarized the importance of Walls and Brian Stanley to African Christianity when he testified to their efforts on the dedication page: "Many have bemoaned the collapse of Christian scholarship in Africa; you both have done something about it."[4]

Africa as a Christian Heartland

In 1970, contrary to the fear at Edinburgh 1910 that Africa might develop as a "Muhammadan continent," David Barrett observed that given the phenomenal growth of Christianity on the continent, "African Christians might well tip the balance and transform Christianity permanently into a non-Western religion."[5] Kwame Bediako points us to the fact that it was Andrew F. Walls who drew out the fullest implications of Barrett's observation with his suggestion that "what happens within the African Churches in the next generation will determine the whole shape of church history for centuries to come; what sort of theology is most characteristic of the Christianity of the twenty-first century may well depend on what has happened in the minds of African Christians in the interim."[6] The shift in the center of gravity of the Christian faith to the South, Bediako explains, does not mean that the church in the North ceases to matter. Rather, he concurs with an assertion by Mbiti that it was essential to recognize the theological significance of the concerns of the church in the South, not merely for the sake of the South but for the fact that it was only in that way that the universality

---

3. See Andrew F. Walls, "Foreword" to Kwame Bediako, *Christianity in Africa: The Renewal of a Non-Western Religion* (Maryknoll, N.Y.: Orbis Books, 1995), xi.

4. Ogbu U. Kalu, ed., *African Christianity: It's an African Story* (Trenton, N.J.: Africa World Press, 2007).

5. David B. Barrett, "AD 2000: 350 Million Christians in Africa," *International Review of Mission 59*, no. 233 (1970): 39–54.

6. Andrew F. Walls, "Towards an Understanding of Africa's Place in Christian History," in *Religion in a Pluralistic Society,* ed. John S. Pobee (Leiden: E. J. Brill, 1976), 180–89.

of the church would be meaningful both evangelistically and theologically.[7] If understood in that way, the strong affirmations of the church in Africa as signifying hope for World Christianity in the face of the recession of the faith in the modern West would not be understood as an exercise in theological and ecclesial triumphalism.

Rather, as Walls consistently observes in his writings, this would be seen as a call to mission from the South to the West, for the former heartlands of Christianity that sent out so many missionaries in the nineteenth century now stand in need of missionaries themselves. The observation that the heartlands of the Christian faith will shift southward with Africa as a leading player has proven very prophetic. This chapter looks at the contribution of Andrew F. Walls to the body of scholarly publications on the nature, growth, and implications of Christianity as a non-Western religion with African Christianity as a major player in this field. Although he never set out to write a book on a single theme, the first collection of his articles into one volume brought together under the title *The Missionary Movement in Christian History* gives some good idea of how Walls's thoughts have developed as a scholar in Christian history and mission. The first section is a reflection on the nature of the Christian faith, seen from the perspective of its historical transmission. The second focuses on the transmission process in relation to the special case of Africa, and the third dwells on the missionary movement from the West as a model of what happens as the transmission of faith takes place.[8]

This book, which as we have noted brings together some of the most important articles written by Walls over almost four decades of an illustrious career as a church historian, tells of his early graduate studies in patristics. His work in Sierra Leone and Nigeria as a missionary theological educator, which opened Walls's eyes to the southern shift in the demographic center of Christianity to Asia, Latin America, and Africa and its implications for his own career:

> The abundant evidence was on every hand of the decline of Christianity in Britain; but how would these future ministers ever realize that the Christian faith was actually expanding in most of the rest of the world, that most Christians would soon be living in the southern

---

7. Kwame Bediako, *Christianity in Africa: The Renewal of a Non-Western Religion* (Maryknoll, N.Y.: Orbis Books, 1995), 156.

8. Andrew F. Walls, "Introduction," in *The Missionary Movement in Christian History: Studies in the Transmission of Faith* (Maryknoll, N.Y.: Orbis Books, 1996), xiii.

continents? . . . Gradually I found myself drawn into a new discipline, to which Africa had induced the first faltering steps. From church history, Christian duty led to the history of religions.[9]

Subsequently Walls became a historian of religions whose interest was Christianity and especially the Christianity of where the faith now was, Africa. He placed African church history on the church history agenda of Europe and went on to supervise many African scholars now serving in various theological institutions and departments for the study of religions burgeoning across the continent. A second book, which like the first is a collection of previously published essays, also pays considerable attention to African Christianity. Part II is titled "Africa in Christian History" and deals with matters relating to the growth and character of Christianity when it transitioned from Western into African hands.[10] Through these and other writings on Christianity in Africa, Walls has paid considerable attention to primal worldviews because of his position that all Christians are "primalists" underneath and in any case that Christianity has grown in places where primal religions still make strong showings.

African Christianity and the Primal Imagination

In the process of transformation of Christianity into a primarily non-Western religion, Andrew Walls was one of those who recognized early that in the process of transmission the Christian faith reinforced the African worldview of the inseparability of the sacred and secular realms of the universe. African Christians have on the whole avoided any significant secularization of their outlook.[11] With reference to his definition of conversion as a process of "turning," it could be said that what the Gospel has done in Africa, as far as the primal imagination is concerned, is to affirm a spirituality that was already there "even if it has also pruned off some of its features and sharpened its focus, this time, upon Christ."[12] "Primal" is not a euphemism

---

9. Ibid., xv.
10. Andrew F. Walls, *The Cross-Cultural Process in Christian History* (Maryknoll, N.Y.: Orbis Books, 2002).
11. Bediako, *Christianity in Africa*, 176.
12. Ibid.

for "primitive," he notes. Rather it underlines its historical anteriority and its basic elemental status in human experience.[13]

For example, whereas none of the divinities of the Greco-Roman world — Zeus or Jupiter — could be described as God, the experience of African Christians has been different. The bearers of the Christian message, even when they assumed that they were addressing polytheistic primal societies in Africa, found the recognition of a Creator God who was also the moral governor of the universe. To make the point that the God of the primal world was also encountered as the Father of our Lord Jesus Christ, Walls cites various examples from the Mende of Sierra Leone who call him Ngewo, the Akan of Ghana who call him Onyame, the Yoruba of Nigeria who call him Olorun, and the Igbo among whom he is known as Chukwu or Chineke. For these people and others like them, he notes, "there was thus an absolute class difference between the Supreme Being and lower orders of divinity and that is why it was natural to use Ngewo, Nyame, Olorun for the God of the Bible."[14] Elsewhere Walls refers to such beliefs as spiritual causation and the continuing influence of the ancestors in the lives of the living to make the point that the principal evidence for the ongoing life of African traditional religion lies within African Christianity. As I will note, the place to look for this evidence, is the spirituality and ritual practices of the indigenous independent churches that emerged as alternative spiritual homes to the historic mission churches.

Incarnation as Translation and Conversion

The sort of Christian history that Andrew Walls represents is one that pays considerable attention to the way in which Jesus Christ is translated into cultural relevance for all peoples and nations. The bewildering paradox at the heart of the Christian confession, Walls writes, is not just the obvious one of the divine humanity. Rather, it is what he refers to as "the two-fold affirmation of the utter Jewishness of Jesus and of the boundless universality of the Divine Son." In Jesus Christ, God "made humanity his own" and so for Walls, "the divine saving activity can be understood in terms of

---

13. See Andrew F. Walls, "Primal Religious Traditions in Today's World," in *The Missionary Movement in Christian History: Studies in the Transmission of Faith* (Maryknoll, N.Y.: Orbis Books, 1996).

14. Andrew F. Walls, "The Evangelical Revival, the Missionary Movement, and Africa," in *The Missionary Movement in Christian History: Studies in the Transmission of Faith* (Maryknoll, N.Y.: Orbis Books, 1996), 95.

translation."[15] Through the incarnation, he writes, "divinity is translated" into *specific* humanity that is at home in specific segments of social reality. If the incarnation of the Son represents a divine act of translation, Walls argues, then "it is a prelude to repeated acts of retranslation as Christ fills the Pleroma again — other aspects of social reality."[16]

If incarnation is translation, then when God in Christ became man, Divinity was translated into humanity, as though humanity were a receptor language. Every language, Walls argues from this position, is specific to a people or an area and so "when Divinity was translated into humanity, he did not become generalized humanity but rather a *person* in a particular locality and in a particular ethnic group, at a particular place and time."[17] From this argument, Walls slowly builds up a case for Africa as critical to God's salvific scheme by pointing to Christ as "God's translated speech" that has been "translated from the Palestinian Jewish original." And this requires that the various nations of the world are to be made Disciples of Christ. For, as he points out, if the Christian faith is about translation then it is about conversion.[18]

> At the heart of Christian faith is the Incarnate Word — God became human. The divine Word was expressed under the conditions of a particular human society; the divine Word was, as it were, *translated*. And since the Divine Word was for all humanity, he is translated again in terms of every culture where he finds acceptance among its people.[19]

At the present time when the Christian faith seems to be under siege in the modern West as it was under Herod at the birth of Jesus, Christianity has returned home to Africa where, to use the words of Walls, the faith has "found acceptance among its peoples." Thus in primal societies such as those of Africa, missionaries found God ahead of them in the cultures. He was known by different vernacular names, and these names were affirmed as referring to the God and Father of the Lord Jesus Christ when they were deployed in the translation of Yahweh into the vernacular Scriptures. Where

---

15. Walls, "Introduction," xvi.
16. Ibid., xvii.
17. Andrew F. Walls, "The Translation Principle in Christian History," in *The Missionary Movement in Christian History: Studies in the Transmission of Faith* (Maryknoll, N.Y.: Orbis Books, 1996), 27.
18. Ibid., 28.
19. Andrew F. Walls, "Culture and Conversion in Christian History," in *The Missionary Movement in Christian History: Studies in the Transmission of Faith* (Maryknoll, N.Y.: Orbis Books, 1996), 47.

these vernacular names of God have been used in the Bible, "the coming of Christianity has not been . . . bringing God to the people, so much as bringing him near."[20] It is the translatability of both the Divine in the *Person* of Christ and the corresponding translatability of the written word that enabled African cultures to serve as recapture cultures to the God of the Bible and allowed people to hear the good news in their own mother tongues.

Conversion and Discipling of the Nations

The proper response to such activity is conversion, which Walls defines as "turning," and so for him Christian conversion becomes a process of "turning toward Christ" what is already there. These are thoughts he develops further in his article "Converts or Proselytes? The Crises over Conversion in the Early Church."[21] The essay refers to the various linguistic and conceptual complexities of the word "conversion," but as Walls states, it focuses on the meaning of conversion as "turning," noting that there is adequate biblical warrant for that meaning.[22] The decisions of the early church through the Jerusalem Council and the attitude of St. Paul in not requiring Gentile believers to undergo Jewish customary rituals such as circumcision underscores for Walls the fact that the followers of Jesus were not expected to be proselytes but converts. This approach to conversion "marked the church's first critical departure from Jewish tradition and experience" because "it built cultural diversity into the church forever."[23] The point of the article, we stated earlier, is that in conversion we turn "what is already there" toward Christ. If Hellenistic backgrounds had to be turned toward Christ then so must the African or primal backgrounds of the peoples and cultures of where the Christian faith now is, Africa.

> Converts have to be constantly, relentlessly turning their ways of thinking, their education and training, their ways of working and doing things, toward Christ. They must think Christ into the patterns of

---

20. Andrew F. Walls, "Origins of Old Northern and New Southern Christianity,' in *The Missionary Movement in Christian History: Studies in the Transmission of Faith* (Maryknoll, N.Y.: Orbis Books, 1996), 71.

21. Andrew F. Walls, "Converts or Proselytes? The Crisis over Conversion in the Early Church," in *Speaking about Things We Have Seen*, ed. Jonathan J. Bonk, Dwight P. Baker, Daniel J. Nicholas, and Craig A. Noll (New Haven: Conn.: OMSC Publications, 2007), 1–12. This article was originally published in the *International Bulletin of Missionary Research* 28, no. 1 (2004): 14–19.

22. Ibid., 2.

23. Ibid., 9.

thought they have inherited, into their networks of relationships and their processes for making decisions.[24]

This understanding of Christian faith is built on what Walls refers to as the "indigenizing principle," which is based on the hypothesis that on the basis of the work of Christ, God accepts people as they are. At the same time, he argues, God does not take people as isolated beings who are self-governing units. People are conditioned by "a particular time and place, by our family group and society" and by culture. The inseparability of individuals from their social relations or society is what leads to the human desire to indigenize, which he explains to mean, "to live as a Christian and yet as a member of one's own society" so that the church becomes "a place to feel at home."[25] Walls concludes from this that "no group of Christians has therefore any right to impose in the name of Christ upon another group of Christians a set of assumptions about life determined by another time and place." Not only does God in Christ take people as they are, he continues, but he takes them in order to transform them into what he wants them to be.[26] He proceeds then to affirm Third World Christian theology, of which African Christianity is a part, and the theology that has arisen out of that context as the representative Christian theology of the twenty-first century. It is therefore important when thinking of African theology, Walls counsels, "to remember that it will act on an African agenda."[27]

Understanding Africa's Place in Christian History

We have already quoted extensively from Andrew F. Walls's *The Missionary Movement in Christian History* to indicate how his studies in the "transmission of faith" attempt to establish the critical place that the Third World in general and Africa in particular occupies in Christian history. The first essay dealing with "Africa's place in Christian History" in that collection makes the following observation that summarizes his thoughts:

[Taking] it as a whole, in its Catholic as well as its Protestant aspect, the missionary movement has changed the face of Christianity. It has

---

24. Ibid., 11.
25. Andrew F. Walls, "The Gospel as Prisoner and Liberator of Culture," in *The Missionary Movement in Christian History: Studies in the Transmission of Faith* (Maryknoll, N.Y.: Orbis Books, 1996), 7.
26. Ibid., 8.
27. Ibid. 11.

transformed the demographic and cultural composition of the church, with consequences not yet measurable for its future life and leadership and theology and worship. The most remarkable feature of this transformation has been in the African continent, minimal in Christian profession when the missionary movement began, but now, when so much of the West is in the post-Christian period, moving to the position where it may have more professing Christians than any other continent.[28]

Walls concludes from this that the sheer size of its Christian community must be one reason why Africa should be taken seriously as significant in the history of Christianity.[29] Not only has the demographic future of the church moved to Africa but African Christianity — both at home and in the Diaspora — continues to be the focus of religious anthropology, history, and theological study and writing. More importantly, however, Walls observes that in spite of the contributions of the missionary enterprise, modern African Christianity is the result of movements among Africans and has been sustained principally by Africans and so has on the whole been "the result of African initiatives."[30] The fathers of the missionary movement had expected that Christianity would assimilate Africans to a European style of life, but as Walls demonstrates from his discussions of religious innovation on the continent, the gaps between cerebral Christianity and a Christianity that is experiential were realized early.

African Christians, Walls points out, "face situations where integrity requires them to find a solution in Christian terms — that is by the application of the word about Christ and of Scripture — where Western Christianity, the source from which Christian tradition has come, has no answers, because it has no parallel experience."[31] That is why one of the most noticed features of modern Christian history in Africa, according to Walls, "has been the emergence of churches that owe little to Western models of how a church should operate, and much to African readings of Scripture, for which the conditions of African life often provide a hall of echoes."[32]

---

28. Walls, "The Evangelical Revival," 85.
29. Ibid.
30. Ibid., 86.
31. Ibid., 94.
32. Andrew F. Walls, "A History of the Expansion of Christianity *Reconsidered,*" in *The Cross-Cultural Process in Christian History* (Maryknoll, N.Y.: Orbis Books, 2002), 17.

Christian Religious Innovation in Africa

The missionary movement "changed the face of Christianity" and "transformed the demographic and cultural composition of the church," and the most remarkable feature of this transformation has been in Africa.[33] Walls underscores the fact that modern African Christianity is not simply the result of movements among Africans, but it has been principally sustained by Africans and is indeed the result of African initiatives. To begin with, even under Western missionaries, the principal carriers of the message to the hinterlands were ordinary African Christians going about their normal duties as farmers, small-scale artisans, and petty traders. The story is illustrated by Walls as follows:

> I recall a survey of how the numerous congregations within one densely populated area of Nigeria had come into being. Time after time the seminal figure was a new court clerk who was a Christian, or a worker on the new railway, or a tailor, carrying his sewing machine on his head, or some other trader. Some such stranger, or a group of strangers, had arrived and had started family prayers, stopped work on Sunday, and sang hymns instead, and some local people got interested. Or the initial impetus came from people from that village who had gone elsewhere — to school, to work, to trade, in more than one case to jail — and on return home sought the things they had found in their travels.[34]

Even today there are very few historic mission churches that were started through deliberate official policies. Most churches are started by lay people who then request a pastor when resources are enough to pay the emoluments of one and to ensure the constant celebration of the sacraments, the performance of confirmation rites, and burial of the departed.

In reaction to the staid, silent, orderly, and overly cerebral nature of historic mission Christianity, with its Western liturgical orientation, African Christians led by indigenous prophets, took their spiritual destinies into their own hands. Garrick S. Braide of the Niger Delta, William Wade Harris of Liberia and the then Gold Coast (Ghana), Simon Kimbangu of the DR Congo, and Isaiah Shembe of South Africa are all indigenous prophets who at the turn of the twentieth century led local revival movements culminating in the formation of African independent churches (AICs). When

---

33. Walls, "The Evangelical Revival," 85.
34. Ibid., 87.

Walls, talking about factors accounting for the expansion of Christianity in Africa, refers to "the emergence of dynamic figures who owed little in any direct way to church mission and nothing to any commission from one," these are the people he is referring to.[35] Harold W. Turner, who was a pioneering investigator of these churches, referred to them as "prophet-healing churches" on account of their dependence on charismatic prophets and the centrality of healing to their ministries.[36] All the prophets were charismatic figures who had the same message. They called on people to abandon traditional gods and follow the one God of the Christian Scriptures who has revealed himself in Christ. Walls quite rightly refers to Prophet Harris as the most celebrated of these figures and gives the following account of his orientation to Christian ministry:

> He called people to repentance; he persuaded thousands to abandon traditional African religious practices; he pointed them to the God of the Scriptures, which as yet they could not read, sometimes leaving King James Bibles as a sign of the source of the teaching to follow; he baptized with water and, by prayer and exorcism, triumphed over the spirits.[37]

The AICs that emerged from the efforts of these prophets constitute the most extensively studied new religious movements in African Christian history and scholarship.[38] The stress on the syncretistic aspects of these churches, mostly in Western scholarship in the observation of Walls, tends to obscure the extent to which they are also radical, innovative, and revolutionary movements.[39] African initiatives in Christianity has continued since the decline of the AICs from the 1960s as their charismatic leaders started ageing and dying. There are clear continuities between the religious practices and theological beliefs of the new African Pentecostal or charismatic churches and their older compatriots, the AICs. Again Walls was one of the first people to point us to these continuities:

---

35. Ibid.
36. Harold W. Turner, *Religious Innovation in Africa: Collected Essays on New Religious Movements* (Boston: G. K. Hall, 1979).
37. Walls, "The Evangelical Revival," 88.
38. See for instance the essays and bibliography in *Exploring New Religious Movements: Essays in Honor of Harold W. Turner,* ed. Andrew F. Walls and Wilbert R. Shenk (Elkhart, Ind.: Mission Focus Publications, 1990).
39. Walls, "A History of the Expansion of Christianity *Reconsidered,*" 17–18.

Until recently these prophet-healing churches could be held the most significant and fastest-growing sector of the indigenous churches. This is no longer so certain. Nigeria and Ghana, to name but two countries, are witnessing the rise of another type of independent church. Like many prophet-healing churches, they proclaim the divine power of deliverance from disease and demonic affliction, but the style of proclamation is more like that of American Adventist and Pentecostal preaching. Gone are the African drums and the white uniforms of the aladuras; the visitor is more likely to hear electronic keyboards and amplified guitars, see a preacher in elegant *agbada* or smart business suit, and a choir in bow ties. Yet these radical charismatic movements are African in origin, in leadership, and in finance. They are highly entrepreneurial and are active in radio and television and cassette ministries as well as in campaigns and conventions.... All the new movements share with the prophet-healing churches a quest for the demonstrable presence of the Holy Spirit and a direct address to the problems and frustrations of modern African urban life.[40]

The very differences between these churches and historic mission denominations and especially their attempts at responding to what Walls has referred to as "a direct address to the problems and frustrations of modern African urban life" permit these churches to be studied as "African." A high proportion of studies of African Christianity has centered on the older independent churches, but in the last two decades several others have appeared that focus on the new charismatic churches in Africa.

Christian Scholarship in Africa

A major area of importance for Andrew Walls, as far as the phenomenal growth of Christianity in Africa is concerned, is for corresponding attention to be given to Christian scholarship. Christian scholarship follows and derives from Christian mission, he writes, and the demand for scholarship occurred as soon as the Gospel crossed its first cultural frontier — that between Israel and the Hellenistic world.[41] Thus Christian mission from the

---

40. Walls, "The Evangelical Revival," 93.
41. Andrew F. Walls, "Christian Scholarship in Africa in the Twenty-First Century," *Journal of African Christian Thought* 4, no. 2 (2001): 44.

inception of that process has been a history of scholarship and documentation, and this is true also of the early planting of Christianity in Africa. Early Ethiopian Christianity developed "its own distinctive literature and tradition of scholarship," using its own distinctive writing system," Andrew Walls points out, and this enabled the recovery of Ethiopian Christianity from near disaster.[42] The tradition of Christian scholarship continued with the modern missionary movement in Africa. Out of its essential concern to communicate the Gospel, the missionary movement was forced into what Walls refers to as "innovative scholarship."[43] The new fields of study that were invented in the languages and literatures of worlds beyond Europe in the process of mission included comparative linguistics, anthropology, comparative religion, and tropical medicine.

Walls draws links between innovative Christian scholarship and mission as incarnation and conversion. Christian scholarship arises out of the exercise of cross-cultural Christian mission, which entails living on someone else's terms or taking the risk of entering another person's world. This is analogous to the incarnation, he explains, as the Gospel itself is about God living on someone else's terms. In the incarnation, "divinity was expressed in terms of humanity."[44] This has implications for conversion because, according to Walls, "cross-cultural diffusion...has to go beyond language, the outer skin of culture, into the processes of thinking and choosing, and all the networks of relationship that lie beneath language, turning them all towards Christ."[45] Such deep translation, as he refers to the process, is necessary to deep mission and so periods of active mission need to be periods of active scholarship. When the sense of mission is dulled or diverted, Walls concludes from this, then "the death knell sounds for Christian scholarship."[46]

The implications of this proposition for the revival of appropriate and relevant Christian scholarship for Africa as a major heartland of Christian mission are clear. Although demographically the composition of the Christian church has shifted to southward, Walls bemoans the fact that the "thought processes and cultural awareness" of mission have not yet moved proportionately with this demographic shift. The gaps need to be bridged. The development of an effective Christian scholarship in a tradition that

---

42. Ibid., 45.
43. Ibid., 46.
44. Ibid.
45. Ibid.
46. Ibid.

transitioned from Paul through Justin to Origen and beyond, enabled the conversion of the Greek past and made it possible for Christians nourished in Hellenistic culture to relate Christ to their pre-Christian inheritance. This example from early church history, Walls notes, makes the "conversion of the African past" toward Christ an urgent theological task. Africa, he continues, stands in need of Origens, of people who, brought up in the Christian faith and rooted in the Christian Scriptures, are certain of their Christian identity, and yet are also confident of their African identity, confident enough to handle the African past as Christians and as Africans.[47]

It does make sense in terms of twenty-first-century Christian mission that, if Africa has become a major heartland of the Christian faith, then what happens on the continent will be an important part in the determination of the nature of contemporary Christianity. What happens in the modern West, as we are beginning to realize with African immigrant Christianity, will matter less and less. In the words of Walls, "it is Africans and Asians and Latin Americans who will be the representative Christians, those who represent the Christian norm, the Christian mainstream, of the twenty-first and twenty-second centuries."[48] The point is that Third World Christian theology is gradually shifting to the center as mainstream theology and the call is for Christian scholarship in Africa to realize the dawn of that new theological era and rise up to the occasion. African and Asian theological scholarship, Walls prophesies, will help determine the shape and quality of World Christianity. This point is worth stressing, Walls notes, because in the area of theological scholarship leadership may shift into African hands.

In most of the scientific, medical, and technological spheres, leadership will remain with the West, or with Asia in those departments where East Asia can outstrip the West. And in the humanities and social sciences, the stockpiled resources of the West will continue to give it great strength.[49]

> But authentic theological scholarship must arise out of Christian mission and, therefore, from the principal theatres of mission. Theology is about making Christian decisions in critical situations, and it is on the southern continents that those decisions will be most pressing, and the key theological developments are accordingly to be looked for. If

---

47. Ibid., 47.
48. Ibid.
49. Ibid.

appropriate scholarship does not emerge to give guidance and discipline to that process of decision, those key theological developments are likely to be stunted and ineffectual. In a word, if Africa, Asia, and Latin America do not develop a proper capacity for leadership in theological studies, there will be, for practical purposes, no theological studies anywhere that will be worth caring about.[50]

Redeeming Our Heritage

The demand for Christian scholarship that is relevant to the needs of Africa and its place in global Christianity is paramount because, in the assessment of Walls, the Western theological academy is sick. Although the university developed as a product of Christian concern, the Enlightenment mind-set has edged out the supernatural from theological studies. The greater part of the Western academy, he points out, "brackets out the whole of the 'other' world, the world of spirit, even in the study of religion."[51] This has turned theology into a mere academic discipline in which people engage for reasons of promotion and self-aggrandizement. Professors have become a guild, a profession, he notes, and the academy a mere career. While human life is devastated across Africa, Walls boldly chides, sponsors can be found to research the most effective way of dunking cookies, and universities will take money and provide the laboratory space. This approach to university research goes against the original purposes for the establishment of such institutions as places for "the promotion of learning for the glory of God."[52] In response, what we need according to Walls, is a cleansing of theological scholarship, a reorientation of academic theology to Christian mission, a return to the ideal of scholarship to the glory of God, a return to the ideal of the academic life as a liberating search for truth.[53]

Much of African life operates with a worldview quite different from that of the Enlightenment, as was noted earlier, and according to Walls the contemporary strength of Christianity in Africa may derive from a number of factors: first, its independence of Enlightenment views; second, its openness to the accommodation of other visions of reality, visions in which the frontier with the spiritual world is crowded with traffic in both directions,

---

50. Ibid.
51. Ibid., 49.
52. Ibid., 48.
53. Ibid.

visions that involve communal solidarity and do not take the autonomy of the individual as a defining category.[54] As Western theological scholarship leaves out whole worlds that are familiar to Africans untouched by Christ, Walls calls for a new approach that deals with such African concerns as witchcraft, demon possession, the interface between emerging African neo-Pentecostal prosperity theology and suffering, ethnic conflicts and genocide, and salvation as a communal affair. Some of these theological issues and challenges are what brought into being the African independent churches and neo-Pentecostal movements, and Walls gives some attention to these movements and the incalculable contributions they are making to relevant theological scholarship in Africa.

Conclusion

I began this essay with some reference to the deliberations at the first World Missionary Conference, Edinburgh 1910, which felt that Africa was going to turn Islamic. For Andrew F. Walls, the most astonishing difference in the Christian world between 1910 and the present lies in Africa. The report read at Edinburgh, he notes, spoke of the evangelization of the interior of Africa as hardly begun. Yet during the twentieth century, the expansion of the churches of sub-Saharan Africa has been phenomenal. It is a century that saw the emergence of sub-Saharan Africa as a Christian heartland, with Africa quietly slipping into the place in the Christian world once occupied by Europe. At the forefront of this expansion, we learn from Walls, has been the innovative Christianity led by indigenous African prophets and the independent and charismatic churches that their religious efforts have spawned. These are churches that took the primal imagination seriously in the formulation of Christian teaching and practices and subsequently developed new forms of church life that differed markedly from those offered by enlightenment Christianity. Walls concludes from all this that "it is as though sub-Saharan Africa has crammed several centuries of Christian history and experience into the single century that separates us from the World Missionary Conference."[55] Christian mission in and from Africa is likely to widen the theological agenda; the consequent benefit could be of more than African significance.[56]

---

54. Walls, "Ivory Towers and Ashrams," 2.
55. Andrew F. Walls, "Christian Mission in a Five-Hundred-Year Context," in *Mission in the Twenty-First Century: Exploring the Five Marks of Global Mission,* ed. Andrew F. Walls and Cathy Ross (Maryknoll, N.Y.: Orbis Book, 2008), 202.
56. Ibid., 203.

15

Gospel and Culture:
Andrew F. Walls in Africa,
Africa in Andrew F. Walls

GILLIAN BEDIAKO

Introduction

"I still remember the force with which one day the realization struck me that I, while happily pontificating on that patchwork quilt of diverse fragments that constitutes second-century Christian literature, was actually living in a second-century church."[1] With these words from Andrew Walls's introduction to his first major collection of essays, but repeated in other contexts and to different audiences around the world,[2] Walls describes his moment of illumination in Sierra Leone, an illumination that revolutionized not only his perspectives on church history and Christian scholarship, but also the range and scope of the historical study of Christianity; "real church history" in Africa was now found to include "work on the African materials," namely, "the forms of African religion and society," in the same way that patristic studies required study of the "literatures, history and religion of the later Roman Empire." What began as a hobby, a sideline, soon became fundamental to his scholarship.[3]

In addition to this intellectual revolution there was occurring something deeper, "a very definite movement from depression to hope"[4] concerning Africa and the future of Christianity. The depressing picture of the local church Walls had received from fellow Britons living in Freetown gave way to a new hope, founded on the recognition of a great *kairos* moment for

---

1. Andrew F. Walls, "Introduction," in *The Missionary Movement in Christian History, Studies in the Transmission of Faith* (Maryknoll, N.Y.: Orbis Books, 1996), xiii.
2. See, for example, Tim Stafford, "A Historian Ahead of His Time," *Christianity Today* (2007): 87–89; James A. Ault, Interview with Andrew F. Walls, Yale (July 2001), communication of transcript from videotape in email, dated January 5, 2006.
3. Walls, "Introduction," xiv.
4. Quoted by Stafford, "A Historian Ahead of His Time," 88.

the Gospel of Jesus Christ in Africa that paralleled similar moments in the earlier mission history of Christianity. The impact of these realizations upon him was such that Andrew Walls has been at pains to stress ever since that, "All I know, I learned in Africa."[5]

Andrew F. Walls in Africa

Andrew Walls spent nine years in Africa from 1957 to 1966. For the first five years he taught church history to Anglican ministerial candidates at Fourah Bay College, Freetown, Sierra Leone. From there he moved to the new University of Nsukka in Nigeria to set up a Department of Religion that should "provide for the study of all the religious traditions of Nigeria." It "developed programs in Christian and Muslim studies in parallel," as well as courses in the primal religions of Africa.[6]

While his subsequent bases have been in Scotland, first in Aberdeen (1966–86) and then in Edinburgh (1986–97), in the United States, at Princeton Theological Seminary (1997–2001), and latterly at Liverpool Hope University, U.K., there is a sense in which Andrew Walls has never left Africa. Quite apart from the fact that Africa frequently came to him in the form of graduate students studying in all four places, Walls's curriculum vitae details regular visits to Africa as a visiting lecturer in theological institutions and universities. In particular, since 1998 he has been an adjunct faculty member and emeritus professor of the Akrofi-Christaller Institute of Theology, Mission and Culture, Akropong-Akuapem, Ghana, where he continues to lecture and supervise doctoral students, making several visits each year.

Similarly, the new learning he acquired in Sierra Leone and Nigeria led him to pioneer new directions for the study of Christian history and the history of religions, not just in the African contexts, but also in Aberdeen, Edinburgh, Princeton, and everywhere else that he has taught. For it has become his conviction that the living contexts of World Christianity require it.

I have been in academic life for over fifty years, in African countries and in the West, in institutions of ministerial training and in public universities. Within my lifetime, the demography of the Christian church has undergone a far-reaching transformation, involving recession from

5. Andrew F. Walls, "Editorial," *Journal of African Christian Thought* 9, no. 2 (2006): 2.
6. Walls, "Introduction," xiv.

faith in the West and accession to faith in the non-Western world. As a consequence, African Christianity is becoming more important and Western Christianity less important in the general situation of Christianity in the world. Yet neither the Western churches nor the African churches, including the theological academy as a whole, appear to have understood the implications of this shift.... Ministers in the West are still being trained without any thought of what the Christian church has now become. [They are] deprived by not being given the opportunity to... realize that the Western Christianity that they have known is not a universal, normative version of the faith.... And African and Asian students, so often trained on a curriculum designed for the West, receive a distorting view of Christian history.[7]

This learning marked also the beginning of a vocation, intensifying with the years, which one can only describe as prophetic. Andrew Walls's time in Africa and engagement with Africa has made him something of a lone voice in the wilderness pointing to the decay in the modern academy.

We cannot escape the fact that the Western academy is in desperate straits. It has been corrupted by money... by competitiveness, careerism and the race for promotion. The theological academy is no exception. For... it has been said that the majority of [theological] research projects are about the advancement of academic careers. Such a situation sounds the death knell for the academy.[8]

However, his tone is not one of despair but of hope. For his vision is for a renewal of the academy through Christian scholarship, seen as a vocation in the service of mission. Just as the Greek academy of the early centuries was revived through the Greek Christian academy, so hope for the future of the theological academy will lie in a vigorous African Christian scholarship.

We may thus hope that the academy may yet again be saved by developments in scholarship among Christians in the non-Western world. For this to happen, there is a need for scholarship to be perceived and lived as a Christian vocation.... Christian scholarship needs to be rooted in Christian life, focussed on mission, drawing inspiration

7. Andrew F. Walls, "Scholarship, Mission and Globalization: Some Reflections on the Christian Scholarly Vocation in Africa," *Journal of African Christian Thought* 9, no. 2 (2006): 34–37 (36).
8. Ibid., 36–37.

from a common life of worship and service. One may hope that African Christian scholarship may recover something of the ideal of the early monastic communities, where scholarship was pursued not in isolation, nor in competition, but in co-operation, as the community shared and worshipped together.[9]

His voice has also been one of encouragement and challenge, calling African Christian scholars to develop an "adequate" and "effective" Christian scholarship,[10] with the following ingredients: a renewal of the sense of Christian vocation to scholarship, a research climate, exacting standards, collegial attitudes, a pioneering spirit, dual education (biblical and contextual), a catholic attitude to knowledge, and a lively interactive sense of World Christianity.[11] A later work elaborates these characteristics: Christian scholars in Africa are called to be "encyclopaedic and wide-ranging" in focus, "creative in the integration of disciplines and fields of study," "prepared to do fundamental, ground-breaking research," to develop new "specializations, a wide range of languages, including biblical, international, and indigenous languages, and archival skills," "to take risks in producing pioneering studies and to be ready to venture into areas that no one has explored before," to engage in "mutual critique" and "networks of co-operation across Africa (including the African diaspora) and beyond."[12] The challenge has also included warnings against loss of hope, against dependency and "Micawberism" that is, not venturing to do anything substantial until the resources somehow turn up.[13]

It will be seen from this catalogue of tasks and challenges that Andrew Walls has not been in Africa to promote himself. His overriding concern has been the empowerment of a new generation of non-Western, and particularly African, Christian scholars, on the understanding that theirs is the responsibility for the future.

Above all, African Christian scholars should not be content to be, or allow themselves to be treated as, pensioners or clients of world Christian scholarship. They are called to be full participants in a task

---

9. Ibid., 37.

10. Andrew F. Walls, "Christian Scholarship in Africa in the Twenty-First Century," *Journal of African Christian Thought* 4, no. 2 (2001): 44–52 (46).

11. Ibid., 51.

12. Walls, "Scholarship, Mission and Globalization," 37.

13. Walls, "Christian Scholarship in Africa in the Twenty-First Century," 52.

that has never been more necessary to the work of the Kingdom of God.[14]

There are many African Christians, whether theologians, ministers, or active lay Christians, who can testify to his impact upon them. It has not been his formidable intellect or breadth of knowledge that has touched them most deeply, but rather, his humility, generosity, and spirituality, and the fact that he has also exemplified the qualities that he has desired to see emerge in others.[15] Through their association of over thirty years, Kwame Bediako came to describe Andrew Walls, and dedicate one of his books to him, as "Teacher, Encourager, Friend."[16] In this, Kwame Bediako has not been alone.

Africa in Andrew F. Walls

Andrew Walls not only discovered new things in Africa, he also learned much from Africa and from Africans that made a deep impact upon him. Indeed, Africa both affirmed and changed him.

In the first place, Africa affirmed his interest in, and love for, the patristic era by bringing it to life, helping him to "understand the second-century material in the light of all the religious events going on around me."[17] It was as if Africa introduced him to "the community that informed the texts" he had been studying for years.[18]

> As I looked at the surviving literature of the early second century, I could see all the examples of that literature around me. You read the first letter of Clement, and, yes, I'd hear sermons like that, and just as long. You read Ignatius, and though I had not actually seen anybody going to martyrdom, you saw the same sort of intensity.[19]

He was able to develop further his research and archival instincts in Nigeria, unearthing and collecting, together with Nigerian colleagues, a vast

---

14. Walls, "Scholarship, Mission and Globalization," 37.
15. See the comments by the whole range of staff and students of Akrofi-Christaller Institute, "In Appreciation of Professor Emeritus Andrew F. Walls," *Journal of African Christian Thought* 9, no. 2 (2006): 51–55.
16. Kwame Bediako's comments as Rector of ACI, "In Appreciation of Professor Emeritus Andrew F. Walls," 55. The dedication is found in his *Christianity in Africa, The Renewal of a Non-Western Religion* (Maryknoll, N.Y.: Orbis Books, 1995).
17. Walls, "Introduction," xiii.
18. Stafford, "A Historian Ahead of His Time," 88.
19. Ibid.

array of church records going back to the 1880s, revealing "an African church with African executives, keeping its records with varying degrees of efficiency, according to the degree of education of the people involved ...worshipping, sinning, repenting; all this going on for a 70- or 80-year period."[20] With respect to research, "the crying need seemed to be to be able to understand the local situation. Why were there 331 churches in a five-mile radius in one small town?...What was the significance of the fact that in recounting the origins of any congregation in the area hardly anyone ...ever mentioned a missionary?"[21]

He was affirmed in another, and perhaps unexpected direction. His study of the primal religions of Africa led him to another realization,

> that texts still existed...that reflected...the process of interaction between the Christian faith and the primal religions of Europe. What was the process by which my own ancestors...came to appropriate the Gospel? What were the structures of the old primal religions of Europe and how parallel were they to the primal religions of today? More importantly, was it possible to understand those old texts...better in the light of the encounters of religions presently visible in Africa? Might the same texts...help to understand what was going on in Africa now?...It was a revelation to see how African Christians responded to these documents...and the insights they brought to them.[22]

The exploration of Europe's primal past and mission history gave the "Dark Ages" a new significance, underscoring the common humanity shared by Christians around the world, as well as the common workings of the grace of God that have opened the way for Christian mission through the ages.

Probably the most fundamental affirmation has been the fruit of his labors in the scholarship of his African students. So many have flourished under his tutelage and in ways that have affirmed his essential insights. Kwame Bediako must be one of the most notable of these, exploring and vindicating intuitions first aired by Walls.[23]

---

20. Ibid.
21. Walls, "Introduction," xiv.
22. Ibid., xvi.
23. See Kwame Bediako's major works: *Theology and Identity: The Impact of Culture upon Christian Thought in the Second Century and Modern Africa* (Oxford: Regnum Books, 1992); *Christianity in Africa: The Renewal of Non-Western Religion*, Studies in World Christianity (Edinburgh: Edinburgh University Press, and Maryknoll, N.Y.: Orbis Books, 1995); *Jesus in*

Africa also changed Andrew Walls. We have already noted the new learning that broadened his horizons on the study of Christian history and set him on a trajectory that would be immensely fruitful for Christian scholarship. Perhaps what we should note here is that the way to that learning was "to stop pontificating and observe what was going on."[24] Or, as he expressed it elsewhere more graphically, to "shut up, look around, and listen,"[25] the point being, having the humility to recognize the need to learn and to be open to receiving something new from Africa. For, while the initial realization was sudden and dramatic, the process of learning, of working through the implications, occurred "very stumblingly, it took a long time."[26]

Andrew Walls was changed also by his exposure to African Christian worship. He cites as "the most obvious fruit of cultural contact...the opportunity to refresh our own experience of Christian worship" as it is enriched through new patterns. "Now we have got more than we ever had before...and we don't have to give anything up!"[27]

> It is one of the most extraordinary things — you don't know the language, and yet you know you are in a Christian congregation, and gradually you find your place in this form of worship. And gradually you learn to pray and sing. You are reading the Scriptures together, as human beings together, looking to one Christ for salvation.... I don't think anyone brought up in the thin-blooded North can go to Africa and attend African churches without something happening to give them new insights into Christian worship — that expression of joy, that enormous vitality that comes through the African setting, with all the poverty, all the distress that people have.... When people pray with you, you realize why the New Testament talks about praying with the bowels! I would hope other Christians would be similarly enriched. We are one body.[28]

If we wish to understand why Andrew Walls is so much loved and respected by African Christians, and non-Western Christians generally, part

---

Africa: The Christian Gospel in African History and Experience (Akropong: Regnum Africa, 2000); reissued by Orbis Books in 2004 as *Jesus and the Gospel in Africa, History and Experience.*

24. Walls, "Introduction," xiii.
25. Ault, Interview with Andrew F. Walls.
26. Ibid.
27. Ibid.
28. Ibid.

of the answer lies here — that Africa changed him, and that he has been ever ready to acknowledge it with gratitude.

Gospel and Culture

Two of the key discoveries in and from Africa that Andrew Walls has spent his scholarly life exploring, have been the cultural component in Christian history and the significance of the primal substructure of Christianity. In bringing to bear upon these discoveries his "deep historical and theological vision,"[29] they, in turn, enriched it.

The Cultural Component in Christian History

In the first place, the incarnation takes on new significance as a cultural event.

> The bewildering paradox at the heart of the Christian confession is not just the obvious one of the divine humanity; it is the twofold affirmation of the utter Jewishness of Jesus and the boundless universality of the Divine Son. The paradox is necessary to the business of making sense of the history of the Christian faith. On the one hand it is a seemingly infinite series of cultural specificities — each in principle as locally specific as that utterly Jewish Jesus. On the other hand, in a historical view, the different specificities belong together. They have a certain coherence and interdependence in the coherence and interdependence of total humanity in the One who made humanity his own.[30]

Christian mission and expansion are seen in terms of "the process of diffusion across cultural boundaries," where "the distinctive nature of the Christian faith becomes manifest in its developing dialogue with culture."[31] Thus Christianity's claim to universality is tested supremely in its ability to inhabit and transform new cultures, through the possibility of fresh incarnations of the Savior, who "grows through the work of mission."[32] The New Testament writings come to be seen as the documents emerging out of the first cultural crossing, from Jewish to Hellenistic culture, as the paradigm

---

29. Stafford, "A Historian Ahead of His Time," 87
30. Walls, "Introduction," xvi.
31. Ibid.
32. Ibid., xvii.

for new images of Jesus and for dealing with the issues arising in subsequent crossings in Christian history.[33]

Along with this come new dimensions to Christian conversion, now understood to involve a cultural conversion, clarified in contrast to proselytization.

> To become a convert, in contrast, is to turn, and turning involves not a change of substance but a change of direction ... to *turn what is already there in a new direction* ... turning it in the direction of Christ. That is what the earliest Jerusalem believers had already done with their Jewish inheritance. Turning that inheritance toward Messiah Jesus transformed the inheritance but did not destroy its coherence or its continuity.... Conversion opened up Hellenistic social and family life to the influence of Christ. It forced people to think of the implications of daily life in terms of social identity and Christian identity, disturbing, challenging, altering the conventions of that life, *but doing so from the inside* ... a risky process. Risk, tension, and controversy are essential to the process of conversion.[34]

As the quotation above indicates, intrinsically bound up with the process of conversion are questions of Christian identity — how one may be truly Christian within one's native culture. The realization that conversion is a cultural process led Walls to identify "two opposing tendencies" being worked out in Christian history, each of which "has its origin in the Gospel itself."[35] The "indigenizing principle" is grounded on the fact that God accepts us as we are in our cultures and that Jesus desires to make his home among us in our cultures. Thus,

> "if any man is in Christ he is a new creation," does not mean that he starts or continues his life in a vacuum, or that his mind is a blank tablet. It has been formed by his own culture and history, and since God has accepted him as he is, his Christian mind will continue to be influenced by what was in it before. And this is as true for groups as for persons. All churches are culture churches — including our own.[36]

---

33. Ibid., xvi–xvii.

34. Andrew F. Walls, "New Mission, New Scholarship: Exploring the Old Faith in New Terms," *Journal of African Christian Thought* 9, no. 2 (2006): 23–29 (24–25).

35. Andrew F. Walls, "The Gospel as Prisoner and Liberator of Culture," in *The Missionary Movement in Christian History: Studies in the Transmission of Faith* (Maryknoll, N.Y.: Orbis Books, 1996), 3–15 (7).

36. Ibid., 8.

The other "force in tension with this indigenizing principle" that Walls identifies is "the pilgrim principle, which whispers to [the Christian] that he has no abiding city and warns him that to be faithful to Christ will put him out of step with his society; for that society never existed... which could absorb the word of Christ painlessly into its system."[37] For "God in Christ... takes people [as they are] in order to transform them into what he wants them to be," and transformation of persons and societies does not come without a struggle.

Another way of looking at this process is to see the indigenizing principle as "associat[ing] Christians with the particulars of their culture and group" and the pilgrim principle as "a universalizing factor," "by associating them with things and people outside the culture and group."[38] It is in this respect that Christians of every nation connect with the history of Israel, "the curious continuity of the race of the faithful from Abraham."

The adoption into Israel becomes a "universalizing" factor, bringing Christians of all cultures and ages together through a common inheritance, lest any of us make the Christian faith such a place to feel at home that no one else can live there; and bringing into everyone's society some sort of outside reference.[39]

Seeing Christian history from the perspective of Gospel and culture dynamics throws new light on our understanding of what it means to be one body in Christ, the ideal toward which the Gospel has always tended being described by Walls as "the Ephesian moment."[40] He is referring to that brief period in the earliest church when "the social coming together of people of two cultures [Jewish and Hellenistic] to experience Christ"[41] was to some extent realized, a fruit of the vision and ministry of the apostle Paul in particular, which finds its most extensive exposition in his Epistle to the Ephesians. The moment passed when the church became predominantly Hellenistic. That early achievement, however, now points us to the significance and the challenge of the times in which we live, for "in our own day the Ephesian moment has come again, and come in a richer mode

---

37. Ibid.
38. Ibid., 9.
39. Ibid.
40. Andrew F. Walls, "The Ephesian Moment, at a Crossroads in Christian History," in *The Cross-Cultural Process in Christian History: Studies in the Transmission and Appropriation of Faith* (Maryknoll, N.Y.: Orbis Books, 2002), 72–81.
41. Ibid., 78.

than has ever happened since the first century," with "no longer two, but innumerable, major cultures in the church."[42]

> The Ephesian metaphors of the temple and of the body show each of the culture-specific segments as necessary to the body but as incomplete in itself. Only in Christ does completion, fullness, dwell. And Christ's completion, as we have seen, comes from all humanity, from the translation of the life of Jesus into the lifeways of all the world's cultures and subcultures through history. None of us can reach Christ's completeness on our own. We need each other's vision to correct, enlarge, and focus our own; only together are we complete in Christ.[43]

There is an inherent eschatological dimension to this vision. Walls sees "the work of salvation [as] a historical process that stretches out to the end of the age,"[44] in which Christ's followers are to "disciple the nations" (Matt. 28:19).[45] Just as "discipleship involves the word of the master passing through the disciple's memory and into all the mental and moral processes; the ways of thinking, choosing, deciding," so "discipling a nation involves Christ's entry into the nation's thought, the patterns of relationship within that nation, the way society hangs together, the way decisions are made."[46] Walls makes explicit the eschatological range of this "cultural significance of the Great Commission":

> And the end of the age itself is not . . . an act unrelated to the historical process. . . . It is possible . . . to see the end of the age in terms of summary: the completion of the process of "summing up" the work of redemption in Christ. Thus, the Ephesian letter speaks of "the power that is working in us" (i.e., in the midst of the believing community) being the same as the "mighty strength" demonstrated in Christ's resurrection and exaltation.[47]

The end in view is Revelation 7:

---

42. Ibid.
43. Ibid., 79.
44. Ibid., 73.
45. Andrew F. Walls, "Culture and Conversion in Christian History," in *The Missionary Movement in Christian History: Studies in the Transmission of Faith* (Maryknoll, N.Y.: Orbis Books, 1996), 43–54 (48).
46. Ibid., 50–51.
47. Walls, "The Ephesian Moment," 73–74.

Never before has the Church looked so much like the great multitude whom no man can number out of every nation and tribe and people and tongue. Never before, therefore, has there been so much potential for mutual enrichment and self-criticism, as God causes yet more light and truth to break forth from his word.[48]

The Significance of the Primal Substructure of Christianity

For Andrew Walls, "the conversion of culture entails conversion of religion." "Since religion is bound up with culture, religions have to be converted, as well as cultures."[49] Here we come to one of the unique insights of Andrew Walls, shared with his colleague Harold Turner[50] and taken up and developed particularly with respect to Africa by Kwame Bediako,[51] that "the majority of Christians have always come from a primal background."[52] Lest the term "primal" be misunderstood, Walls is at pains to explain that

it was not intended as a euphemism for "primitive" but rather to designate their historical priority, anteriority to other religions, as well as taking account of their fundamental and elemental character, as they deal with the most basic issues of religion. Such a perspective is to be understood as being devoid of evolutionary undertones. Generally speaking, for example, pastoralists have a firmer idea of the Transcendent God than cultivators, who focus more on land and territorial spirits. Was this why Abraham, a city dweller in Haran, had to be called out into nomadic life before he could hear clearly the call of the Living God? . . . But we need to understand also that primal settings include the Egyptian, Greek, and Roman civilizations, as well as the Inca and Maya, with the implication that primal does not mean necessarily preliterate or lacking in sophisticated technology.[53]

---

48. Walls, "The Gospel as Prisoner and Liberator of Culture," 15.

49. Comments of Andrew F. Walls included in the Editorial of the *Journal of African Christian Thought* 11, no. 2 (2008): 1–2.

50. See Harold Turner, "The Primal Religions of the World and Their Study," *Australian Essays in World Religions* (Bedford Park, Adelaide, South Australia: Australian Association for the Study of Religions, 1997), 27–37.

51. See Kwame Bediako, *Christianity in Africa: The Renewal of a Non-Western Religion* (Maryknoll, N.Y.: Orbis Books, 1995).

52. Comments of Andrew F. Walls included in the Editorial of the *Journal of African Christian Thought* 12, no. 1 (2009): 2.

53. Ibid., 2.

The discernment of this consistent pattern of conversion in Christian history and of affinity between primal and biblical traditions,[54] led to the further realization that "the primal underlay is vital."[55] It continues to be vital from the point of view of both mission and discipleship in the times in which we now live.

> The Christian consciousness of Africa and Asia is likely to reflect the pre-Christian cultural processes, including the pre-Christian religious processes, of these continents.... Christian theology — active, *working* Christian theology — is constructed under the Spirit's guidance from pre-Christian materials. The vessels and hangings of the tabernacle, while divinely directed in the making, consist of Egyptian gold and Egyptian cloth. The most urgent reason for the study of the religious traditions of Africa and Asia, of the Amerindian and the Pacific peoples, is their significance for Christian theology; they are the substratum of the Christian faith and life of the greater number of the Christians of the world.[56]

This is particularly important because

> in the recent past, Christianity and traditional religion operated along parallel tracks, with the result that the primal traditions were only partially converted. What we need to be working for is total conversion, the interpenetration of the two traditions. In other words, we are working for conversion *within* primal religion, rather than conversion *from* it.[57]

His emphasis on the conversion of the primal past, "including the mental maps of the universe with which we all operate,"[58] is not just for Christians from a primal background, but for the benefit of those who operate with world-view maps that reflect "the small-scale, pared-down view of the universe that was characteristic of the European Enlightenment," in its "insistence on the autonomy of the individual self and its sharp distinctions between the empirical world and the world of spirit."[59] Walls's exposure to,

---

54. Andrew F. Walls, "African Christianity in the History of Religions," *Studies in World Christianity* 2, no. 2 (1996): 116–35 (130–31).
55. Walls's comments, "Editorial," (2008): 2.
56. Walls, "New Mission, New Scholarship," 28.
57. Walls's comments, "Editorial," (2009): 2.
58. Ibid., 2.
59. Walls, "Scholarship, Mission and Globalization," 35.

and reflection on, the Christian story in Africa showed him clearly that the Enlightenment world-view map that has informed Western theology for several centuries is inadequate for the theological and missionary tasks of the world church of today. This is one reason why, in Walls's view, the responsibility for the mission theology of the future lies with Christians and churches of the non-West.

> Disciplined, scholarly theology must now venture where the informal theologians have led, bringing an integrated Christian theology and a deep grasp of Scripture to a view of the universe that is shared by a great part of humanity.[60]

This task "has implications for the good and the benefit of the whole body of Christ world-wide...for the sake of the mission of the Gospel of Christ in the world,"[61] as "further expansions of the understanding of Christ are emerging from his present engagement with the cultures of Africa and Asia."[62] In view of this, he sees a new responsibility on the wealthy Western churches to share their resources so that the poorer churches of the non-West may reach their full potential in the task of Christian scholarship.

> It will be a test for the Western church how far these new centers [of Christian scholarship] are granted access to the stockpile of resources in the West. For in Christian scholarship, the cultural generations need each other in the construction of the new temple.[63]

In all these observations calling for deep and far-reaching theological scholarly endeavor and sharing of resources, Andrew Walls is never far from the eschatological vision, that is, the awareness "that the coming of the New Jerusalem means also the revealing of the full stature of Christ,"[64] in which Christians from a primal background have a key role.

Conclusion

In a feature article in *Christianity Today,* Tim Stafford describes Andrew Walls as "probably the most important person you don't know."[65] This

---

60. Ibid., 36.
61. Walls's comments, "Editorial" (2008): 3.
62. Walls, "New Mission, New Scholarship," 28.
63. Walls, "Scholarship, Mission and Globalization," 36.
64. Walls, "New Mission, New Scholarship," 29.
65. Stafford, "A Historian ahead of His Time," 87.

may be truer of the Western Christian and theological scene than of the non-Western Christian scene. The insights that have emerged from Walls's exposure to Africa, the application of scholarly rigor to the elaboration of those insights, and his consistent encouragement of non-Westerners to pursue a vocation in Christian scholarship, have all contributed to making him a revered and respected elder in the far-flung corners of the world to which invitations take him. His insights into Gospel and culture dynamics have the quality of truth that sets people free. For they point to the nonpartial patterns of God's working in history; they encourage Christians of all cultures, and particularly from primal backgrounds, to believe that Jesus wishes to find a home among them; they inspire hope that it is possible to work for the conversion of their cultures and so realize the biblical and eschatological vision. In Andrew Walls's view, the story of World Christianity constitutes a call to us all to embrace the unprecedented Ephesian moment in which we now live:

> The full-grown humanity of Christ requires all the Christian generations, just as it embodies all the cultural variety that six continents can bring. As the writer to the Hebrews puts it, Abraham and the patriarchs have even now not yet reached their goal. They are waiting for "us" (Heb. 11:39–40).[66]

---

66. Walls, "Introduction," xvii.

16

Migration and the
Globalization of Christianity

JEHU J. HANCILES

*It is important to recognize that the missionary is a form of migrant....
The great new fact of our time — and it has momentous consequences
for mission — is that the great migration has now gone into reverse.
There has been a massive movement, which all indications suggest will
continue, from the non-Western to the Western world.*[1]

In the last three to four decades, few scholars have done more than Andrew
Walls to explicate the changing contours of global Christianity and highlight
the dynamic of cross-cultural transmission intrinsic to its global spread. In
one of his most seminal contributions, Walls argues that Christianity owes its
survival as a separate faith to its capacity to expand across cultural frontiers
in a *serial* manner: a process involving successive cross-cultural penetration that renders "each new point on the Christian circumference...a
new potential Christian center."[2] Historically, this means that the faith
has had no fixed "center" but successive "centers" corresponding to several major historical phases or epochs. Thus, unlike the global spread of
Islam, which has been progressively outward from a set geographical and
cultural location, Christianity's serial expansion has produced "a principal
presence in different parts of the world at different times." He identifies six historical phases, each of which stamped its cultural imprint on
the faith:[3]

---

1. Andrew F. Walls, "Mission and Migration: The Diaspora Factor in Christian History,"
Journal of African Christian Thought 5, no. 2 (2002): 6, 10.

2. Andrew F. Walls, "Culture and Coherence in Christian History," *The Missionary Movement in Christian History: Studies in the Transmission of Faith* (Maryknoll, N.Y.: Orbis Books,
1996), 22.

3. Andrew F. Walls, "Christianity," in *A Handbook of Living Religions,* ed. John R.
Hinnells (London: Penguin Books, 1991), 58–73.

1. The Jewish age, marked by *Jewish* practices and ideas.

2. The Hellenistic-Roman age, marked by the idea of *orthodoxy.*

3. The barbarian age, marked by the idea of a *Christian nation.*

4. The western European age, marked by the primacy of the *individual.*

5. The age of expanding Europe and Christian recession, marked by *cross-cultural transplantation* but also accompanied by massive recession from the faith among European peoples.

6. The Southern age, featuring *extensive penetration of new cultures* in Africa, Latin America, the Pacific, and parts of Asia.

Interestingly, when Walls expounds on the interrelatedness of migration and mission in the two-thousand-year history of Christianity, he does so without reference to his six ages thesis. It seems to me, however, that, Walls's theory of Christianity's serial expansion implicitly points to the central role of human migration in the faith's global spread, at least to the extent that each of the six historical phases emerged through extensive cross-cultural penetration and large-scale movement.

Globalization and Migration

In the vigorous debate that continues to whirl around the phenomenon of globalization, it is the economic aspects that invariably generate the most heat and often the least light. Much of the contention and spilling of ink over the nature and impact of globalization has roots in two poorly understood characteristics of the phenomenon.[4] First, that it is intrinsically paradoxical, incorporating countervailing trends or movements — perhaps most evident in the fact that global manifestations are inextricably tied to local expressions. Second, that globalization is multidimensional, which is to say that it is marked by simultaneous processes (economic, cultural, political, and so on) that are both differentiated and interrelated. Most important, patterns or outcomes evident in one dimension, say economic, are not necessarily replicated in the others.

For all the preoccupation with economic globalization, the cultural dimensions of globalization arguably represent the most pervasive and (in

---

4. Definitions of globalization abound. One of the most basic describes it as "the intensification of worldwide social relations which link distant localities in such a way that local happenings are shaped by events occurring many miles away and vice versa." Anthony Giddens, *The Consequence of Modernity* (Stanford, Calif.: Stanford University Press, 1990), 64.

terms of contemporary experience) the most unprecedented dimension of the phenomenon.[5] Undoubtedly, no dimension of globalization is entirely separate and self-sustained. Critical elements of the economic and political are deeply entangled with, and inseparable from, cultural forms. But attentiveness to cultural processes most effectively exposes the role of religious expansion and human migrations in global transformations. Not only are the two profoundly linked but, taken together, they are also among the most potent forms of (cultural) globalization.[6]

The worldwide spread of Christianity in the last five hundred years, from its heartlands in Europe, is a major case in point. The pivotal role of the Western missionary movement in this development — complicated by extensive overlap and collusion with the Western colonial project — is undeniable, though it is often emphasized at the expense of extensive indigenous agency. Undoubtedly, however, this period of global Christian expansion (from 1500 to roughly 1950) marked a new era of global migration movements, mainly dominated by European initiatives and projects. But like all processes of globalization the outcomes were paradoxical and, for the most part, unanticipated. Most significantly, the globalization of Christianity has led not to the worldwide dominance of Western Christendom but to the *reemergence of Christianity as a non-Western religion.*

The Migrant Factor in Christian History

The critical and central role of human migrations in Christianity's worldwide expansion from its modest beginnings to the present remains a surprisingly ignored issue in historical studies of Christian missions. This negligence is partly attributable to the nature of Western missionary enterprise from the early sixteenth century. The Western missionary project was mainly orchestrated through formal organizational structures and extensively aligned with the structures of empire. It also promoted an ideal of the "missionary" as a trained individual sent to a foreign territory by a political sovereign or self-designated missionary body. This specialist model became so entrenched that the image of a "missionary" as a white person sent to a distant land remains universal. Yet, as Mennonite theologian John Yoder argued, "throughout the history of the Christian faith, migrant Christians who settle in new areas

---

5. Cf. David Held et al., *Global Transformations: Politics, Economics and Culture* (Stanford, Calif.: Stanford University Press, 1999), 327.

6. Ibid., 329, 333.

and form settled fellowships that provide long-term witness have formed the main thrust of cross cultural expansion, not the few gifted specialists serving in distant lands, dependent on the superior resources of their church and country."[7]

Andrew F. Walls on Migration and Christian Mission

In an article that appeared in the *Journal of African Christian Thought,* Walls provides a panoramic and penetrating portrayal of the history of global Christian expansion using the framework of migration and mission.[8] Drawing on the biblical account, Walls offers a twofold typology of migration (from the perspective of the migrant): namely, the "Adamic" and the "Abrahamic." The *Adamic* model stands for "disaster, deprivation, and loss," exemplified by the expulsion of the first couple from the Garden of Eden or the Exile. The *Abrahamic* model represents "escape to a superlatively better future," epitomized by the call of Abraham to leave his Mesopotamian city for the land of promise. Where the former is generally "punitive" the latter is "redemptive"; but the two models can overlap, for within the divine economy, disaster can have redemptive purpose.

The article's subtext revolves around the question of whether migration favors or hinders Christian mission. Walls insists that history does not offer a single clear answer. In some historical situations, such as the rapid spread through extensive Jewish Diaspora networks in the first century, migration clearly advanced the spread of the faith. But in other situations migration inhibited or reversed Christian expansion, such as when established Christian communities were crushed or overwhelmed by invasions involving people of other faiths — the spread of Islam providing an obvious case in point.

I would argue, however, that Walls's careful argument can be refined in one sense: migration, generally speaking, may rightly be said to have had a mixed impact on the fortunes of Christianity; but migration *of Christians* has typically contributed to the spread of Christianity.[9] This is true even in some extraordinary instances involving either a single individual or a handful of Christian migrants. When, in the middle of the third century, Dionysius of

---

7. See John Howard Yoder, "Christian Missions at the End of an Era," *Christian Living* 8 (1961): 12–15.

8. Walls, "Mission and Migration," 3–11.

9. Massive out-migration of Christians can contribute to the decline of Christian presence in a particular locale, but the migrants also take their religious beliefs and practices with them, potentially extending its impact.

Alexandria was banished to the remote Libyan desert, his preaching led to a number of conversions among people who had never heard the Gospel. In a better known example, the shipwrecked Lebanese Christians Frumentius and Aedesius played a key role in the evangelization of Aksum (modern Ethiopia) in the fourth century.

By making the case that migration is often a crucial factor in Christian expansion, Walls's overview enriches our understanding of the tremendous capacity of migrant movement to advance the spread of Christianity. Thus, it was the dispersion of Christians through persecution that triggered the first Gentile mission, an event that took the faith outside the quite distinct Jewish world in which it was born. The spread of Christianity within the Roman Empire, both east and west, often involved violent migrant displacement through persecution, captivity of Christians by invaders, or, more peaceably, use of extensive trade networks traversing land and sea. The remarkably extensive silk route connecting Europe and Asia allowed Christian families from the church of the East to journey across the Asian land mass; while sea routes placed Christian diaspora groups as far away as India. Missionary migration, explains Walls, was a prominent characteristic of the church of the East, not least because Eastern Christian spirituality "produced a corps of devoted people able and willing to travel immense distances and live under the harshest conditions."[10]

In time, large-scale Mongol invasions and the purposive spread of Islam eclipsed much of Eastern and Asian Christianity. By 1500 Europe — where the last Muslim stronghold of Granada was reconquered in 1492 — had emerged as the dominant expression of the Christian faith. Remarkably, this development coincided with the European age of overseas exploration and the "discovery" of lands and peoples whose existence was previously unknown to the European world.

European migration over the next four and a half centuries — labeled "the great migration" by Walls — was unprecedented in its scale and velocity. From 1800 to 1925, between 50 and 60 million, or one-in-five, Europeans moved to overseas destinations. By 1915, some 21 percent of Europeans resided outside Europe, and Europeans effectively occupied or settled in over a third of the inhabited world.[11] Technological advancement (notably in ocean travel), economic ambition, population explosion, missionary purpose

---

10. Walls, "Mission and Migration," 6.
11. W. M. Spellman, *The Global Community: Migration and the Making of the Modern World* (Stroud: Sutton Publishing, 2002), 73, 75.

and sheer adventurism all played their part. By the time the dust settled, Europeans had appropriated and occupied huge portions of the Americas, Africa, Asia, and Oceania. European colonial and industrial needs also saw the intercontinental transfer of sizeable African and Asian populations to colonial possessions in Africa and the Americas.

These phenomenal European migrations provide powerful illustration of the link between migration and mission. Walls sees the European missionary movement as "a semi-detached appendix to the great migration."[12] This may be an understatement. It is hugely significant that the largest migration movement on record coincided in direction and duration with the most extensive missionary movement in history. European missionaries unquestionably formed a segment of the massive surge of European movement which characterized the seventeenth to early twentieth centuries. As I have argued elsewhere, the tide and flow of European missionary activity was a significant undercurrent in the much broader sweep of migration movements.[13]

Migration and the Growth of Non-Western Christianities

The nature and extent of the European missionary contribution to the extraordinary growth of Christianity in the non-Western world remains a matter of debate. Exaggeration of the impact of Western missionary involvement is common, and usually a corollary of the mistaken notion that European hegemony or empire was indispensable for spread of the Gospel. In reality, the Western missionary movement acted as the initial stimulus (a "primary detonator," as Walls puts it) rather than a singular driving force in the growth of the indigenous church. "The foreign missionary," Walls argues, "was sent to persuade, to demonstrate, to offer — but could not compel." Indeed, "some substantial segments of the accession occurred without the presence of [Western] missionaries, or . . . after the missionary presence had ceased."[14] Western missionary agents brought the message of the Gospel to most parts, but it was largely non-Western agents (who quickly outnumbered foreign missionaries by a significant margin) that carried it forward and secured the establishment of Christianity.

---

12. Walls, "Mission and Migration," 8.
13. Jehu J. Hanciles, *Beyond Christendom: Globalization, African Migrations, and the Transformation of the West* (Maryknoll, N.Y.: Orbis Books, 2008), 167–69.
14. Walls, "Mission and Migration," 8.

Non-Western initiatives too, as Walls attests, were bolstered by migration movements that typically occurred outside the European orbit. Among the most remarkable was the missionary impulse that emerged within the black church in America in the late eighteenth and early nineteenth centuries. America's first overseas missionary was Rev. George Liele (1750–1825), a former slave and black Baptist preacher who settled in Kingston, Jamaica, in 1783. Demobilized black soldiers who had fought with the British army during the American Revolutionary War ended up in various parts of the West Indies, where they evangelized black (plantation) populations and established churches. In 1792, a group numbering more than a thousand set sail from Nova Scotia for Sierra Leone, where they established the first Protestant church in tropical Africa and sent out evangelists among the indigenous population. A vision of missionary emigration among black Christians in America also contributed to the creation of Liberia and stimulated numerous missionary efforts. Between 1880 and 1900 the African Methodist Episcopal Church, the largest black denomination in America, had at least sixty missionaries in Africa.[15]

Within Africa itself, internal migrations, voluntary and involuntary, augmented the spread of Christianity. In West Africa, for instance, the Sierra Leone colony (which became home to tens of thousands of recaptured slaves under a British abolition scheme) became a major source of missionary migrants, as Christianized former slaves and their descendants returned to their homelands (or traveled further afield) with the Christian message. Elsewhere on the continent, migrant movement and population displacement linked to the colonial economy also fostered considerable African migrations that contributed to the emergence of new African renewal movements and missionary initiatives. Often, as traditional coping mechanisms were overwhelmed by the social upheavals engendered by urbanization and intensified migration, prophet-healing movements proliferated as one means of handling the traumas associated with rapid change. These too expanded the range and reach of Christianity.

The strong link between migration and mission was also manifest in other parts of the world. Under the brutal crush of Japanese rule (1907–57), the Korean Church sent many missionaries outside the Korean peninsula to Manchuria, Shanghai, Peking, Mongolia, and even California, often to work

---

15. Walter L. Williams, *Black Americans and the Evangelization of Africa, 1877–1900* (Madison: University of Wisconsin Press, 1982), 44; William E. Phipps, *William Sheppard: Congo's African American Livingstone* (Louisville: Geneva Press, 2002), 58.

among Korean immigrants.[16] Within the vast expanse of China, the migration movement of Chinese Christians and families was a major factor in the spread of the Gospel. Indeed, the remarkable Watchman Nee (1903–72) championed "evangelism by migration," whereby Christian families would move to unreached areas of China and beyond, and establish local churches. Pacific Christianity, adds Walls, "is closely linked with the activity of Polynesian Christians, moving not only between islands of their region, but from Polynesia to Melanesia."

Post-1960 Global Migrations and the Non-Western Missionary Movement

As mentioned previously, the globalization of Christianity has also witnessed its transformation into a non-Western religion. The story is now all too familiar. Christianity's rate of expansion over the last hundred years exceeds any other period in its two-thousand-year history, and, significantly, much of this growth has taken place in parts of the world where Christian presence or representation was marginal to start with. In Africa, for instance, the percentage of Christians grew from roughly 9 percent in 1900 to 45 percent by 2000. The same period witnessed a dramatic erosion of Christian faith and presence in the Western world, hitherto the standard-bearer of the faith. Of the ten countries with the fastest growth between 1910 and 2010, six are in Africa and four in Asia.[17] By the closing decades of the twentieth century Africa and Latin America had emerged as the new heartlands of the faith. This stupendous development was not only unimaginable as late as the mid-twentieth century, but it also remained largely undetected until the late 1960s. Andrew Walls was one of a handful of Western scholars, all engaged in assessing emergent forms of African Christianity at the time, who first called attention to the dramatic shift taking place in global Christianity.

It would take a few more decades before the capacity of the new heartlands of the faith to produce a missionary movement of extraordinary scale and vigor became apparent. But by the start of this century it was increasingly evident that transformations within global Christianity combined

---

16. Timothy Kiho Park, "Korean Christian World Mission: The Missionary Movement of the Korean Church," in *Missions from the Majority World: Progress, Challenges, and Case Studies*, ed. Enoch Wan and Michael Pocock (Pasadena, Calif.: William Carey Library, 2009), 100–101.

17. "World Christianity, 1910–2010," *International Bulletin of Missionary Research* 34, no. 1 (2010): pages.

with a new era of global migratory flows had given rise to unprecedented non-Western missionary activity, including forms of outreach into Western societies. Some of this involved bold formal initiatives by the burgeoning churches and ministries in West Africa, South Korea, and Latin America. But, partly due to the pivotal role of migration, vast dimensions of the movement are unstructured, haphazard, and somewhat clandestine.

Since the 1960s the world has witnessed an extraordinary upsurge of migrations and people movements, to unprecedented levels.[18] By 2009, according to U.N. estimates, there were 214 million international migrants (people living outside their country of birth) in the world[19] — up from 191 million in 2005. Significantly, the vast majority of international migrants come from the non-Western world and the main destination countries include the European nations that had been the main source of international migrants in previous centuries. U.N. data further indicates that up to 60 percent of international migrants are to be found in developed countries; with Europe and North America home to more than half (or 56 percent). The United States, with 42.8 million international migrants, has the highest of any country — more than the next four (Russian Federation, Germany, Saudi Arabia, and Canada) combined.[20] The fact that the more developed regions of the world continue to show the largest increases in migrant stock substantiates the fact that South-North migration movement (in a reversal of pre-1960s flows) remains a major strand within global migrations. And, given the nature of global demographic imbalances and global economic disparities, this trend is unlikely to change significantly in the near future.

Even more important, to the extent that this reversal of global migration flows occurred at roughly the same time as the momentous "shift" in global Christianity's demographic and cultural center of gravity to the southern continents, we are confronted with a confluence of historical developments that add up to a striking reality. As in the previous five centuries, the predominant strands of global migratory flows are oriented so as to foster missionary movement from the heartlands of the faith; in this case from major centers in Africa, Latin America, and Asia to Europe, North America, and the Middle East. To put it more clearly, the nature and direction of current global

---

18. Stephen Castles and Mark J. Miller, *The Age of Migration: International Population Movements in the Modern World* (New York: Guilford Press, 1998).

19. *Trends in International Migrant Stock: The 2008 Revision* (United Nations, 2009).

20. *International Migration 2009: Wall Chart* (United Nations, 2009).

migratory flows are such that massive numbers of non-Western Christian migrants in Western countries are thrust into missionary action.

Many, for instance, have been drawn to the wealthy oil-producing states in the Middle East, including the Arab Gulf States. By the early 1990s, foreign workers in these oil rich states (mainly from Africa and Asia) numbered over 7 million.[21] Enoch Wan and Joy Tira point out that thousands of household Filipino maids, many of whom are Christian, are entrusted with the welfare and oversight of children in affluent Arab families[22] — with at least notional missionary possibilities. Writes Peruvian theologian Samuel Escobar:

> In our time..., travelers from poor countries who migrate for economic survival bring the Christian message and missionary initiative with them. Moravians from Curaçao have gone to Holland, Baptists from Jamaica emigrated to Central America and to England, Christian women from the Philippines work in Muslim countries, Haitian believers have gone to Canada, and Latin American missionaries are going to Japan, Australia, and the United States. This missionary presence and activity has been significant even though it rarely reaches reports and stories in the media of institutional missionary activity.[23]

The Missionary Encounter with a Post-Christendom West

It is impossible to gain an adequate grasp of the nature, scope, and crucial agents in the burgeoning non-Western missionary movement without paying close attention to global migratory flows. As Walls attests, "the missionary is a form of migrant."[24] Of even greater import is the understanding that every Christian migrant is a potential missionary. Extraordinary immigrant influx into Western societies has brought with it an unprecedented volume and diversity of religious expressions and practices. Among the swelling tide of guest workers, students, labor migrants, asylum seekers, family reunification migrants, political and economic refugees who constitute the new immigrant population and their descendants are numerous Christians. And, in a context where homegrown Christianity is experiencing dramatic decline in adherents

---

21. Spellman, *The Global Community,* 163.
22. Wan and Pocock, *Missions from the Majority World,* no. 17, 401.
23. Samuel Escobar, *Changing Tides: Latin America and World Mission Today* (Maryknoll, N.Y.: Orbis Books, 2002), 163.
24. Walls, "Mission and Migration," 6.

and influence, the understanding that each Christian immigrant is (biblically speaking) a potential missionary is of singular importance.

For now, the significance of Christian migrants is typically overlooked in the heated public debate about immigration. In Europe and the United States (the two top destinations of international migrants), the public discourse on immigration focuses almost exclusively on Muslim immigrants and illegal immigration, respectively. Yet in both contexts, the dramatic rise in the numbers of Christian immigrants not only augments Christian existence, albeit in ways that trouble or contrast sharply with homegrown forms, but also signifies missionary movement.

In the case of Europe, a 2003 study found that almost half (48.5 percent) of the estimated 24 million migrants in the EU were Christian or "belonged to Christian churches."[25] While it is true that new Muslim immigrants are more prominent in some countries, the same is also true of Christian immigrants. In Italy, for instance, the latter represent at least half the Protestant population.[26] In the event, the flood of Christian immigrants has infused moribund churches and denominations throughout Europe with new vitality. For the most part, however, Christian immigrants have established independent congregations, often in major cities. Presently, the largest and fastest-growing churches were established by African migrants: notably, Sunday Adelaja's twenty-thousand-member-strong Embassy of God in the Ukraine (the largest church in Europe) and Matthew Ashimolowo's Kingsway Christian Center in England. In truth, Adelaja's Embassy of God is clearly exceptional in rate of growth (from seven members to twenty-five thousand members in seven years) and composition (it is 99 percent white).[27] But research indicates that most immigrant churches, notably those founded by African migrants, subscribe to a strong missionary vision and harbor firm commitment to cross-cultural outreach.

In a groundbreaking study of the missionary outlook and approaches of non-Western Christian migrants in Europe, Währisch-Oblau confirms that the idea of being sent by God as missionaries to Europe is prominent in the immigrant pastors' "expatriate narratives."[28] In a context where

---

25. Darrell Jackson and Alessia Passarelli, *Mapping Migration: Mapping Churches' Response* (Brussels: World Council of Churches, 2008), 29. An estimated 30.9 percent were Muslims, and about 20.5 percent belonged to other religions.

26. Ibid., 29.

27. Sunday Adelaja, *Church Shift* (Lake Mary, Fla.: Charisma House, 2008), 99.

28. Claudia Währisch-Oblau, *The Missionary Self-Perception of Pentecostal/Charismatic Church Leaders from the Global South in Europe: Bringing Back the Gospel* (Boston: Brill, 2009), 226–27, 239–42, 278–83.

anti-immigrant sentiments are widespread and attitudes to the presence of nonwhite is generally hostile, the immigrants' missionary outlook directly challenges popular sentiment. Whereas public discourse depicts immigrants as a threat to society and an unwelcome burden, the Christian immigrants' strong sense of missionary purpose explicitly projects immigration as a source of blessing rather than a problem and recasts the migrant as an agent of positive change.[29]

Even so, immigrant churches in Europe, or "new mission churches" as they are termed, must reckon with formidable challenges. Some are self-inflicted, as in the case of migrant pastors whose brand of spiritual warfare precludes meaningful cross-cultural preparation or adequate language learning, thus forestalling cultural integration and, by extension, cross-cultural missionary engagement. But even for the most adaptable and missionary-conscious, successful cross-cultural outreach must overcome daunting obstacles: including racial rejection, social marginalization, and aggressive secularism.[30] That said, there is an argument to be made that, in some instances, the most insidious barrier that new mission churches must overcome comes not from the non-/post-Christian population but from homegrown churches. In the German context, for instance, a striking clash of worldviews between immigrant Christianity (marked by charismatic leadership, evangelistic emphasis, and a preoccupation with spiritual power/warfare) and homegrown Christianity (defined by cultural identity, formalized structures, and Enlightenment rationality) is palpably evident. In many cases, this disparity has engendered "mutual disqualification" and barriers of mistrust that all but preclude meaningful collaboration or harmonious engagement in the mission of God.[31]

The American experience provides striking contrast with Europe's in certain details; but the overall trends are not entirely different. America is the definitive immigrant nation. Not only does it owe its existence to Christian migration, its religious heritage and remarkable foreign missions tradition also reflect the fervent religiosity and dynamism instilled by a recurrent cycle of immigration. Massive Christian immigration throughout the nineteenth century is perhaps the most important single reason why the decline of Christianity in America at the end of the twentieth century is less substantial

---

29. Ibid., 260, 317, 333.
30. Cf. Jackson and Passarelli, *Mapping Migration*, 29; Währisch-Oblau, *The Missionary Self-Perception*, 317, 333.
31. Währisch-Oblau, *The Missionary Self-Perception*, 312.

than Europe's. America, as Andrew Walls comments, simply "started its Christian decline from a much higher base that Europe did."[32] Even with this exceptional history, the impact on the American religious landscape of rapidly proliferating immigrant congregations since the 1970s is nothing short of extraordinary.

The Christian element in post-1960 migration to the United States was more substantial than that in any other Western nation. Research indicates that up to two-thirds of American's new immigrants self-identify as Christian;[33] and this finding correlates with the fact that the main source countries of immigration (notably Mexico, the Philippines, and Jamaica) are overwhelmingly Christian. Through massive immigration, Hispanic, Chinese, and African congregations are also growing vigorously. The impact is most striking within the Roman Catholic Church. Not only do Hispanics now account for a third of all Catholics in the United States,[34] they have also infused American Roman Catholicism with Hispanic forms of piety and greater emphasis on charismatic practices. But across all Protestant groups (mainline or evangelical), congregations or "ethnic" churches formed by the new immigrants are the main centers of vitality and growth.

Perhaps the most obvious impact of large-scale Christian immigration is the de-Europeanization of American Christianity.[35] In thousands of churches and Christian communities across the country, the language of worship, theological orientation, and modes of interaction draw on decidedly foreign elements and seek to replicate non-Western preferences. The extent of cross-cultural impact is less easy to determine. Missionary consciousness and commitment to cross-cultural outreach is stronger among some groups than others. Korean immigrants in the United States have formed churches at a faster rate than any other immigrant group — up to thirty-five hundred churches throughout the country by 2007. But Korean churches tend to be monocultural, though second-generation church plants generally reflect

32. Walls, "Mission and Migration," 10.

33. Guillermina Jasso et al., "Exploring the Religious Preferences of Recent Immigrants to the United States: Evidence from the New Immigrant Survey Pilot," in *Religion and Immigration: Christian, Jewish, and Muslim Experiences in the United States*, ed. Yvonne Yazbeck Haddad, Jane I. Smith, and John L. Esposito (Walnut Creek, Calif.: AltaMira Press, 2003), 221; also R. Stephen Warner, "Coming to America," *Christian Century* (February 10, 2004): 20–23.

34. *Changing Faiths: Latinos and the Transformation of American Religion* (The Pew Research Center, 2007), 12; see also Robert D. Putnam, *Bowling Alone: The Collapse and Revival of American Community* (New York: Simon & Schuster, 2000), 76.

35. See Fenggang Yang and Helen Ebaugh, "Transformations in New Immigrant Religions and Their Global Implications," *American Sociological Review* 66 (2001): 269–88.

higher levels of cultural adaptation and a multiethnic composition. Here, as in Europe, immigrant congregations have flourished because they help to preserve ethnic identity. But they have also flourished as sites of religious conversion and religious renewal.

Due in some measure to committed evangelism among fellow immigrants, church attendance within many immigrant groups is higher than within the same group in their homeland. Roughly one in three Hispanic Christians (31 percent) report that they "share their faith at least weekly" — among the subset of Hispanic Pentecostals the rate is 70 percent.[36] My own research among African immigrant churches also revealed high levels of evangelistic commitment. Moreover, the most gifted among African immigrant pastors inevitably internationalize their ministries and often adopt a vision for cross-cultural outreach.[37]

The Limitations of Old Measurements

The long-term missionary impact, if not the _missionary function,_ of the hordes of Christian migrants and their descendants in Western societies remains unclear. While the missionary-mindedness of immigrant Christians and congregations is well attested, the challenges to cross-cultural mission are just as significant. The outlook remains complex. There is also strong indication that the outreach capacity of new mission churches increases over time with critical adaptation to the cultural environment and naturaliza-tion, which in turn indicates that the next generation may hold the key to greater missionary effectiveness. Yet the point needs to be made that even by evangelizing other immigrants — most of whom are beyond the outreach of Western churches in the countries they now reside — the new immigrant congregations are making a significant contribution to the growth of Christianity in the Western world.

Much confusion about the nature and potential impact of this non-Western missionary movement arises from assessments that are dependent on models and strategies associated with the much better known Western missionary movement. But the new reality and its unique elements call for fresh assessments. The long-term preoccupation with numerical quotients (numbers of agents, churches, baptisms, etc.) so dominant within Western

---

36. _Changing Faiths,_ 29.
37. Cf. Hanciles, _Beyond Christendom,_ 344–49.

missiological assessments was acceptable because it mainly applied to structured, planned, efforts. It remains helpful; but, by itself, it can yield data that is profoundly misleading. As a case in point, the claim that North America and Europe "continue to send the bulk of cross-cultural missionaries (over 65 percent)"[38] only makes sense if "cross-cultural" means "international," given the fact that the vast majority of non-Western missionary agents do not have to leave their country of birth to engage in "cross-cultural" missionary activity.

The complexity and multiplicity of the new missionary initiatives emerging out of the non-Western world defy straightforward analysis, in part because so much of it is informal and covert but also because of embeddedness in complex global migratory flows. In truth, empirical assessment of a phenomenon as dynamic and organic as missionary action will always be subject to profound limitations. But in part due to forces of globalization, the Christian missionary landscape has never looked more complex and impenetrable. The combination of extraordinary transformations within global Christianity, the sheer multiplicity of initiatives that characterize new missionary movements, and the limitations of traditional instruments of measurement means that a true picture remains beyond reach. It is God's mission after all and, in that sense, it will always be bigger than any particular assessment of it.

More than the work of any other scholar in our time, Andrew Walls's perceptive assessment of these global trends from both a biblical and a historical perspective furnishes us with an invaluable interpretative framework. As he makes clear, the current age of migration links the Western and non-Western worlds more concretely than ever before and raises the possibility that the initiatives and ministries associated with new Christian migrants will "advance Christian mission" in both worlds. This, he points out, "opens the dazzling possibility that the fullness of the stature of Christ, that . . . is reached as people of diverse ethnicities and cultures are united in the body of Christ, could be realized in our time."[39] Alas, as he recognizes almost wistfully, the new trends may also lead to further fracture of the Body of Christ through "self-seeking and neglect." What is certain is that the future of the Christian faith, as it was in the past, is bound up with that most basic of traits of the human condition: migration.

38. "Missionaries Worldwide, 1910–2010," *International Bulletin of Missionary Research* 34, no. 1 (2010): 31.

39. Walls, "Mission and Migration," 11.

Conclusion

The Emergence of World Christianity and the Remaking of Theology

KWAME BEDIAKO

A Changed Christian World: A Fully World Religion

In 1974 John Mbiti of Kenya, probably the most influential theologian of Africa in the twentieth century, observed that "the centers of the Church's universality are no longer in Geneva, Rome, Athens, Paris, London, New York, but Kinshasa, Buenos Aires, Addis Ababa, and Manila."[1] I do not think he was attaching any particular significance to the specific cities he cited; what was important were the terms in which he stated his observation. It was "the Church's universality" that has found new centers elsewhere, beyond the West. Christianity, a religious faith that has been universal in principle from its origins, has become universal in history for the first time, a fact that makes Christianity "unique among the world's religions and is a new feature of the Christian faith itself."[2]

In other words, a situation that had subsisted for a millennium of history and gave rise to the perception that the Christian faith was the religion of the West has now been succeeded by a new realization that the faith is to be more accurately understood as a "non-Western religion," in that we are now able to describe Christianity as a truly world faith, present on all continents and in virtually all countries. In what was probably the last published work under his name, *A World History of Christianity,* which he edited, the late Adrian

This essay was presented as a public lecture at Calvin College on July 19, 2007. It is used with permission from the Nagel Institute at Calvin College.

1. John Mbiti, "Theological Impotence and the Universality of the Church," *Lutheran World* 21, no. 3 (1974); republished in *Mission Trends 3: Third World Theologies,* ed. Gerald Anderson and Thomas Stransky (Grand Rapids: Eerdmans, 1976) 6–18. For a discussion of Mbiti's idea, see Kwame Bediako, *Christianity in Africa — The Renewal of a Non-Western Religion* (Maryknoll, N.Y.: Orbis Books, 1995), 154ff.

2. Andrew F. Walls, "The Christian Tradition in Today's World," in *Religion in Today's World,* ed. F. B. Whaling (Edinburgh: T. & T. Clark, 1987), 76.

Hastings commented: "One could reasonably claim that it [Christianity] is in historical reality, the one and only fully world religion."[3] What Dr. Mbiti discerned thirty years ago has now entered general consciousness and is no longer controversial.

Understanding Our New Christian Reality

All this means it is important that as Christian scholars and committed Christians engaged in the witness to the Christian faith and in the affirmation of Christian action in the world, we understand the phenomenon of this new Christian reality and what lessons it may hold for our vocation. In particular, as those who affirm divine providence in human history, it is important that we understand our new Christian world in a way that is consistent with Christian history and which, by illuminating that history, helps point us into our future. This is because it is also possible to misread and misunderstand.

It is undeniable that what has occurred is a reconfiguration of the cultural manifestation of the Christian faith in the world, a phenomenon that one may also describe as a shift in the center of gravity of Christianity. The notion of shifts in the center of gravity of Christianity in the course of Christian history, as I use it, I owe to Dr. Andrew F. Walls, who in our time, is widely regarded as the most perceptive interpreter of Christian history. A recent article in *Christianity Today* described him as "a historian ahead of his time" and "probably the most important person you don't know!"[4] Derived from the evidence of Christian history itself, the notion of shifts refers to a series of dominant cultural shifts.

The very first disciples who gathered around our Lord Jesus and were constituted into the faith community on the Day of Pentecost were all, with only a few exceptions, Jews. They did not even call themselves Christians. Yet by the time that the last apostle was dying in the late first century, the majority of the followers of Christ were from a Hellenistic background. Whatever one thought of the immoral Corinthians or the fickle Galatians or the unstable Colossians in the pages of the New Testament, they were the future. From the second century onward, for nearly three centuries, Christianity, now the name of their peculiar movement, became associated with

---

3. Adrian Hastings, "Introduction," in *A World History of Christianity*, ed. Adrian Hastings (Grand Rapids: Eerdmans, 1999), 1.

4. Tim Stafford, "A Historian Ahead of His Time," *Christianity Today* (February 2007): 86–89 (87).

the Graeco-Roman world of the Mediterranean, outside of Palestine, though it also expanded eastward into Iran and southward into Upper Egypt and Ethiopia, where Christianity has remained unbroken till our time.

Then, following the sack of Rome and the collapse of the Western Roman Empire, the center of gravity would shift to the tribal peoples of northern and western Europe, whom the Greeks and Romans called "Barbarians." The subsequent phases of Christian history to our time, marked by the migration of European peoples, various missionary enterprises and their interweaving with the histories of economic, political, and imperial interests are familiar to us.

In our own time, it is a shift from North to South, from the northern continents of [Western] Europe and North America, or the North Atlantic, to the southern continents of Latin America, parts of Asia and the Pacific, and Africa. It is generally accepted that over 60 percent of all professing Christians now are found in the South, and that percentage continues to grow.

In the preface to the collection of essays titled *The Changing Face of Christianity — Africa, the West and the World,* which he edited with Lamin Sanneh, Joel Carpenter notes:

> Today, Christianity is a global faith but one that is more vigorous and vibrant in the global South than among the world's richer and more powerful regions. It presents a remarkable case of "globalization from below" rather than imposition from the world's great powers.[5]

Joel Carpenter's insight points to a significance in the present shift beyond the obvious demographic evidence. It has to do with the recognition that Christianity now lives through other cultures, in other historical, social, economic and political realities than those that appear to prevail in the West. This means that we may not too easily assume that the present universalizing of Christianity partakes in all respects in the Western-driven project of globalization, which would reduce the acceptance of Christianity to little more than the consumption of a "cultural product honed in the West over centuries,"[6] as some analysts argue.

---

5. Joel Carpenter, "Preface," in *The Changing Face of Christianity — Africa, the West and the World,* ed. Lamin Sanneh and Joel C. Carpenter (New York: Oxford University Press, 2005), vii.

6. Paul Gifford, *African Christianity — Its Public Role* (London: Hurst & Co., 1998), 322.

Our Changed Christian World
as the Logic of Christian History

In a lecture here at Calvin a few years ago, I suggested that the evidence of Christian history indicates a correlation between each shift in Christianity's center of gravity and some critical and decisive religious, cultural, social and other developments within the matrix of Christianity's dominance at the time that threaten the survival of the faith.[7] I wish to recall this argument and take the discussion a little further. On this understanding, the first cultural shift enabled the faith to escape being extinguished as a sect within Judaism when the Jewish state and its religious structures were demolished with the fall of Jerusalem in A.D. 70. The next major shift made it possible for the faith to outlast the fall of the Western Roman Empire, so that it would not be identified as simply the religion of the "civilized" Mediterranean basin, as against the "barbarian" world of the ancient northern and western Europeans. Similarly, the present shift in the center of gravity may have secured for Christianity a future that would otherwise be precarious in the secularized cultural environment of the modern West. It has given the faith a new lease on life in the predominantly religious worlds of Africa, Latin America, the Pacific and parts of Asia.

In these regions of the world, shared world-views have retained affinities with the living world of the Bible and the experience of the reality and actuality of the Living God, as Jesus and the apostles experienced them as recorded in the Bible. These affinities should not be understood to mean that these societies are "premodern," or "unsophisticated," as some observers conclude.[8] Rather, modern conceptual maps used to interpret and understand existence, community, and our place in the universe, which are based on a severely pared-down Enlightenment, secular view of life, may need to be revised.

As far back as 1974, German theologian Karl Rahner, in *The Shape of the Church to Come,* wrote that the modern Western world, as "a milieu that has become unchristian," was in need of reevangelization. Thus, when we consider the successive shifts in the center of gravity of Christianity,

---

7. See, for a published version, Kwame Bediako, "Africa and Christianity on the Threshold of the Third Millennium: The Religious Dimension," *African Affairs* (Centenary Edition) 99, no. 395 (2000): 303–23.

8. See, for instance, Philip Jenkins, *The New Faces of Christianity — Believing the Bible in the Global South* (New York: Oxford University Press, 2006).

it becomes evident that both *accession* and *recession* belong within Christian religious history and that there is accordingly no permanent center of Christianity. Every center is a potential periphery and every periphery is a potential center.

But another way to describe recession and accession within Christian history is to speak of Christian *decay* and Christian *vitality.* Decay does not necessarily mean an absence of Christian manifestations, but an attrition of robust discipleship. Alongside Christian vitality, there is always the phenomenon of counterfeit, to which Jesus refers in the Parable of the Weeds (Matt. 13:24–30). Thus the history of Christian mission and of Christian churches in all places and periods gives ample evidence to show that the name "Christian" covers a considerable diversity of phenomena. The content and meanings derived from the application of the name have not always been uniform, or even mutually recognizable among various groups of Christians. We may not presume that the Christian world of our time is any different. We may not be worse than earlier generations, but it helps to be attentive to the distortions and discrepancies of our time too.

The Scandal of the Evangelical Conscience: Why Are Christians Living Just Like the Rest?[9] a book published a couple of years ago, does not give a flattering account of Christian faith and conduct in North America. But the phenomenon described is not limited to North American Christianity. With regard to my own home country, Ghana, one analyst who describes the country as having "a recognisably Christian" ethos,[10] has identified preachers in whose sermons " 'Take up your cross daily and follow me' does not exist and is unthinkable"; and he calls them "Ghana's new Christianity."[11] It is important to understand these apparently similar phenomena in their specific contexts. The first describes a situation of Christian decay. The second describes the counterfeit backlash to Christian vitality. The point, then, is not that the new centers of Christian vitality are without imperfections; rather, their imperfections are diverse. And yet they disclose recognizable features of Christian history.

In this connection, what the present reality of the Christian world discloses above all, and on a scale not seen before, is that no Christian history

---

9. Ron Sider, *The Scandal of the Evangelical Conscience: Why Are Christians Living Just Like the Rest?* (Grand Rapids: Baker Books, 2005).

10. Gifford, *African Christianity,* 110.

11. Paul Gifford, "A View of Ghana's New Christianity," in *The Changing Face of Christianity,* ed. Lamin Sanneh and Joel Carpenter, 85. See also Gifford, *Ghana's New Christianity: Pentecostalism in a Globalising African Economy* (London: Hurst & Co., 2003).

anywhere ever ceases to be a *missionary* history, in which Christians never cease to be called upon to apply the mind of Christ to the realities, questions and dilemmas of that time. Accordingly, in the present situation it becomes less helpful to speak of a "global Christianity" whereby, presuming a contest for "global" hegemony, the new centers of Christian vitality are represented as "the next Christendom" — a relocation of power from Western churches, and therefore a global threat to the West.[12] Rather, it is more helpful and indeed more accurate, to recognize the emergence of a "World Christianity," the result of diverse indigenous responses to the Christian faith in various regions of the world, the emergence of a positive polycentrism, in which the many centers have an opportunity to learn from each other.[13] It is possible, therefore, to see in the emergence of the "World Christianity" of our time the logic of Christian history itself. This leads us to recognize a connection between Christian history and Christian theology.

Christian History as Mission and the Birth of Theology

If the World Christianity of our time discloses the logic of Christian history, it is the logic of Christian history as mission. In other words, it is mission as the effort to establish the credentials and validity of the Christian faith, not only in terms of the religious and spiritual universe in which Christians habitually operate, but also and especially in terms of the religious and spiritual worlds that persons of other faiths inhabit,[14] which produces theology. This means that it is mission that engenders theology, which, in turn, should sustain mission. There is, then, a symbiotic relationship between mission as "cultural crossing" and theology as the process whereby the faith appropriated is lived, embodied, and communicated. Inasmuch as the several historical shifts of the heartlands of the Christian faith, as noted earlier, have been cultural crossings, they are privileged moments for understanding the meanings inherent in the faith, that is, for the development of theology.

---

12. See Philip Jenkins, *The Next Christendom: The Coming of Global Christianity* (New York: Oxford University Press, 2002).

13. Stafford, "A Historian Ahead of His Time," 86; Kwame Bediako, "Whose Religion Is Christianity? Reflections on Opportunities and Challenges for Christian Theological Scholarship as Public Discourse — The African Dimension," *Journal of African Christian Thought* 9, no. 2 (2006): 43–48.

14. Kwame Bediako, "How Is Jesus Christ Lord? Aspects of an Evangelical Christian Apologetics in the Context of African Religious Pluralism," *Exchange, Journal of Missiological and Ecumenical Research* 25, no. 1 (1996): 27–42.

It would not take extensive argument to demonstrate that this is the consistent picture in the New Testament. Certainly, what we regularly understand as the theology of the New Testament is inconceivable apart from the cultural crossing from the Jewish world into Hellenistic culture. In fact, it is possible to describe the books of the New Testament as the authoritative documents illustrative of the major mission activity of the apostolic era; without that mission activity, the books and the theological teachings they have imparted to succeeding Christian generations would not exist.

The Reformation in World Christian History

It would be possible to study and understand, for example, the Reformation of the sixteenth century as also involving in some important respects a "cultural crossing," even if it was largely confined to the European arena. It involved a cultural crossing of the Christian faith from the "civilized" and hallowed meanings framed, learned, and transmitted only in Latin, to the universe of vernacular mother-tongue meanings inhabited by the northern "barbarians."

Everyone familiar with the history of the church in Europe knows of the long dominance of Latin in the Christian history of the ancient peoples of northern and western Europe. Since Latin was not for them a vernacular language, but rather a "special" language for Christians — the "language for Scripture, liturgy, and learning" — this meant that as people were brought into Christianity, Latin functioned not so much as the "motor for the penetration of their cultures; rather it was a vehicle for learning to appropriate and express a new identity,"[15] which originally had not belonged to them. In effect, as people accepted Christianity, they were stepping outside their indigenous cultures, and it would take several centuries for this situation to change.

Therefore we can understand why Anton Wessels, the former professor of theology at the Free University of Amsterdam, should pose the question in the title of his book *Europe — Was It Ever Really Christian? The Interaction between Gospel and Culture,*[16] thinking of pre-Reformation Europe. We

---

15. Andrew F. Walls, "The Translation Principle in Christian History," in *Bible Translation and the Spread of the Church — The Last 200 Years,* ed. Philip Stine (Leiden: E. J. Brill, 1990), 24–39; quotation on p. 38. The article is reprinted in Andrew F. Walls, *The Missionary Movement in Christian History: Studies in the Transmission of Faith* (Maryknoll, N.Y.: Orbis Books, 1996), 26–42.

16. Anton Wessels, *Europe — Was It Ever Really Christian? The Interaction between Gospel and Culture* (London: SCM Press, 1994).

are generally accustomed to thinking of the Reformation as a contest of theological positions. We may be considerably less aware of it as a religious and cultural renewal movement, in which the translation of the Scriptures into indigenous European languages came to play a major role. This is what engendered a much more profound interaction between Gospel and culture, having far-reaching effects in many areas of life, including the inauguration of the Christian academy in a new form. It is perhaps not always realized that the impact of the major work of John Calvin, *The Institutes*, came about not through the Latin version, but through the French, his mother tongue!

There is also a general view that the fuller missionary implications of this internal cultural crossing appear to have escaped the first generation of Reformers. But whatever the merits of that view, it overlooks the tremendous effort that was required to overcome the prolonged Latin captivity of the northern European Christian mind. Some may even wonder whether that Latin captivity has been effectively overcome in all Protestant theological discourse!

Be that as it may, it is also possible to recognize that in the Evangelical Revival and Great Awakening of two centuries later, as well as in the world-wide missionary movement that they inspired, it was the delayed learning from that earlier cultural crossing that was then catching up with European Christians.

By and large, the Christian histories of the South, insofar as they are connected with the modern West, have not followed the earlier European model. What one finds instead is the link between the vernacular principle and religious and cultural renewal through the Gospel. Allowing for unevenness in the details of specific histories, it is this early predominance of the Scriptures in many mother tongues, enabling deep connections to be made with indigenous world-views, that goes to explain, in large measure, the expansion of Christianity in the South. It has been the Bible in the hands of indigenous preachers, not Western missionaries as such, that has won the South for Christ.[17]

Looked at in this way, the sixteenth-century Reformation and its lessons come to look strangely familiar to Christians elsewhere. Since it illustrates a cultural crossing in Christian history, albeit in a particular sense, all Christians can share in it, as, indeed, in all the other cultural crossings. For if

---

17. Kwame Bediako, "Epilogue — The Impact of the Bible in Africa," in Ype Schaaf, *On Their Way Rejoicing: The History and Role of the Bible in Africa*, trans. Paul Ellingworth with an epilogue by Kwame Bediako (Carlisle, U.K.: Paternoster Press, 1994), 243–54.

we maintain an organic view of Christian history, then the whole tradition of the whole church belongs to the church in every time and place. By the same token, when some of the Reformation's fruit turns sour, as it did in the apartheid theology in South Africa, we are able to formulate a Christian critique of the distortion or, as in this case, the heresy,[18] without being dismissive or destructive of Christian tradition as a whole.

The emergence of a World Christianity in our time, therefore, has brought us into a larger heritage of shared space than ever before, as the church looks now more like what it will look like at the end, the "multitude that no one can count, from every nation, tribe, people and language" (Rev. 7:9).

The Remaking of Theology: Embracing the Task Afresh

What, then, might the "remaking" of theology involve in an era of post-Western World Christianity? Remaking here is not to be understood as an attempt to provide a once-for-all revision or reformation of what has so far been achieved in Christian articulation. It would be a mistake to imagine "that we are about to usher in the eschatological age in theology."[19] The remaking that is meant is simply the recognition that our changed Christian world presents opportunities and challenges for Christian theology that are not generally available in the Western context, for the task of Christian articulation has now been taken "into areas of life where Western theology has no answers because it has no questions."[20] This is another way of saying that since the significant cultural crossings of the Christian Gospel are taking place in the churches of the South, it is to these theaters of Christian interaction that we must turn for the reorientation that is needed for embracing the task of theology afresh in our time. Among several challenges

---

18. See *Apartheid Is a Heresy*, ed. John de Gruchy and Charles Villa-Vicencio (Grand Rapids: Eerdmans, 1983).

19. Maurice Wiles, *The Making of Christian Doctrine: A Study in the Principles of Early Doctrinal Development* (Cambridge: Cambridge University Press, 1967), 174. For this essay I have reread Dr. Wiles's two books, *The Making of Christian Doctrine* and *The Remaking of Christian Doctrine* (London: SCM Press, 1974). Though Dr. Wiles intended to apply the "principles" from "early doctrinal development" to "the present task of doctrine," his treatment took no account of the emergence of a World Christianity beyond the West, and he stayed within the boundaries of a Western discussion, apart from one reference to the Indian theologian Raymond Panikkar. See *The Remaking of Christian Doctrine*, 58–59.

20. Andrew F. Walls, "Structural Problems in Mission Studies," in *The Missionary Movement in Christian History: Studies in the Transmission of Faith* (Maryknoll, N.Y.: Orbis Books, 1996), 143–59 (146).

that might be addressed, I shall confine myself to three: first, a recovery of the religious dimension to theology that can provide a confident basis for courageous Christian witness amid religious pluralism; second, the recognition of the critical importance of the living church for doing theology; and third, a recovery of spirituality in theology.

Adrian Hastings's observation that Christianity is "the one and only fully world religion," while accurate, also conceals the fact that Christians are now more dispersed than ever before. Territorial Christianity, Christendom, the supreme achievement of Charlemagne (742–814), which endured in Europe and in the extensions of Europe until relatively modern times, has come to an end. Now virtually all Christians the world over live in pluralistic societies, comprising persons of diverse religious faiths or of none. How persons in such situations may live in harmony and contribute to a common human intellectual space has become a crucial testing of the public theology of every religious faith.

In this connection, the modern West has less to offer than may be readily recognized. There are two main reasons for this. The prolonged experience of Christendom in the West meant that Western Christian thought lacked the regular challenge to establish its conceptual categories in relation to alternative religious claims. Then the secularized environment that followed the Enlightenment has tended to suggest that specifically religious claims are no longer decisive. As a result of this two-fold Western handicap, the encounter with religious pluralism may lead to either religious polarization or else the diminishing of religious conviction. This latter is what Lamin Sanneh has described as "a situation that tolerates people to be religiously informed so long as they are not religious themselves."[21]

The lived experience of the new heartlands of the Christian faith, by contrast, constitutes a remarkable achievement. In general, Christian expansion has taken place in the midst of other religious faiths, compelling Christian thought to establish its categories in the interface of Christian convictions, on the one hand, and the local alternatives, on the other.[22] In the midst of other faiths, Jesus remains Lord, and Gospel distinctives do not have to be imposed or surrendered, as one is so often tempted to do in a Western

---

21. Lamin Sanneh, *Piety and Power: Muslims and Christians in West Africa* (Maryknoll, N.Y.: Orbis Books, 1996), x.

22. On this subject, see my *Christianity in Africa: The Renewal of a Non-Western Religion,* chapter 6, "The Primal Imagination and the Opportunity for a New Theological Idiom," 91–108.

setting. If Christian theologians of the South and indeed ordinary Christians too became more aware of what their Christian interaction with their religious and cultural environment has done for them, they would realize what a significant gain this is for Christian theology. It is this character of the theologies of the South that Dutch theologian and missiologist the late Dr. Johannes Verkuyl saw when he described them as "communicative, evangelistic, and missionary" and focused on the question: "How can we best do our theology so that the Gospel will touch people most deeply?"[23]

Second, Christian theology as public discourse relates primarily to the fortunes of Christianity as a living faith. This means that the emergence of vigorous and vibrant Christian communities in the new World Christianity of our time provides the opportunity to do "scientific theology again," as in the midst of "Christianity in its most dynamic forms, the theologian has a whole living range of contemporary data on which to work."[24] It is not helpful, therefore, for Western scholars who show interest in understanding the Christian manifestations in the South to stress how "different," or how uncongenial they may appear, fixating on what seems aberrant, as some do. Diversity need not mean difference, and to be stuck on that is to be wrong-footed. We all know that the complex intellectual processes that we call the Enlightenment in Europe have something to do with our present situation. By its exaltation of reason over against revelation, of the autonomous individual self over against community and collective consciousness, of the present and so-called modernity over against the past and tradition, the Enlightenment turned much of European traditional thought, informed by Christian teaching and practice, upside down. The Western Christian theology that emerged from that bruising struggle was Enlightenment theology, a Christian theology shaved down to fit the Enlightenment world-view.

But it is with the southward shift in Christianity's center of gravity that the profound undermining of the Christian faith by the Enlightenment can now be seen, and perhaps one should agree with Andrew Walls that "part of the strength of Christianity in the South today is the fact that it is independent of the Enlightenment."[25] There is so much that happens in Christian

---

23. Johannes Verkuyl, *Contemporary Missiology: An Introduction,* trans. and ed. Dale Cooper (Grand Rapids: Eerdmans, 1978), 277.

24. H. W. Turner, "The Contribution of Studies on Religion in Africa to Western Religious Studies," in *New Testament Christianity for Africa and the World: Essays in Honour of Harry Sawyerr,* ed. Mark Glasswell and E. W. Fasholé-Luke (London: SPCK, 1974), 169–78 (177–78).

25. Andrew F. Walls, "Christian Scholarship in Africa in the Twenty-First Century," *Journal of African Christian Thought* 4, no. 2 (2001): 50.

life and thought, particularly where the Transcendent impinges upon every-day human existence, that the Enlightenment marginalized, discounted, or simply ignored in earlier Western Christian experience. We can understand how Andrew Walls, writing about Africa, comes to suggest that, as a consequence, "Western theology is not big enough for Africa." It may not be big enough for the church in the North either.

To take, for instance, the field of biblical studies, which we would consider to be vital in the curriculum of theological formation, the historical-critical method of exegesis, a legacy of Enlightenment methodology, which belongs to just a segment of Western intellectual history, continues to hold sway, however modified it may seem to be. And yet it will not take exhaustive research to demonstrate that neither the Old Testament prophets, nor our Lord Jesus, nor his apostles, are models of that method of Scriptural exegesis. Other cultural traditions in the treatment of sacred lore and heritage, indigenous to the southern continents where the majority of the Christians now are, could prove immensely helpful in freeing our Scriptures from this persisting Western hegemony and liberate the living Word of God for our time, so that our theology can communicate God's authoritative truth to our societies. We are now able to recognize, in a way that we were not able to before, that there are, in the ancient cultures of the southern continents, persisting indigenous cultural traditions of wisdom, knowledge, and spiritual insight that make the world of the Christian Scriptures and the depths of Christian apprehension of reality so evidently luminous with meaning.

This brings me to my third and final observation. Does theology have a place and a role in public discourse, bringing its unique contribution to the shaping of a shared human intellectual space? Emmanuel Katongole (from Uganda, now teaching at Duke Divinity School), in an article, spoke of theology being tempted to succumb to what he called "Christian theology's false humility," the "tendency to allow its social contribution to be shaped and defined by the secular disciplines of political science, economics, and sociology,"[26] and therefore disabling theology from speaking in its own terms as the discernment of the manifestations and acts of God. Almost twenty years ago, Lesslie Newbigin indicated what he thought would be

---

26. Emmanuel Katongole, "Hauerwasian Hooks and the Christian Social Imagination," in *God, Truth, and Witness: Essays in Conversation with Stanley Hauerwas*, ed. L. Gregory Jones, Reinhard Hütter, and C. Rosalee Velloso Ewell (Grand Rapids: Brazos Press, 2005), 137

needed to overcome the destructive dichotomies injected by the Enlightenment that weaken the impact of Christian affirmations, making them into private opinion rather than public truth in a "unified view of things."

> This calls for a more radical kind of conversion than has often been thought, a conversion not only of the will, but of the mind, a transformation by the renewing of the mind so as not to be conformed to this world, not to see things as our culture sees them, but — with new lenses — to see things in a radically different way.[27]

By "our culture," he meant modern Western culture. In my *Christianity in Africa: The Renewal of a Non-Western Religion,* I suggest that in the cultural worlds of the Christian communities of the Southern continents, there is opportunity to recover the ancient Christian unity of theology and spirituality and so restore to theology the vital dimension of living religiously for which the theologian need make no apology.[28]

Conclusion: A Reverse Pilgrimage

I drew attention earlier on to the observation by Joel Carpenter that our changed Christian world "represents a remarkable case of 'globalization from below,' rather than imposition from the world's great powers." There is a further insight in that comment: Christian history is the theater not of the imposition of human will upon the world, but the disclosure of the initiative and sovereignty of the living God. And now the trend toward the South is well nigh irreversible.

So I end as I began, with John Mbiti, writing over thirty years ago. Two sentences further on from the statement I cited, he makes the further observation and raises a question:

> Theologians from the new (or younger) churches [of the South] have made their pilgrimages to the theological learning of the older churches [of the North]. We had no alternative. We have eaten theology with you; we have drunk theology with you; we have dreamed theology with you. . . . We know you theologically. The question is: Do you know us theologically? Would you like to know us theologically?[29]

---

27. Lesslie Newbigin, *The Gospel in a Pluralist Society* (Grand Rapids: Eerdmans, 1989), 38.
28. Kwame Bediako, *Christianity in Africa: The Renewal of a Non-Western Religion* (Maryknoll, N.Y.: Orbis Books, 1995), 105.
29. Mbiti, "Theological Impotence and the Universality of the Church."

Bibliography of the Writings of Andrew F. Walls

MARK R. GORNIK

The following bibliography is intended as a working resource for continued study of the themes of this book. From biblical studies to what is today called disability studies, from Austen to the Zionists, and from Patristics to poetry, the range of contributions and interests is profound. Yet the reader will also find threaded throughout the themes of a life's calling, topics that were accepted and embraced. This material is organized chronologically under the following headings:

- books
- booklets
- entries in encyclopedias and dictionaries
- chapters in books
- chapters in booklets
- articles in journals
- book reviews and notices
- articles in newsletters
- bibliographies
- introductions and forewords to books
- interviews
- unpublished papers on CD
- unpublished papers

Additionally, one can find, in a more limited way

- video links and documentation
- select works about Andrew F. Walls

For the final section, the order follows the author alphabetically.

Although the bibliography has sought to be comprehensive, no such claim is possible, for it seems there is always one more encyclopedia article to be documented or essay yet remaining in active process. Please note these are only works published in English. In addition to the help of Andrew Walls, for help along the way, gratitude is extended to Margaret Acton, Janice McLean, Rebekah Ramsay, and Wilbert Shenk. Any errors most certainly are mine.

Please send any corrections or additions to *Mark@Cityseminaryny.org.*

Books

The First Epistle General of Peter, co-author with A. M. Stibbs. Tyndale New Testament Commentary. London: Tyndale Press, 1959.

A Guide to Christian Reading: A Classified List of Selected Books, editor. 2nd ed. London: Inter-Varsity Fellowship, 1961.

Mission Studies and Information Management, jointly edited with Willi Henkel. Leiden: International Association for Mission Studies, 1981.

Exploring New Religious Movements: Essays in Honour of Harold W. Turner, jointly edited with Wilbert R. Shenk, and with one chapter. Elkhart, Ind.: Mission Focus Publications, 1990.

Christianity in Africa in the 1990s, edited with Christopher Fyfe, and with Introduction and conclusion. Edinburgh: Center of African Studies, University of Edinburgh, 1996.

The Missionary Movement in Christian History: Studies in the Transmission of Faith. Maryknoll, N.Y.: Orbis Books; Edinburgh: T. & T. Clark, 1996.

The Cross-Cultural Process in Christian History: Studies in the Transmission and Appropriation of Faith. Maryknoll, N.Y.: Orbis Books; Edinburgh: T. & T. Clark, 2002.

Mission in the Twenty-First Century: Exploring the Five Marks of Global Mission, jointly edited with Cathy Ross, with one chapter. London: Darton, Longman and Todd, and Maryknoll, N.Y: Orbis Books, 2008.

Crossing Cultural Frontiers: Studies in the History of World Christianity. Maryknoll, N.Y.: Orbis Books, forthcoming.

Booklets

Needs and Opportunities in Christian Literature. 1962.

Some Personalities of Aberdeen Methodism, 1760–1970. Aberdeen, 1973.

The History of Christian Expansion Reconsidered. New Haven, Conn.: Yale Divinity School Library, Occasional Publication No. 8, 1996. Also published in *The Cross-Cultural Process in Christian History,* 3–26.

The Morning Star of Africa. Church Missionary Society in Sierra Leone, 2004. Private Circulation.

Entries in Encyclopedias and Dictionaries

"Deification," "Essenes," "Hermetic Literature," "Logia," "Logos," "Mystery," "Peter," "Word." In *Baker's Dictionary of Theology*. Ed. Everett F. Harrison and G. W. Bromiley. Grand Rapids: Baker 1960.

"Apostles," "Epistles to the Corinthians," "Gnosticism," "New Testament Apocrypha," "Peter," "First Epistle," "Maccabees." In *The New Bible Dictionary*. Ed. J. D. Douglas. Grand Rapids: Eerdmans, 1962.

"Bunting, Jabez"; "Clowes, William"; "Kilham, Alexander"; "Methodist New Connexion"; "Peake, A. S."; "Porteus, Beilby"; "Rastafarians"; "Testamentum Domini"; "Venn, Henry"; "Venn, John"; "Watson, Richard." In *New International Dictionary of the Christian Church*. Ed. J. D. Douglas. Grand Rapids, Mich: Zondervan, and Exeter: Paternoster, 1974.

"Gambia," "Sierra Leone." In *The Encyclopedia of World Methodism*. Ed. Nolan B. Harmon. Nashville: United Methodist Publishing House, 1974.

"African Independent Churches," "Samuel Ajayi Crowther," "David Livingstone" "Missionary Societies," "Outposts of Empire." In *The History of Christianity*. Ed. Tim Dowley. London: Lion, 1977.

"Maccabees." In *Illustrated Bible Dictionary*. InterVarsity Press, 1980.

"World Christianity." In *The Guinness Encyclopedia*. Middlesex: Guinness Publishing, 1990.

"Missiology." In *Dictionary of the Ecumenical Movement*. Ed. Nicholas Lossky. Geneva: WCC Publications; Grand Rapids: Eerdmans, 1991.

"Paris Evangelical Missionary Society." In *Encyclopedia of the Reformed Faith*. Ed. Donald K. McKim. Louisville: Westminster John Knox Press, 1992.

"Anderson, John"; "Arthur, John William"; "Ballantyne, James Robert,"; "Campbell, Andrew"; "Cargill, David"; "Christie, Dugald"; "Dobson, Thomas"; "Farquhar, John Nicol"; "Hastings, Harry"; "Hislop, Stephen"; "Hitchcock, John William"; "Johnston, Robert"; "Kerr, George McGlashan, and Kerr, Isabel Gunn"; "Kilham, Alexander"; "Legge, James"; "Macdonald, Andrew Buchanan"; "Mackenzie, Peter"; "Matthews, Thomas Trotter"; "Missions"; "Mitchell, John Murray"; "Ross, John"; "Scott, George"; "Slessor, Mary Mitchell"; "Thom, William"; "Wilkie, Arthur West". In *Dictionary of Scottish Church History and Theology*. Ed. Nigel M. de S. Cameron. Andrew F. Walls Advisory Editor. Edinburgh: T. & T. Clark, 1993.

"Aggrey, James Emman Kwegyir"; "Arthur, John William"; "Bishop, Isabella Lucy (Bird)"; "Bogue, David"; "Bosshardt, R(udolf) Alfred"; "Bourgeoys, Margurite"; "Buxton, Thomas Fowell"; "Cargill, David"; "Christie, Dugald"; "Colenso, John William"; "Crowther, Samuel Adjai (or Ajayi)"; "Crummell, Alexander"; "Dobinson, Henry Hughes"; "Duff, Alexander"; "Falkner, Thomas"; "Fraser, Alexander Garden"; "Gardiner, Allen Francis"; "Gogerly, Daniel John"; "Gollmer, Charles Andrew (Carl Anders)"; "Graham, John Anderson"; "Groves, Charles Pelham"; "Hardy, Robert Spence"; "Haweis, Thomas"; "Hinderer, David and Anna (Martin)"; "Hislop, Stephen"; "Ibiam (Francis)

Akanu"; "Johnson, Samuel"; "Kerr, George McGlashamn, and Isabel (Gunn)"; "Lyall, Leslie Theodore"; "Matthews, Thomas Trotter"; "Mitchell, John Murray"; "Moshoeshoe (Moshesh and various other spellings)"; "New, Charles"; "Oppong (Kwame) Sam(p)son"; "Origen"; "Parrinder (Edward) Geoffrey (Simons)"; "Price, Roger"; "Townsend, Henry"; "Wakefield, Thomas." In *Bibliographical Dictionary of Christian Mission.* Ed. Gerald H. Anderson. Grand Rapids: Eerdmans, 1998.

"Allen, Roland"; "Ghana, Christianity in" "Harris, William Wade"; "Nigeria, Christianity in;" "Sierra Leone." In *The Oxford Dictionary of the Christian Church.* Ed. F. L. Cross. 3rd ed. Ed. E. A. Livingstone. Oxford: Oxford University Press, 1997.

"Missionaries." In *Concise Encyclopedia of Language and Religion.* Ed. J. F. A. Sawyerr and J. M. Y. Simpson. Oxford: Pergamon, 2001.

"Shamanism," "New Religious Movements." In *Dictionary of Contemporary Religion in the Western World: Exploring Living Faiths in Postmodern Contexts.* Ed. Christopher Partridge. Downers Grove, Ill.: InterVarsity Press, 2002.

"Kigozi." In *Who's Who in World Religions.* Ed. John R. Hinnells. New York: Holiday House, 1992.

"Aesir and vanir; African Independent Churches; African Religions; Afro-Brazilian Religions; Aladura; Algonquin (Algonkin) Religion; Anaconda; ancestors, African; apu; atua; Australian Aboriginal Religion; angakok; Aztec Religion; ball-game; Black Elk; calendar (Meso-American); calmecac; calumet; Cargo; Cernunnos; Cheyenne Religion; Christian Fellowship Church; Christianity in Africa; Christianity in Australasia; Christianity in Latin America; Christianity in the Middle East; Dagda, the; Dinka religion; divinization (Africa): Druids; Dry Paintings; Fenrir; fetish; Frigg; frost giants; fylgia; Harris, William Wade; head cult (Celtic); Hopi Religion; Huaca; human sacrifice (Meso-American); Illapa; Inca Religion; Iroquois Religion; Kachinas; Land of youth; Lenshina, Alice Mulenga; Loki; Mabinogion; Mamaccha; Mana; Manitou; Maori Religion; Maria Legio; matres, matrones; Maya religion; medicine bundle; medicine lodge; Melanesian religion; Modimo; Mulungu; Mwari; Navajo Religion; Nuer religion; Olmec Religion; Ometeoti; Pachacamac; Pachacuti; Pachamama; priesthood (Mes-America); Providence Industrial Religion; Pueblo religion; Quetzalcoatl; Tezcatlipoca; saga; shamanism; Shilluk religion; ship burial; Sioux religion; tabu; Taqui Ongoy; Toltec religion; Templo mayo; Tollan; Tyr, Tiwaz, Tu; Viracocha; Voluspa; Volva; windigo; witchcraft and sorcery, African; wondjina; Zionist churches." In *Chambers Encyclopedia of Religion.*

"British Missions." In *The Encyclopedia of Christianity.* Vol. 1, ed. Erwin Fahlbusch et al., 1999.

"Kilham, Hannah," "Kirchenbau Afrika." In *Religion in Geschicte und Gegenwart.* Vol. 4. Ed. Hans-Dieter Betz (Tübingen: Mohr Siebeck, 2001).

"Azariah, V. S.; Clapham Sect; Crowther, Samuel; Ghana; Harris, William Wade; Inculturation; Jabavu, Davidson Don Tengo; Kilham, Hannah; Koelle, Sigismund W., Liang A-Fa (Liang-Fa; Leang A-Fa); Luthuli, Albert John; Matthews,

Z. K.; Pilkington, George Lawrence; Schon, James Frederick; Sharp, Granville; Sierre Leone; Studd, Charles Thomas; Tutu, Desmond." In *Encyclopedia of Protestantism.* Ed. Hans J. Hillerbrand. New York: Routledge, 2004.

"History." In *Dictionary of Mission Theology.* Ed. John Corrie. Nottingham: Inter-Varsity Press 2007.

"Alexandria and Early Christianity — Egypt." In *Encyclopedia of African History.* Vol. 1. Ed. Kevin Shillington. London: Fitzroy Dearborn, 2005.

"Allen, Roland." In *New Dictionary of Theology.* Ed. Martin Davie, Tim Grass, Stephen R. Holmes, John McDowell, and Tom Noble. Nottingham: Inter-Varsity Press, forthcoming.

"Kilham, Hannah." In *Religion Past and Present.* Vol. 7. Leiden: Brill, 2009, 182–83.

"Newbigin, Lesslie." In *New Dictionary of Theology.* Ed. Martin Davie, Tim Grass, Stephen R. Holmes, John McDowell, and Tom Noble. Nottingham: Inter-Varsity Press, forthcoming.

Chapters in Books

"Proverbs." In *New Bible Commentary.* 1st ed. [1953]. Revised in 1969. Ed. Donald Guthrie, J. A. Motyer, and Francis Davidson. Grand Rapids: Eerdmans, 1970.

"The Theological Faculty and Local Studies in Africa." In *Christian Theology in Independent Africa,* ed. H. Sawyerr. Freetown, 1961.

"A Christian Experiment: The Early Sierra Leone Colony." In *The Mission of the Church and the Propagation of the Faith: Papers Read at the Seventh Summer Meeting and the Eighth Winter Meeting of the Ecclesiastical History Society,* Studies in Church History 6. Ed. G. J. Cumming, 107–29. Cambridge: Cambridge University Press, 1970.

"The First Chapter of the Epistle to the Romans and the Modern Missionary Movement." In *Apostolic History and the Gospel: Biblical and Historical Essays Presented to F. F. Bruce on His 60th Birthday,* ed. W. W. Gasque and R. P. Martin, 346–57. Exeter, U.K.: Paternoster, 1970. Also published in *The Missionary Movement in Christian History,* 55–67.

"Missionary Vocation and the Ministry: The First Generation." In *New Testament Christianity for Africa and the World: Essays in Honour of Harry Sawyerr,* ed. Mark E. Glasswell and Edward W. Fasholé-Luke, 141–46. London: SPCK, 1974. Also published in *The Missionary Movement in Christian History,* 160–72.

"A Colonial Concordat: Two Views of Christianity and Civilization." In *Church, Society and Politics,* ed. Derek Baker, 293–302. Oxford: Blackwell, 1975.

"The Nineteenth-Century Missionary as Scholar." In *Misjonskall og Forskerglede: festskrift til professor Olav Guttorm Myklebust,* ed. Nils E. Bloch-Hoell, 209–21. Oslo: Universitetsforlaget, 1975.

"Towards Understanding Africa's Place in Christian History." In *Religion in a Pluralistic Society: Essays Presented to C. G. Baëta*, ed. J. S. Pobee, 180–89. Leiden: Brill, 1975.

"Access Considerations for Handicapped Visitors," in *Museums and the Handicapped*, ed. D. S. Sorrell, 27–29. Leicester: Leicestershire Museums Art Galleries and Reco, 1976.

"Religious Studies, the Universities and the Schools." In *Common Ground*, ed. A. R. Rodger, 18–24, 38–44. Dundee, 1976.

"Towards Understanding Africa's Place in Christian History." In *Religion in a Pluralistic Society*, ed. J. S. Pobee, 180–89. Leiden: Brill, 1976.

"Outposts of Empire," "Missionary Societies," "African Independent Churches," "Samuel Ajayi Crowther," and "David Livingston." In *The History of Christianity*. Ed. Tim J. Dowley London: Lion Publishing, 1977.

"The African Missionary and the Household of Caesar in the 19th Century." In *Church in a Changing Society*. Uppsala: Swedish Sub-Commission of CIHEC, 1978, 353–63.

"Black Europeans, White Africans: Some Missionary Motives in West Africa." In *Religious Motivation: Biographical and Sociological Problems for the Church Historian*, Studies in Church History, 14, ed. Derek Baker, 339–48. Oxford: Blackwell, 1978. Also published in *The Missionary Movement in Christian History*, 102–10.

"Religion and the Press in 'the Enclave' in the Nigerian Civil War." In *Christianity in Independent Africa*, ed. Edward Fasholé-Luke, Richard Gray, Adrian Hastings, Godwin O. M. Tasie, 207–15. London: Collins, 1978.

"The Canon of the New Testament," in *The Expositor's Bible Commentary*, vol. 1, ed. Frank E. Gaebelein, 631–43. Grand Rapids: Zondervan, 1979.

"Missionary Vocation and the Ministry: The First Generation." In *The History of Christianity in West Africa*, ed. Ogbu U. Kalu, 22–35. London: Longman, 1980.

"Ruminations on Rainmaking: The Transmission and Receipt of Religious Expertise in Africa." In *Experts in Africa: Proceedings of a Colloquium at the University of Aberdeen*, ed. J. C. Stone, 146–51. Aberdeen: University of Aberdeen African Studies Group, 1980.

"The Best Thinking of the Best Heathen: Humane Learning and the Missionary Movement." In *Religion and Humanism*, Studies in Church History 17, ed. Keith Robbins, 341–53. Oxford: Blackwell, 1981. Also published in *The Missionary Movement in Christian History*, 199–210.

"British Missions." In *Missionary Ideologies in the Imperialist Era: 1880–1920*, ed. Torben Christensen and William R. Hutchison, 341–53. Copenhagen, Denmark: Aros, 1982.

"The Heavy Artillery of the Missionary Army: The Domestic Importance of the Nineteenth-Century Medical Missionary." In *The Church and Healing*, Studies in Church History 19, ed. W. J. Shiels, 287–97. Oxford: Blackwell, 1982. Also published in *The Missionary Movement in Christian History*, 211–20.

"The Old Gods: Religions of Northern Europe." In *The World's Religions*. Ed. Robert Pierce Beaver et al. Tring, U.K.: Lion Publishing, 1982.

"Stewardship." In *A Shaftesbury Project Handbook on World Development*. London, Overseas Aid and Development Group of the Shaftesbury Project, 1983.

"Such Boastings as the Gentiles Use: Thoughts on Imperialist Religion." In *An African Miscellany for John Hargreaves*, ed. R. C. Bridges, 109–16. Aberdeen: University of Aberdeen African Studies Group, 1983.

"Christianity." In *A Handbook of Living Religions*, ed. John R. Hinnells, 56–122. Harmondsworth: Penguin, 1984.

"Christian Expansion Reconsidered." In *How to Plant Churches*, ed. Monica Hill, 34–43. London: MARC Europe, 1984.

"The Christian Tradition in Today's World." In *Religion in Today's World: The Religious Situation of the World from 1945 to the Present Day*, ed. Frank Whaling, 76–109. Edinburgh: T. & T. Clark, 1987.

"Primal Religious Traditions in Today's World." In *Religion in Today's World: The Religious Situation of the World from 1945 to the Present Day*, ed. Frank Whaling, 250–78. Edinburgh: T. & T. Clark, 1987. Also published in *The Missionary Movement in Christian History*, 119–39.

"On the Origins of Old Northern and New Southern Christianity." In *Bilanz und Plan: Mission an der Schwalle zum dritten Jahrtausend: Festschrift für George W. Peters zu seinem achtzigsten Geburtstag*, ed. Hans Kasdorf and W. Müller, 243–55. Bad Liebezell: Verlag der Liebezeller Mission, 1988. Also published in *The Missionary Movement in Christian History*, 68–75.

"The American Dimension of the Missionary Movement." In *Earthen Vessels: American Evangelicals and Foreign Missions, 1880–1980*, ed. Joel A. Carpenter and Wilbert R. Shenk, 1–25. Grand Rapids: Eerdmans, 1990. Also published in *The Missionary Movement in Christian History*, 221–40.

"Building to Last: Harold Turner and the Study of Religion." In *Exploring New Religious Movements: Essays in Honour of Harold W. Turner*, ed. Andrew F. Walls and Wilbert R. Shenk, 1–17. Elkhart, Ind.: Mission Focus Publications, 1990.

"Religious Studies in the University: Scotland." In *Turning Points in Religious Studies: Essays in Honour of Geoffrey Parrinder*, ed. Ursula King, 32–45. Edinburgh: T. & T. Clark, 1990.

"The Translation Principle in Christian History." In *Bible Translation and the Spread of the Church*, ed. Philip C. Stine, 24–39. Leiden: E. J. Brill, 1990. Also published in *The Missionary Movement in Christian History*, 6–42.

"World Christianity, the Missionary Movement and the Ugly American." In *World Order and Religion*, ed. Wade C. Roof, 142–72. Albany: State University of New York, 1991.

"The Western Discovery of Non-Western Christian Art," In *The Church and the Arts, Studies in Church History* 28. Ed. Diana Wood, 541–85. Oxford: Blackwell, 1992. Also published in *The Missionary Movement in Christian History*, 173–86.

"Carrying the White Man's Burden: Some British Views of National Vocation in the Imperial Era." In *Many Are Chosen: Divine Election and Western Nationalism*, ed. William R. Hutchinson and Hartmut Lehmann, 29–50. Minneapolis: Fortress Press, 1994. Also published in *The Cross-Cultural Process in Christian History*, 177–93.

"The Evangelical Revival, the Missionary Movement, and Africa." In *Evangelicalism: Comparative Studies of Popular Protestantism in North America, the British Isles, and Beyond, 1770–1990*, ed. Mark A. Noll, David W. Bebbington and George A. Rawlyk, 310–30. Oxford: Oxford University Press, 1994. Also published in *The Missionary Movement in Christian History*, 79–101.

"William Robertson Smith and the Missionary Movement." In *William Robertson Smith: Essays in Reassessment*, JSOT Supplement Series 189, ed. William Johnstone, 101–17. Sheffield: Sheffield Academic Press, 1995.

"Introduction: African Christianity in the History of Religions." In *Christianity in Africa in the 1990s*, ed. Christopher Fyfe and Andrew Walls, 1–16. Edinburgh: Center of African Studies, University of Edinburgh, 1996.

"Africa and the Future of Christianity: A Summary and Reflection." In *Christianity in Africa in the 1990s*, ed. Christopher Fyfe and Andrew Walls, 139–48. Edinburgh: Center of African Studies, University of Edinburgh 1996. Slightly revised version in *Studies in World Christianity*, 2, no. 2 (1996): 183–203, and *The Cross Cultural Process in Christianity History*, 116–35.

"Missiological Education in Historical Perspective." In *Missiological Education for the Twenty-First Century: The Book, the Circle, and the Sandals*, ed. J. Dudley Woodberry, Charles Van Engen, and Edgar J. Elliston, 11–22. Maryknoll, N.Y.: Orbis Books, 1996.

"Christianity." In *New Handbook of Living Religions*, rev. ed. John R. Hinnells, 55–161. Oxford: Blackwell, 1997.

"Isibongo." In *Rethinking African History*, ed. Simon McGrath, Charles Jedrej, Kenneth King and Jack Thompson, vii–xi. Edinburgh: Center of African Studies, University of Edinburgh, 1997.

"Meditations among the Tombs: Changing Patterns of Identity in Freetown, Sierra Leone." In *Rethinking African History*, ed. Simon McGrath, Charles Jedrej, Kenneth King, and Jack Thompson, 489–504. Edinburgh: Center of African Studies, University of Edinburgh, 1997.

"The Gospel as Prisoner and Liberator of Culture." In *New Directions in Mission and Evangelization*, ed. James A. Scherer and Stephen B. Bevans, 17–28. Maryknoll, N.Y.: Orbis Books, 1999.

"The Mission of the Church Today in the Light of Global History." In *Mission at the Dawn of the Twenty-First Century: A Vision for the Church*, ed. Paul Varo Martinson, 384–88. Minneapolis: Kirk House Publishers, 1999.

"The Eighteenth-Century Protestant Missionary Awakening in Its European Context." In *Christian Missions and the Enlightenment*, ed. Brian Stanley, 22–44. Grand Rapids: Eerdmans, 2001.

"Rethinking Mission: New Direction for a New Century," "Proselytes or Converts: Gospel and Culture in the New Testament," and "Converting the Past: Gospel and Culture in the Early Church." In *World Mission in the Twenty-First Century*, ed. Kwang Soon Lee, 69–80; 81–90; 91–98. Seoul: Center for World Mission, Presbyterian College and Theological Seminary, 2001.

"Christian Scholarship and the Demographic Transformation of the Church." In *Theological Literacy for the Twenty-First Century*, ed. Rodney L. Peterson with Nancy M. Rourke, 166–83. Grand Rapids: Eerdmans, 2002.

"Enlightenment, Postmodernity, and Mission." In *A Scandalous Prophet: The Way of Mission after Newbigin*, ed. Thomas F. Foust, George R. Hunsberger, J. Andrew Kirk and Werner Ustorf, 145–52. Grand Rapids: Eerdmans 2002.

"The Multiple Conversions of Timothy Richard: A Paradigm of Missionary Experience." In *The Gospel in the World: International Baptist Studies*, Studies in Baptist History and Thought, ed. David W. Bebbington, 271–94. Carlise, U.K.: Paternoster Press, 2002.

"Sierra Leone, Afroamerican Remigration and the Beginnings of Protestantism in West Africa (18th–19th Centuries)." In *Transcontinental Links in the History of Non-Western Christianity*, ed. Klaus Koschorke, 45–56. Wiesbaden: Harrassowitz Verlag, 2002.

"The Missionary Movement: A Lay Fiefdom?" In *The Rise of the Laity in Evangelical Protestantism*, ed. Deryk W. Lovegrove, 167–86. London: Routledge, 2002.

"Wesleyan Missiology Theories, the Case of Richard Watson." In *The Global Impact of the Wesleyan Traditions and Their Related Movements*, ed. Charles Yrigoyen Jr., 27–47. Lanham, Md.: Scarecrow Press, 2002.

"Missions and Historical Memory: Jonathan Edwards and David Brainerd." In *Jonathan Edwards at Home and Abroad: Historical Memories, Cultural Movements, Global Histories*, ed. David W. Kling and Douglas A. Sweeney, 248–65. Columbia: University of South Carolina Press, 2003.

"Geoffrey Parrinder (1910) and the Study of Religion in West Africa." In *European Traditions in the Study of Religion in Africa*, ed. Frieder Ludwig and Afe Adogame, 207–15. Wiesbaden: Harrassowitz Verlag, 2004.

"The Future of Shari'ah and the Debate in Northern Nigeria: A Commentary on the Contribution of Abdullahi An-Naim." In *Comparative Perspectives on Shari'ah in Nigeria*, ed. Philip Ostien, Jamilla M. Nasire, and Franz Kogelmann, 373–81. Ibadan: Spectrum Books, 2005.

"The Great Commission 1910–2010." In *Considering the Great Commission: Evangelism and Mission in the Wesleyan Spirit*, ed. W. Stephen Gunter and Elaine Robinson, 7–22. Nashville: Abingdon Press, 2005.

"Rethinking Mission: New Directions for a New Century"; "Proselytes and Converts: Gospel and Culture in the New Testament"; "Converting the Past: Gospel and Culture in the Early Church." In *World Mission in the Twenty-First Century*, ed. Kwang Soon Lee, 69–80; 81–89; 92–98. Seoul: Center for World Mission, Presbyterian College and Theological Seminary, 2005.

"Evangelical and Ecumenical: The Rise and Fall of the Early Church Model." In *Evangelical, Ecumenical and Anabaptist Missiologies in Conversation: Essays in Honor of Wilbert R. Shenk,* ed. James R. Krabill, Walter Sawatsky, and Charles E. Van Engen, 28–37. Maryknoll, N.Y.: Orbis Books, 2006.

"Globalization and the Study of Christian History." In *Globalizing Theology: Belief and Practice in an Era of World Christianity,* ed. Craig Ott and Harold A. Netland, 70–82. Grand Rapids: Baker Academic, 2006.

"The Society for Promoting Christian Knowledge and the Missionary Movement in Britain." In *Halle and the Beginning of Protestant Christianity in India: The Danish-Halle and the English-Halle Mission,* vol. 1, ed. Andreas Gross, Y. Vincent Kumaradoss, and Heike Liebau, 107–28. Halle: Franckesche Stiftungen zu Halle, 2006.

"India's Place in Christian History." In *Uniting in Christ's Mission,* ed. Enos Das Pradhan, Sudipta Singh, and Kasta Dip, 22–46. Delhi: ISPCK, 2006.

"The Ephesians Moment in Worldwide Worship: A Meditation on Revelation 21 and Ephesians 2." In *Christian Worship Worldwide: Expanding Horizons, Deepening Practices,* ed. Charles E. Farhadian, 27–37. Grand Rapids: Eerdmans 2007.

"Methodists, Missions and Pacific Christianity: A New Chapter in Christian History." In *Weaving the Unfinished Mats: Wesley's Legacy, Conflict, Confusion and Challenge in the South Pacific Proceedings of the Wesley Historical Society,* ed. Peter Lineham, 9–32. Oreza, N.Z.: Wesley Historical Society of New Zealand, 2007.

"Theology and Scholarship in a Global Church." In *Antioch Agenda: Essays on the Restorative Church in Honor of Orlando E. Costas,* ed. Daniel Jeyeraj, Robert W. Pazmino and Rodney L. Petersen, 41–48. New Delhi: ISPCK 2007.

"Afterword: Christian Mission in a Five-hundred-year Context." In *Mission in the Twenty-First Century: Exploring the Five Marks of Global Mission,* ed. Andrew Walls and Cathy Ross, 193–204. London: Darton, Longman and Todd; Maryknoll, N.Y.: Orbis Books, 2008.

"English Neo-Calvinism and the Early Protestant Missionary Movement." In *Calvinism on the Peripheries: Religion and Society in Europe.* Ed. Abraham Kovacs and Bela Levente Barath. Paris: L'Harmattan, 2009.

"World Parish to World Church: John and Charles Wesley on Home and Overseas Mission." In *Missions in the Wesleyan Spirit.* Ed. Gerald H. Anderson and Darrell Whiteman. Nashville: Providence House Publishers, 2009.

"Commission One and the Church's Transforming Century." In *Edinburgh 2010: Mission Then and Now,* ed. David A. Kerr and Kenneth R. Ross, 27–40. Oxford: Regnum Books; Pasadena: William Carey International University Press, 2009.

"Christianity across Twenty Centuries." In *Atlas of Global Christianity,* ed. Todd M. Johnson and Kenneth R. Ross, 48–49. Edinburgh: University of Edinburgh Press, 2009.

"Towards a Theology of Migration." In *The African Christian Presence in the West: New Immigrant Congregations and Transnational Networks in North America and Europe,* ed. Freider Ludwig and Kwabena Asamoah-Gyadu, 314–22. Trenton: Africa Word Press, 2010.

"World Christianity and the Early Church." In *A New Day: Essays on World Christianity in Honor of Lamin Sanneh,* ed. Akintunde E. Akinade, 17–30. New York: Peter Lang, 2010.

"Documentation and Ecclesial Deficit: A Personal Plea to Churches." In *Christian Movements in Southeast Asia: A Theological Exploration,* ed. Michael Nai-Chiu Poon, 121–32. Singapore: Genesis Books and Trinity Theological College, 2010.

"Missiology as Vocation." In *Walk Humbly with the Lord: Church and Mission Engaging Plurality,* ed. Viggo Mortensen and Andreas Osterlund Nielsen, 230–37. Grand Rapids: Eerdmans, 2010.

"World Views and Christian Conversion." In *Mission in Context: Conversations with J. Andrew Kirk,* ed. John Corries and Cathy Ross. Aldershot: Ashpate, forthcoming.

Chapters in Booklets

"Mission and Service." In *Viewpoint: Evangelical Views on Mission and Development.* London: Christian Aid, 1975, 1–4.

Articles in Journals

"A Primitive Christian Harvest Festival." *Theology* 58 (1956): 336–39.

"The Apostolic Claim in the Church Order Literature." In *Studia Patristica* 2 (1957): 83–92.

"The Nova Scotian Settlers and Their Religion." *Sierra Leone Bulletin of Religion* 1 (1959): 19–31.

"Documentary Sources for the Study of Sierra Leone Church History." *Sierra Leone Bulletin of Religion* 1, no. 2 (December 1959): 57–61.

"In the Presence of the Angels" (Luke 15:10). *Novum Testamentum* 3 (1959): 314–16.

"James Lee of Shadoxhurst: A Study in Evangelical Religion in the Bleak Age." *Evangelical Quarterly* 32, no. 1 (January–March 1960): 34–44.

"Richard Baxter and Abraham de la Pryme." *Notes and Queries* (NS) 7 (1960): 77.

"Some Attitudes to Sacrifice." *Sierra Leone Bulletin of Religion* 2, no. 2 (December 1960): 69–70.

"Some Recent Studies (1958–1959) Relating to Religion in Sierra Leone." *Sierra Leone Bulletin of Religion* 2, no. 2 (December 1960): 70–72.

"The Latin Version of Hippolytus' Apostolic Tradition." In *Studia Patristica* 3, ed. F. L. Cross, 155–62. Berlin: Texte und Untersuchungen 78, 1961.

"References to Apostles in the Gospel of Thomas." *New Testament Studies* (1961): 266–70.

"The Usefulness of Schoolmasters: Notes on the Earliest Sierra Leone Documents of the Methodist Missionary Society." *Sierra Leone Bulletin of Religion* 3 (1961) 28–40.

"'Stone' and 'Wood' in Oxyrhynchus Papyrus I." *Vigiliae Christianae* 16, no. 1 (1962): 71–76.

"The Acts and Acts." *Tyndale House Bulletin* 12 (April 1963): 4–11.

"The McCall Papers and the Livingstone Inland Mission." *Bulletin of the Society for African Church History* 1, no. 1 (1963): 21–23.

"William Singleton." *Proceedings of the Wesley Historical Society* 34 (1963): 23.

"The Gilbert Family: A West Africa Footnote." *Proceedings of the Wesley Historical Society* 34 (1964): 145.

"The Montanist 'Catholic Epistle' and Its New Testament Prototype." In *Studia Evangelica* III, ed. F. L. Cross, 88, 437–46. Berlin: Texte and Untersuchungen, 1964.

"A Second Narrative of Samuel Ajayi Crowther's Early Life." *Bulletin of the Society for African Church History* 2, no. 1 (1965): 5–14.

"Miss Austen's Theological Reading." *Anglican Theological Review* 47, no. 1 (January 1965): 49–58.

"Papias and Oral Tradition." *Vigiliae Christianae* 21, no. 1 (1967): 137–40.

"Mission Studies: A Must." *Kingdom Overseas* (June 1968): 18–22.

"Some Recent Literature on Mission Studies." *Evangelical Quarterly* 42, no. 4 (1970): 213–29.

"Miss Austen on Sunday." *Trivium* 6 (May 1971): 92–102.

"African Church History: Some Recent Studies." *Journal of Ecclesiastical History* 23, no. 2 (1972): 161–69.

"English Bards and Scottish Reviewers: Some Early Interactions of Scottish and English Methodism." *Journal of the Scottish Branch of the Wesley Historical Society* 3 (1974): 8–14.

"English Bards and Scottish Reviewers: Some Early Interactions of Scottish and English Methodism." *Journal of the Scottish Branch of the Wesley Historical Society* 4 (1974): 2–13.

"The Study of Religion in East, Central and Southern Africa," jointly with Jocelyn Murray. *Religion* (1975): 94–98.

"Africa and Christian Identity." *Mission Focus* 6, 7 (1978): 11–13

"The Anabaptists of Africa: the Challenge of the African Independent Churches." *Occasional Bulletin of Missionary Research* 3 (April 1979): 48–51. Also published in *The Missionary Movement in Christian History*, 111–18.

"A Bag of Neediments for the Road: Geoffrey Parrinder and the Study of Religion in Britain." *Religion* 10 (1980): 141–50.

"Does Christianity Change?" *Religions in Education* 2 (1981): 18–22.

"'The Likes of You': Museums and the Disabled Visitor." *OmniGatherum* (1981): 1–2.

"Evangelization and Civilization: Protestant Missionary Motivation in the Imperialist Era. 4: The British." *International Bulletin of Missionary Research* (April 1982): 60, 62–64.

"The Gospel and Prisoner and Liberator of Culture." *Faith and Thought* 108, no. 1–2 (1982): 39–52. A slightly revised version appeared in *Missionalia* 10, no. 3 (1982): 93–105; *Evangelical Review of Theology* 7, no. 2 (October 1983): 219–33; and is reproduced in *New Directions in Mission and Evangelization 3*, ed. James A. Scherer and Stephen B. Bevans, 17–28. Maryknoll, N.Y.: Orbis Boos, 1999. Also appears in *The Missionary Movement in Christian History*, 3–15.

"Papers of J. W. Westgarth, Qua Iboe Mission." *Bulletin of the Scottish Institute of Missionary Studies* New Series 1 (1982): 6

"Manuscripts of Dr. John Hector of Calcutta." *Bulletin of the Scottish Institute of Missionary Studies* New Series 1 (1982): 7.

"A Missionary Manuscript on Madagascar." *Bulletin of the Scottish Institute of Missionary Studies* New Series 1 (1982): 8.

"Islam and the Sword: Some Western Perceptions 1840–1918." *Scottish Journal of Religious Studies* 5, no. 2 (Autumn 1984): 89–104.

"Culture and Coherence in Christian History." *The Evangelical Review of Theology* 9, no. 3 (1985): 214–25. Also published in the *Scottish Bulletin of Evangelical Theology* 3, no. 1 and in *The Missionary Movement in Christian History*, 43–54.

"Three Unpublished Mission Manuscripts." *Bulletin of the Scottish Institute of Missionary Studies* New Series 2 (1983–84): 17–19

"The Legacy of David Livingstone." *International Bulletin of Missionary Research* 11, no. 3 (1987): 125–29. Also published as "David Livingstone, 1813–1873 — Awakening the Western World to Africa" in *Mission Legacies: Biographical Studies of Leaders of the Modern Missionary Movement*, ed. Gerald H. Anderson, Robert T. Coote, Norman A. Horner, James M. Phillips, 140–47. Maryknoll, N.Y.: Orbis Books, 1994.

"The Old Age of the Missionary Movement." *International Review of Mission* 76, no. 301 (1987): 27–32.

"Missionary Societies and the Fortunate Subversion of the Church." *Evangelical Quarterly* 88, no. 2 (1988): 141–55. Also published in *The Missionary Movement in Christian History*, 241–54.

"Why Missions Studies Librarianship Is Different: Responsibilities and Opportunities." *Bulletin, Association of British Theological and Philosophical Libraries* 2 (November 1990): 25–33.

"Conversion and Christian Continuity." *Mission Focus* 18, no. 2 (June 1990): 17–21.

"Structural Problems in Mission Studies." *International Bulletin of Missionary Research* 15 (1991): 74–77. Also published in *The Missionary Movement in Christian History*, 143–59.

"The Legacy of Samuel Ajayi Crowther." *International Bulletin of Missionary Research* 16 (January 1992): 15–16, 18–21. Also published in *Mission Legacies: Biographical Studies of Leaders of the Modern Missionary Movement*, ed. Gerald H. Anderson, Robert T. Coote, Norman A. Horner, James M. Phillips, 132–39. Maryknoll, N.Y.: Orbis Books 1994, and *The Cross-Cultural Process in Christian History*, 155–64.

The "Legacy of Thomas Foxwell Buxton." *International Bulletin of Missionary Research* 15 (October 1991): 146–55. Also published in *Mission Legacies: Biographical Studies of Leaders of the Modern Missionary Movement,* ed. Gerald H. Anderson, Robert T. Coote, Norman A. Horner, James M. Phillips, 11–17. Maryknoll, N.Y.: Orbis Books 1994.

"Christianity in the Non-Western World: A Study in the Serial Nature of Christian Expansion." *Studies in World Christianity* 1, no. 1 (1995): 1–25. Also published in *The Cross-Cultural Process in Christian History*, 27–48.

"African Christianity in the History of Religions." *Studies in World Christianity* 2, no. 2 (1996): 183–203.

"Old Athens and New Jerusalem: Some Signposts for Christian Scholarship in the Early History of Mission Studies." *International Bulletin of Missionary Research* 21, no. 4 (October 1997): 146–53.

"Africa in Christian History — Retrospect and Prospect." *Journal of African Christian Thought* 1, no. 1 (June 1998): 2–15. Also published in *The Cross-Cultural Process in Christian History*, 85–115.

"In Quest of the Father of Mission Studies." *International Bulletin of Mission Research* 23, no. 3 (1999): 98–102, 104–5.

"Africa as the Theatre of Christian Engagement with Islam in the Nineteenth Century." *Journal of Religion in Africa* 29, no. 2 (1999): 155–74. Also published in *Christianity and the African Imagination: Essays in Honour of Adrian Hastings*, ed. David Maxwell with Ingrid Lawrie, 41–62. Brill: Leiden 2002.

"Christian Advance Is Serial." *Mission Thrust 21* 1, no. 3 (2003): 1–2.

"Re-Visioning Christian History with a Wider Lens." *Religion and Values in Public Life* 7, no. 4 (Fall 1999): 4–6, 8. Slightly different versions are "Eusebius Tries Again: Reconceiving the Study of Christian History," *International Bulletin of Mission Review* 24, no. 3 (July 2000): 105–9, 110–11, and "Eusebius Tries Again: The Task of Reconceiving and Re-visioning the Study of Christian History." In *Enlarging the Story: Perspectives on Writing World Church History*, ed. Wilbert R. Shenk, 1–21. Maryknoll, N.Y.: Orbis Books, 2003.

"Of Ivory Towers and Ashrams, Some Reflections on Theological Scholarship in Africa." *Journal of African Christian Thought* 3, no. 1 (June 2000): 1–4.

"The Mission of the Church Today in Light of Global History." *Word and World* 20, no. 1 (Winter 2000): 17–21. Also published in *Mission at the Dawn of the Twenty-First Century: A Vision for the Church,* ed. P. V. Martinson, 384–88. Minneapolis: Kirk House, 1999.

"Christian Scholarship in Africa in the Twenty-First Century." *Journal of African Christian Thought* 4, no. 2 (December 2001): 44–52. A slightly different version is Andrew F. Walls, "Christian Scholarship and the Demographic Transformation of the Church," in *Theological Literacy for the Twenty-First Century,* ed. Rodney L. Peterson with Nancy M. Rourke, 166–83. Grand Rapids: Eerdmans, 2002. Also appears to be published as "Christian Scholarship in Africa in the Twenty-First Century." *Transformation* 19, no. 4 (2002): 217–28 and *Religion in a World of Change: African Ancestral Religion, Islam and Christianity,* ed. T. L. Okere, 144–66. Owerri: Whelan Research Academy for Religion, Culture and Society, 2002.

"From Christendom to World Christianity: Missions and the Demographic Transformation of the Church." *Princeton Seminary Bulletin* 22, no, 3 (2001): 306–30. Also published in *The Cross-Cultural Process in Christian History,* 49–71. See also *Crux* 37, no. 4 (2001): 9–24.

"Kenneth Scott Latourette, Historian of Six-Continent Christianity." *Christian History* 20, no. 4 (2001): 72.

"Obituaries: Harold W. Turner, 1911–2002." *AASR Newsletter* 19 (2003): 7–9.

"Imperial Evasion." *Christian History* 21, no. 2 (2002): 41–42.

"Mission and Migration: The Diaspora Factor in Christian History." *Journal of African Christian Thought* 5, no. 2 (December 2002): 3–11.

"Cross-Cultural Encounters and the Shift to World Christianity." *Journal of Presbyterian History* 81, no. 2 (2003): 112–16.

"Converts or Proselytes? The Crisis Over Conversion in the Early Church." *International Bulletin of Missionary Research* 28, no. 1 (January 2004): 2–6.

"The Morning Star of Africa." *Yes Magazine* (May–August 2004): 18.

"West African Christian Proclamation: The Early Years." *The Bible Translator* 55, no. 3 (July 2004): 389–400.

"Ecumenical Missiology in Anabaptist Perspective." *Mission Focus: Annual Review* 13 (2005): 191–98.

"Migration and Evangelization: The Gospel and Movement of Peoples in Modern Times." *Covenant Quarterly* 63, no. 1 (2005): 3–28

"The Cost of Discipleship: The Witness of the African Church." *Word & World* 25, no. 4 (2005): 433–43.

"Mission History as the Substructure of Mission Theology." *Swedish Missiological Themes* 93, no. 3 (2005): 367–78.

"Martyrs and Witnesses: Some Chapters of African Christian History." *AICMAR Bulletin* 5 (2006): 1–16.

"New Mission, New Scholarship: Exploring the Old Faith in New Terms." *Journal of African Christian Thought* 9, no. 2 (2006): 23–29. This is a modified version of "Old Athens and New Jerusalem: Some Signposts for Christian Scholarship in the Early History of Mission Studies." *International Bulletin of Missionary Research* 21, no. 4 (October 1997): 146–53.

"Scholarship under the Cross: Thinking Greek and Thinking Christian." *Journal of African Christian Thought* 9, no. 2 (2006): 16–22. This is a slightly modified version of "In Quest of the Father of Mission Studies." *International Bulletin of Mission Research* 23, no. 3 (1999): 98–102, 104–5.

"Scholarship and the Missionary Movement: The China Experience." *Journal of African Christian Thought* 9, no. 2 (2006): 30–33.

"Scholarship, Mission and Globalization: Some Reflections on the Christian Scholarly Vocation in Africa." *Journal of African Christian Thought* 9, no. 2 (2006): 34–37.

"World Views and Theology." *Word and Context* 5 (2006): 72–76.

"Thoughts on Background to the Project" (Primal Religion as the Substructure of Christianity). *Journal of African Christian Thought* 11, no. 2 (2008): 1–4.

"Kwame Bediako and Christian Scholarship in Africa." *International Bulletin of Missionary Research* 32, no. 4 (2008): 188–93.

"The Significance of Global Christianity for Theological Education and Scholarship." *Ogbomoso Journal of Theology* 15, no. 1 (2010): 1–10.

"A Watershed for Translation." *Journal of African Christian Thought*, forthcoming.

Book Reviews and Notices

"N. Q. King." *There's No Such Divinity Doth Hedge a King": Studies in Ruler Cult and the Religion of Sacral Monarchy in Some Late Fourth-Century Byzantine Monuments. Sierra Leone Bulletin of Religion* 3, no. 2 (December 1961): 80.

"The Journey of a Slave Trader (John Newton) 1750–1754." *Sierra Leone Bulletin of Religion* 5, no. 1 (June 1963): 38–40.

The World of Mission by Bengt Sundkler. *Evangelical Quarterly* 41, no. 1 (1969): 52–53.

To Advance the Gospel: Selections from the Writings of Rufus Anderson, ed. with and introduction by R. Pierce Beaver. *Evangelical Quarterly* 41, no. 1 (1969): 54–55.

The Roots of Ghana Methodism, by F. L. Bartels. *Evangelical Quarterly* 41, no. 1 (1969): 55–56.

Theology and Rural Development, by Peter G. Batchelor and Harry R. Boer. *Evangelical Quarterly* 41, no. 1 (1969): 56.

Patterns of Ministry: Theological Education in a Changing World, by Steven Mackie. *Evangelical Quarterly* 42, no. 2 (1970): 121–23.

Covenant and Community: The Life, Writings and Hermeneutics of Pilgram Marpeck, by William Klassen. *Evangelical Quarterly* 42, no. 4 (1970): 244–45.

The Photian Schism: History and Legend, by Francis Dvornik. *Evangelical Quarterly* 43, no. 1 (1971): 48–49.

In Search of the Missionary, by Helen and Richard Exley. *Evangelical Quarterly* 43, no. 1 (1971): 49.

Ecumenicity and Evangelism, by David M. Stowe. *Evangelical Quarterly* 44, no. 1 (1972): 61.

John Wesley's Mission to Scotland, 1751–1790, by Samuel Rogal. *International Bulletin of Missionary Research* 16 (1992): 141–42.

Thomas of Tonga, 1797–1881: The Unlikely Pioneer, by Janet Louisa Luckcock. *Proceedings of the Wesley Historical Society* (1990).

Ashe, Traditional Religion and Healing in Sub-Saharan Africa and the Diaspora: A Classified International Bibliography. In *Journal of Religion in Africa* (August 1993): 292–93.

The Irish Missionary Movement: A Historical Survey, 1830–1980, by Edmund M. Hogan. *International Review of Mission* (1993): 419–20.

Black Christians and White Missionaries, by Richard Gray. *Bulletin, School of Oriental and African Studies* 56, no. 1 (1993): 204–5.

Religion and Politics in Southern Africa, ed. Carl Frederik Hallencreutz and Mai Palmberg. Uppsala, Sweden: Scandinavian Institute of African Studies, 1991.

The Cross and the Rising Sun: The Canadian Protestant Missionary Movement in the Japanese Empire 1872–1931, by A. Hamish Ion. *Journal of Imperial and Commonwealth History* 21, no. 1 (1993).

Northward from Cape Town: The Anglican Church Railway Mission in Southern Africa 1885–1980, by John Roden. *Theology* 104, no. 819 (May–June 2001): 230–31 [44–45].

The Moravian Church and the Missionary Awakening in England, by J. C. S Mason. *English Historical Review* 119, no. 482 (2004): 806–7.

Occupy until I Come: A. T. Pierson and the Evangelization of the World. Journal of Presbyterian History (Fall–Winter 2005): 79–80.

Articles in Newsletters

"His Mission and Ours — John 20:19–21." *Akrofi-Christaller Center Newsletter* (December–January 2002): 8–10.

"What the Kingdom of Heaven Is Like (Matthew 20:1–16)." *Akrofi-Christaller Center Newsletter.*

Bibliographies

"Bibliography of the Society for African Church History-I." *Journal of Religion in Africa* 1, no. 1 (1967): 46–94.

"Bibliography on Mission Studies." *International Review of Mission,* quarterly since 1972.

"Bibliography on Mission Studies," co-author with Margaret M. Acton. *International Review of Mission,* quarterly since 1997.

Introductions and Forewords to Books

Introduction to *South African Records of the Society for the Propagation of the Gospel.* Booklet for microfilm. Bradford, 1973.

Foreword to Harry Sawyerr, *The Practice of Presence: Shorter Writings of Harry Sawyerr,* ed. John Parratt, viii–xvi. Grand Rapids: Eerdmans, 1994 (1996).

Foreword to Kwame Bediako, *Christianity in Africa: The Renewal of a Non-Western Religion*. Edinburgh: Edinburgh University Press and Maryknoll, N.Y.: Orbis Books, 1995, xi–xii.

Foreword to David Smith, *Mission after Christendom*. London: Darton, Longman and Todd, 2003, ix–xv.

Foreword to Anne Kwantes, *She Has Done a Beautiful Thing for Me: Portraits of Christian Women in Asia*. Manila: OMF Literature, 2005.

Foreword to Theodore Gabriel, *Christian Citizens in an Islamic State: The Pakistan Experience*. Aldershot: Ashgate. 2007.

Foreword to Jeanette Hardage, *Mary Slessor — Everybody's Mother: The Era and Impact of a Victorian Missionary*. Eugene, Ore.: Wipf and Stock, 2008.

Foreword to Young-Hoo Lee, *The Holy Spirit Movement in Korea: Its Historical and Theological Development*. Eugene, Ore.: Wipf and Stock, 2009.

Foreword to Victor Ezigbo, *Re-Imagining African Christologies*. Wipf and Stock, 2010.

Foreword to Barabra Bompani and Maria Frahm-Arp, eds., *Development and Politics from Below: Exploring Religious Spaces in Africa*. London: Palgrave-Macmillan, 2010.

Foreword to Theodore Gabriel, *Playing God: Belief and Ritual in the Mutappan Cult of North Malabar*. London: Equinox 2010.

Foreword to Indian edition of *Towards an Intercultural Theology: Essays in Honor of J. A. B. Jongeneel*. Missiological Classics 9, ed. Martha Frederiks, Meindert Dijkstra, and Anton Houtepen. Bangalore: Center for Contemporary Christianity 2010, xi–xii

"A Salute to Lamin Sanneh." In *A New Day: Essays on World Christianity in Honor of Lamin Sanneh*, ed. Akintunde E. Akinade, ix–xiii. New York: Peter Lang, 2010.

Foreword to Julie C. and Wansuk Ma, *Mission in the Spirit: Towards a Pentecostal/Charismatic Missiology*. Oxford: Regnum International, 2010.

Foreword to Mark R. Gornik, *Word Made Global: Stories of African Christianity in New York City*. Grand Rapids: Eerdmans, 2011.

Foreword to Harsha Kumar Kotian. *Christonormative Pluralism: A Critical Appraisal of the Works of Stanley Jones, Stanley Samartha, and Paul Knitter*, ix–xi. Delhi: ISPCK Zoll, 2011.

Interviews

"The Expansion of Christianity: An Interview with Andrew Walls." *Christian Century* 117, no. 22 (August 2–9, 2000): 792–95.

"On the Road with Christianity: A Conversation with Missiologist Andrew Walls." *Books and Culture* 7, no. 3 (2001): 18–19

Unpublished Papers on CD

"Translation and Christian Conversion," 1993, at the Yale Divinity School, Yale-Edinburgh Group: Papers 1992–2005. CD *www.divinity.library@yale.edu*

"From Christendom to World Christianity: Missions and the Demographic Transformation of the Church," No. 146, Currents in World Christianity Collected Papers of North Atlantic Missiology Project and Currents in World Christianity Project, 1996–2001.

"Methodist Missions and the Printed Word": introduction to CD version of Methodist Missions and the Printed Word: Proceedings of the MMS History Project Conference, 2006.

Unpublished Papers

"Missionary Studies and the Scottish Theological Faculties." A paper read on May 5, 1967, at the Conference of the Scottish University Divinity Faculties held at King's College, Aberdeen.

"Missionary Studies — Why and What?" London, January 1968. Personal Collection of Wilbert R. Shenk.

"Can Christianity Authentically Take Root in China? Some Lessons from Nineteenth- and Twentieth-Century Missions."

Video Links and Documentation

James Ault Productions

- Life & Revelations in Sierra Leone. *vimeo.com/10825065*.

- Effects of the Enlightenment on Christianity. *vimeo.com/10825065*.

- With Kwame Bediako on African Christianity and Pentecostalism. *vimeo.com/6270961*.

"A Century of Mission Documentation." Delivered at DABOH Conference, Balaton, Hungary, August 18, 2008. See online *http://cscadocs.blogspot.com/2008/09/video-of-professor-andrew-f.html*.

Select Works about Andrew F. Walls

Akrofi-Christaller Institute of Theology, Mission and Culture, Staff and Students "In Appreciation of Professor Emeritus Andrew F. Walls." *Journal of African Christian Thought* 9, no. 2 (2006): 51–55.

Balcomb, Anthony. "Faith or Suspicion? Theological Dialogue North and South of the Limpopo with Special Reference to the Theologies of Kwame Bediako and Andrew Walls." *Journal of Theology for Southern Africa* 100 (March 1998): 3–19.

Cox, James. 2004. "From Africa to Africa: The Significance of Approaches to the Study of Religions at Aberdeen and Edinburgh Universities from 1970 to 1998." In *European Traditions for the Study of Religion in Africa,* ed. Frieder Ludwig and Afe Adogame, 303–14. Wiesbaden: Harrassowitz Verlag.

———. *A Guide to the Phenomenology of Religion.* New York: Continuum, 2006, 150–59.

Chitando, Ezra. "'For We Have Heard for Ourselves': A Critical Review of T. Ranger's Portrayal of Christianity as an Aspect of African Identity." *Studia Historiae Ecclesiasticae* 28, no. 1 (2002): 218–34.

Ellingworth, Paul, "Interim Unscientific Marginalia." In *Essays in Religious Studies for Andrew Walls,* ed. James Thrower, 10–16. Aberdeen: Department of Religious Studies, University of Aberdeen, 1986.

Gornik, Mark R. "Andrew Walls and the Transformation of World Christianity." *Catalyst* 31, no. 3 (March 2005): 5–6

———. "New Centers of Scholarship: Andrew Walls on World Christianity and Theological Education." *Princeton Theological Review* 11, no. 2 (Spring 2005): 9–12.

Hastings, Adrian. "AFW as Editor." In *Essays in Religious Studies for Andrew Walls,* ed. James Thrower, 5–9. Aberdeen: Department of Religious Studies, University of Aberdeen, 1986.

———. "African Christian Studies, 1967–1999: Reflections of an Editor." *Journal of Religion in Africa* 30, no. 1 (2000): 30–44.

Jennings, Willie James. *The Christian Imagination: Theology and the Origins of Race.* New Haven: Yale University Press, 2010, 155–61.

Noll, Mark. "Translating Christianity." *Books and Culture* (November–December 1996): 6–7, 35–37.

———. "Andrew F. Walls, The Missionary Movement in Christian History." *First Things* 101 (2000): 55–56.

Park, Hyung Jin. "Journey of the Gospel: A Study in the Emergence of World Christianity and the Shift of Christian Historiography in the Last Half of the Twentieth Century." Unpublished Ph.D. dissertation, Princeton Theological Seminary, May 2009.

Poon, Michael Nai-Chiu. "Re-Imagining World Christianity for the Church Universal: Andrew Walls and His Legacy." Paper presented at Princeton Theological Seminary, 2011.

Thrower, James, ed. *Essays in Religious Studies for Andrew Walls.* Aberdeen: Department of Religious Studies, University of Aberdeen, 1986.

Turner, Harold. "Andrew Walls as Scholar." In *Essays in Religious Studies for Andrew Walls,* James Thrower, 1–4. Aberdeen: Department of Religious Studies, University of Aberdeen, 1986.

Stanley, Brian. "Profile: Andrew Walls." *Epworth Review* 28, no. 4 (2001): 17–26.

———. "Review of the Missionary Movement in Christian History." *Journal of Theological Studies,* New Series 49, no. 1 (1998): 486–90.

Sanneh, Lamin, "Walls, Andrew F(inlay)." *Biographical Dictionary of Christian Missions,* ed. Gerald Anderson, 714. New York: Macmillan, 1998.

Sanneh, Lamin, and Grant Wacker, "Christianity Appropriated: Conversion and the Intercultural Process." *Church History* 68, no. 4 (December 1999): 954–61.

Shenk, Wilbert. "Walls, Andrew." In *Evangelical Dictionary of World Mission,* ed. Scott Moreau, Charles Van Engen, and Harold A. Netland Baker, 2000.

Smith, David I. "Cross-Cultural Learning and Christian History." *Journal of Christianity and Foreign Languages* 6 (2005): 3–7.

Stafford, Tim. "Historian Ahead of His Time." *Christianity Today* (February 2007): 86–89.

Young, Richard Fox. "World Christian Historiography, Theological 'Enthusiams,' and the Writing of R. E. Frykenberg's *Christianity in India,*" *Religion Compass* 5, no. 4 (2011): 71–79,

Finlay Anderson

Hymns and Prayers for Aberdeen (and Some Miles Around), privately distributed, 2010.

Contributors

J. Kwabena Asamoah-Gyadu is professor of African Christianity and pentecostal theology and the dean of graduate studies at the Trinity Theological Seminary, Accra, Ghana.

Kwame Bediako is late rector of the Akrofi-Christaller Institute for Theology, Mission and Culture, Akropong-Akuapem, Ghana.

Gillian Bediako is the deputy rector of Akrofi-Christaller Institute for Theology, Mission and Culture, Akropong-Akuapem, Ghana.

Stephen B. Bevans is the Louis J. Luzbetak, SVD, Professor of Mission and Culture at the Catholic Theological Union, Chicago, USA.

Jonathan J. Bonk is the executive director of the Overseas Ministries Study Center in New Haven, USA, and editor of the *International Bulletin of Missionary Research*.

William R. Burrows is managing editor emeritus of Orbis Books and research professor of missiology at the Center for World Christianity at New York Theological Seminary in New York, USA.

Mark R. Gornik is the director of City Seminary of New York in New York, USA.

Jehu J. Hanciles is an associate professor of the history of Christianity and globalization and director of the Center for Missiological Research at Fuller Theological Seminary, Pasadena, USA.

Allison Howell is the dean of accredited studies and senior research fellow at the Akrofi-Christaller Institute for Theology, Mission and Culture, Akropong-Akuapem, Ghana.

Maureen Iheanacho is on the staff at the Akrofi-Christaller Institute for Theology, Mission and Culture, Akropong-Akuapem, Ghana.

Moonjang Lee is the senior pastor of Doorae Church in the City of Guri, South Korea.

I. Howard Marshall is professor emeritus of New Testament exegesis and honorary research professor at the University of Aberdeen, Scotland.

Janice A. McLean is on the faculty of City Seminary of New York in New York, USA.

Mark Noll is the Francis A. McAnaney Professor of History at the University of Notre Dame in Notre Dame, USA.

Michael Poon is the director and Asian Christianity coordinator of the Centre for the Study of Christianity in Asia at the Trinity Theological College, Singapore.

Dana L. Robert is the Truman Collins Professor of World Christianity and History of Mission as well as co-director of the Center for Global Christianity and Mission at Boston University in Boston, USA.

Lamin Sanneh is the D. Willis James Professor of Missions and World Christianity and professor of history at the Yale Divinity School in New Haven, USA.

Wilbert R. Shenk is senior professor of mission history and contemporary culture at the Fuller Theological Seminary, Pasadena, USA.

Brian Stanley is professor of World Christianity and the director of the Centre for the Study of World Christianity at the University of Edinburgh, Scotland.

Index